Second Edition

A SHORT COURSE IN TEACHING READING

PRACTICAL TECHNIQUES FOR BUILDING READING POWER

Beatrice S. Mikulecky

PEARSON
Longman

A Short Course in Teaching Reading: Practical Techniques for Building Reading Power, Second Edition

Copyright © 2011 by Pearson Education, Inc.
Pearson Education, 10 Bank Street, White Plains, NY 10606
Staff credits: The people who made up *A Short Course in Teaching Reading* team—representing editorial, design, production, and manufacturing—are Margaret Antonini, Rhea Banker, Mindy DePalma, Amy McCormick, Lise Minovitz, Joan Poole, Jennifer Stem, and Pat Wosczyk.
Cover design: Jill Lehan
Cover photo: Uppercut/Getty Images
Text design: Pat Wosczyk
Text composition: Rainbow Graphics
Text font: 10.5 pt ITC Caslon 224 Book
ISBN 13: 978-0-13-136385-4
ISBN 10: 0-13-136385-9

Library of Congress Cataloging-in-Publication Data

Mikulecky, Beatrice S.
  [A short course in teaching reading skills]
  A short course in teaching reading : practical techniques for building reading power / Beatrice S. Mikulecky. — 2nd ed.
      p. cm.
  Includes bibliographical references.
  Originally pub.: Reading, Mass. : Addison-Wesley, A short course in teaching reading skills, c1990.
  ISBN-13: 978-0-13-136385-4
  ISBN-10: 0-13-136385-9
  1. English language—Study and teaching—Foreign speakers. 2. English language—Textbooks for foreign speakers 3. Reading comprehension. 4. Books and reading. I. Title.
  PE1128.A2M55 2010
  428.4'07—dc22

                          2010043248

Printed in the United States of America

16 2019

CONTENTS

ACKNOWLEDGMENTS

Thank you to the anonymous reviewers of an earlier draft of this book. I hope they will see that I have responded to many of their concerns. And thanks to a later reviewer, Judy Mendelson; her comments on the final draft helped tighten the organization of the book.

I am grateful to my editors: Lise Minovitz, Supervising Editor, for her patience, encouragement, and support in shepherding this book; Joan Poole, Development Editor *par excellence*, for contributing her knowledge and making so many tactful and useful suggestions; and Mindy DePalma for her support and guidance in producing the book.

Linda Jeffries and I co-authored the *Reading Power* series, and I want to acknowledge her collaboration in developing many of the sample exercises included in this book.

Most of all, thank you to the teachers who have reported that they found the first edition of *Short Course* useful in their work. I hope you like the second edition as well.

Bea Mikulecky

This book is dedicated to Anna and Piper from GB.

INTRODUCTION

This book is intended for teachers and prospective teachers who want to do more for their students in the development of effective reading. Its title (*A Short Course in Teaching Reading*) explains its purpose—those who read the book from the beginning to the end will discover that they have had a "course" of instruction in the teaching of reading. The course begins with an overview of the theory and practice of teaching reading, with special emphasis on meeting the needs of students of English as a second or foreign language and other limited English proficient students. That overview is followed by many sample exercises that are organized according to their role in reading development. This approach is based on the experience of reading instructors in both first and second language reading. The activities and exercises in the book are suitable for a wide variety of students who already have decoding skills in English.

- ESL (English as a Second Language) students who need to learn how to read and think in English for success in academic or business settings in English-speaking countries
- EFL (English as a Foreign Language) students living in non-English-speaking countries who usually rely on written texts for "immersion" in English. They can learn to develop and apply the thinking skills needed to read widely and deeply in English
- Students who may speak English fluently but whose home language is not "mainstream" Standard English. Through the approach detailed in this book, they can master mainstream literacy skills
- Students with language processing disabilities (such as dyslexia) who can benefit from the structured, developmental approach found here
- "Non-mainstream" students in junior or community colleges, who often need to develop the reading skills discussed in this book in order to succeed in their college courses
- Adult native speakers of English in literacy centers and adult basic education (ABE) classes. These students can acquire the advanced reading and thinking skills required for further job training programs and diploma examinations through the approach and methods this book outlines

BACKGROUND

Today, the development of second language reading skills is recognized as an important component of language instruction. But that was not always the case. In the past, second language reading was associated with the grammar/translation approach to instruction, and hence reading was not an important focus of instruction or research. In fact, programs for training TESL/TEFL teachers rarely included a course on the teaching of reading.

In the 1970s and 1980s, research in psycholinguistics and cognitive psychology provided important insights for understanding reading as a psycholinguistic process. Such research was carried out by, to name a few, Anderson, Brown, Goodman, Kintsch, Meyer, Rumelhart, and Smith. Researchers and teachers began to recognize that reading in a second language deserved attention. Some important contributions were made by Alderson; Cates and Swaffar; Coady; Dubin, Eskey, and Grabe; Grellet; Hudelson; Mackay, Barkman, and Jordan; and Nuttall. In addition, the expansion of research and scholarship on second language reading was encouraged by a new journal, *Reading in a Foreign Language,* which began to be published in 1983.

The renewed interest in second language reading development led researchers to examine first language reading research and teaching practices that had been more or less ignored by second language professionals for many years. Scholars such as Alderson, Carrell, Clarke, Connor, Eskey, Grabe, Stoller, and others found that second language professionals could learn a lot from first language reading research and instructional methods.

This led to an interest in research into the nature of second language reading and its relationship to first language reading (e.g., Koda, 2004). Increased contact between researchers and teachers from non-English-speaking countries, where reading is stressed in the foreign language classroom (e.g., at TESOL conventions), has strengthened this interest.

In another development during the 1980s and early 1990s, work by Street, Besnier, Michaels, Cook-Gumperz, Cazden, D'Andrade, Graff, Heath, Gee, and others raised awareness of the relationship between culture and literacy. These scholars' ideas about the social construction of literacy provided another avenue for a deeper understanding of second language reading. More than a psycholinguistic process, reading was seen as an aspect of social literacy; in other words, a sociolinguistic process.

More recent breakthroughs in our understanding of reading have come from a variety of sources. Some researchers have been examining the physiological process involved in the reading process, with new studies on eye movement and reading (Rayner) and brain-based learning (Jensen; Wolf). Others have stressed the importance of phonology and orthography in understanding the development of reading (Birch; McGuinness).

New research on vocabulary learning is yet another area that has had a profound effect on second language reading research and instruction (e.g., Cobb, Coxhead, Nation). Widespread agreement has always existed about the relationship between effective reading and vocabulary size. But it was only with the advance of technology that corpus linguistics research was able to provide information about which words are most important for a student to learn in English in order to be an effective reader. Word frequency lists and technology for analyzing a text for its vocabulary level have brought a revolution to vocabulary teaching and learning.

Together with all the advances in research that have occurred over the past three decades, social forces have also influenced the demand for understanding and developing strong instructional methods for second language reading instruction. First, literacy in both first and second languages has become a burning issue in many parts of the world. The immigration of large numbers of refugees from developing countries into highly industrialized nations and the resettlement of cultural groups in several parts of the world have highlighted the need for effective approaches to developing literacy and reading skills in a second language. In the United States, many school districts have established classes for students who, although born in the United States, use a language other than English in their homes. These students are often fluent speakers of English, but they are learning Standard English as a "second" language.

Another factor in the demand for more reading instruction in English is the explosion of Internet technology. As English has developed into a world language, students, researchers, business people, and many others have had to learn to read well in English in order to have access to online materials available only in English.

Unfortunately, some ESL/EFL teachers remain unaware of the many new approaches to teaching second language reading. Until recently, ESL/EFL teacher training programs often did not include courses in the theories and methods of reading instruction. Moreover, many otherwise excellent books and articles about second language reading have often stopped short of making suggestions about actual lessons and classroom practices.

Consequently, many teachers have continued to teach second language reading based on their own experiences as readers. They may assume that reading skills all transfer automatically from the first language, and they may define reading as the interpretation of texts, neglecting to realize that students need to be able to decode and comprehend before they can become proficient at making interpretations. In some EFL settings, reading continues to be taught as the equivalent of translation, and sometimes the least proficient teachers are assigned to teach these classes. Ironically, although most second and foreign language instructional materials require reading, there is often little systematic instruction in how to comprehend texts.

Effective reading is the basis for all of the components of an English language course: vocabulary development, writing, revising, spelling, grammar, and speaking. Reading instruction in English as a second or foreign language benefits students in many ways. It gives students:

- an increased awareness of the language (metalinguistic awareness).
- immersion in the second language, resulting in increased acquisition.
- models for improving writing in English.
- skills needed for success in academic studies.
- resources for improving vocabulary.
- increased cultural background knowledge.
- opportunities to transfer some first language reading skills.
- chances to improve first language reading abilities.
- a lifelong habit of reading in a second language.

Today, as increasing numbers of English teachers recognize the importance of reading instruction, they are looking for new, effective ways to teach reading. But simple "recipes" are not enough. When instruction is based on an understanding of underlying theories of reading and literacy development, teachers can be more confident and can plan more coherent lessons. Therefore, some connections need to be made between theory and classroom practice.

The Structure of This Book

A Short Course in Teaching Reading is divided into three parts. Part I presents theories and explanations about reading and literacy, including the following: a definition and model of the reading comprehension process; a review of some recent key views about aspects of the reading process; a definition of literacy and a discussion of cultural aspects of reading; and an outline of a model ESL/EFL reading course.

Part II focuses on individualizing student extensive reading for pleasure. It gives a clear rationale for emphasizing extensive reading and presents concrete ideas for promoting literate skills in English. Key features are an up-to-date list of suggested books for extensive reading and numerous examples of activities for building students' motivation to read and eliciting student responses to their books.

Part III —the longest part of the book—introduces an approach to teaching reading comprehension that focuses on the skills students need to learn in order to read effectively in English. The underlying notion is that students should not be asked apply a skill until it has been explained and practiced. Suggested "Intensive Reading Lessons" are interspersed throughout this part of the book to provide an opportunity for the students to learn to apply strategically the skills they have learned. Teachers should feel free to try out the sample exercises with their students and also use them as models for creating their own exercises based on the needs of their students.

The book concludes with helpful appendices and a comprehensive bibliography. The appendices include lists of phonemes and their spelling, high frequency word lists, a table of common collocations found in academic texts, and an answer key for selected skills exercises.

PART I

READING AND LITERACY: Some Connections

This part of the book presents a definition of reading, a discussion of current ideas about the reading process, a definition of literacy, and an examination of the relationship between reading and literacy. It concludes with a discussion of some important implications for an effective approach to teaching reading to ESL, EFL, and other students who need to work on developing their reading skills.

WHAT IS READING?

At the outset, it is important to clarify the definition of reading that this book is based upon. In order to do that, please read the following paragraph. What is this paragraph about and how do you know?

> A newspaper is better than a magazine. A seashore is a better place than the street. At first it is better to run than to walk. You may have to try several times. It takes some skill, but it's easy to learn. Even young children can enjoy it. Once successful, complications are minimal. Birds seldom get too close. Rain, however, soaks in very fast. Too many people doing the same thing can also cause problems. One needs lots of room. If there are no complications, it can be very peaceful. A rock will serve as an anchor. If things break loose, however, you will not get a second chance. (Bransford & Johnson, 1972, p. 717)

What is the topic of the paragraph? If you cannot guess, discuss it with someone. You may find that as you talk about what is in the paragraph, you will come up with a topic that makes sense. (For the answer, see page 245.)

Strategies of Fluent Readers

In order to make sense of the passage, you probably engaged in the following (primarily automatic and subconscious) processes as you read:

- decoding the text.
- predicting what the meaning of the text might be and what would come next.
- testing this prediction by further sampling of the text.
- confirming your prediction or rejecting it and seeking another hypothesis about what the text means.

More specifically, you were consciously and subconsciously employing some or all of the strategies fluent readers use.

1. You read as though you expected the text to make sense.
2. You noticed the distinctive features in letters, words, and meanings.
3. You read to get the meaning rather than to identify individual letters or words.
4. You guessed and took risks to predict meaning.
5. You took an active role and applied your knowledge of the world and of the topic in attempting to understand.
6. You made use of redundancies—orthographic, syntactic, and/or semantic repetitions of information—to reduce uncertainty about meaning.

7. You maintained enough speed to overcome the limitations of visual processing and memory systems.
8. You constantly switched your thoughts back and forth between the text and what you already know in an effort to understand.
9. You discussed the paragraph with someone.
10. You reread parts of the paragraph several times to try to understand.

(Adapted from Cooper & Petrosky, 1976)

In figuring out what the passage was about, you were forced to guess because the topic was *not* stated. You probably had no difficulty with the vocabulary or the sentence structure. You probably made several unsuccessful guesses before you finally came up with a topic that did not seem to be contradicted by anything you could find in the text. In other words, you constructed a meaning based on the contents of the text combined with your prior knowledge as described in the definition of reading below.

A DEFINITION OF READING

Reading is a complex conscious and unconscious mental process in which the reader uses a variety of strategies to reconstruct the meaning that the author is assumed to have intended, based on data from the text and from the reader's prior knowledge.

The Reading Process

And so to completely analyze what we do when we read would almost be the acme of a psychologist's achievement, for it would be to describe very many of the most intricate workings of the human mind, as well as to unravel the tangled story of the most remarkable specific performance that civilization has learned in all its history.

(Sir Edmund Huey, The Psychology and Pedagogy of Reading, 1908, p. 6)

It has taken a century and scores of researchers in a multitude of fields to begin to reach the lofty goals mentioned in this quotation from Sir Edmund's influential book. Recent research allows us to examine the reading process more fully than Sir Edmund might ever have imagined. Much of the new knowledge is the result of advances in technology including ways of tracking parts of the reader's brain with Positron Emission Tomography (PET) scanning and functional Magnetic Resonance Imaging (fMRI), plus a variety of eye tracking systems that are connected to computers. Research is being conducted in a wide array of fields: psychology, cognitive neuroscience, linguistics, psycholinguistics, neurology, psychophysics, optics, education, and more.

The following points about the reading process demonstrate the complexity of learning to read and indicate the enormous challenges that students face in learning to read in a second or foreign language. While most of the research summarized here was based on silent reading in a native language, the conclusions can also apply to reading in a second or foreign language.

The brain is a pattern maker and pattern seeker.

It has long been an accepted fact that learning is based on seeing patterns. Early in human history, for example, navigators looked for patterns in the stars to guide them across vast seas, and farmers relied on the patterns of the seasons to plan their work. Washburn (2009) remarked that the brain constructs meaning via patterns, even occasionally imposing patterns to make meaning from random data—hence conspiracy theories.

Humans begin life with millions of unorganized neurons. These neurons are shaped into networks of patterns through the regularity of experiences in daily life. That is how we make sense of the world. In the late 1960s and early 1970s, scholars began to make connections between prose comprehension and the human brain's capacity for seeking patterns (e.g., Meyer, 1977).

Implications for Teaching: At every level of language learning, an awareness of patterns can facilitate acquisition. In reading, this is especially true. Students who learn to recognize the patterns of English phonemes (the collection of distinctive, permissible sounds in a language), spelling, syntax, and discourse will become better readers. Teaching the strategy of pattern seeking/recognition is therefore an important element in reading instruction.

There is no gene for reading and writing.

Hearing and speaking are based on specific genes and areas of the brain, so those abilities develop naturally. However, in order to learn to read and write, a person's brain has to adapt.

As Wolf (2007) remarked, "Underlying the brain's ability to learn reading lies its protean capacity to make new connections among structures and circuits originally devoted to other more basic brain processes that have enjoyed a longer existence in human evolution, such as vision and spoken language" (p. 5). The brain is altered as it adapts cognitive processes such as shape identification and generalization in order to decode a written language.

Learning to read in a second language requires the brain to make adaptations in the "reading circuit" that are specific to the second language, and so reading in a second language also reshapes the brain. While there are some common regions of the brain that are activated across all writing systems during reading, the specific types and extent of brain adaptations required depend on the reader's native language; the regions of the brain that are most involved will vary from one language to the next based on the writing system. (See Bolger, Perfetti, & Schneider, 2005.)

This is not just a theory. Thanks to PET (Positron Emission Tomography), substantial evidence has been found to support it. Researchers can make a record of the brain's activity and see the different areas of the brain that are involved during reading. For example, written Japanese language employs two types of characters, *kanji* (characters originally borrowed from Chinese that represent ideas, not sounds) and *kana* (characters based on sounds). "When reading *kanji*, Japanese readers use [brain] pathways similar to those of the Chinese; when reading *kana*, they use pathways much more similar to alphabet readers. In other words, not only are different pathways utilized by readers of Chinese and English, but different routes can be used within the same brain for reading different types of scripts" (Wolf, p. 63).

Figure 1.1 on page 7 illustrates the areas of the brain that are involved in reading English, Chinese, and Japanese. Notice how the areas are slightly different in each language. Wolf points out (p. 63) that the English alphabet reader "learns to rely more on the posterior of the left hemisphere" but the reader of Chinese uses many areas of both hemispheres. This is an example of how the brain constructs a reading circuit that is tailored to the language being read.

Implications for Teaching: Wolf reports that it takes about 2,000 days for a child's brain to make the adaptations necessary for reading her first language and many of those adaptations are specific to the child's language (p. 107). It should be clear, therefore, that students who are learning to read in a second language also need time and practice for their brains to adapt and form a new reading circuit in the brain. They need repeated practice to develop the strong neural connections required for effective reading in English.

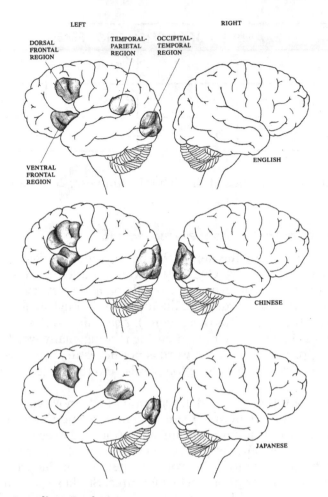

DORSAL FRONTAL REGION

TEMPORAL-PARIETAL REGION

OCCIPITAL-TEMPORAL REGION

VENTRAL FRONTAL REGION

ENGLISH

CHINESE

JAPANESE

Figure 1.1 Three Reading Brains

(From Mary Ann Wolf, Proust and the Squid, *Harper Collins, 2007, p. 62)*

Processing during reading occurs in multiple areas of the brain, including the sections of the brain that process sound.

According to Wolf (p. 63), at least four different areas of the brain are involved in comprehending what we read in English. Part of the frontal region of the brain maps letter information into phonemes. So when we read, our brain is, in a sense, sounding out the phonemes in every word. In proficient readers, the patterns in which these phonemes are found in words are instantaneously available and semantic processing is enhanced.

Implications for Teaching: Students learning to read in English as a second or foreign language do not have a rich "bank" of the phonemes of English, so this area of the brain is not equipped to help in speeding up comprehension.

McGuinness (2005) maintains that ESL/EFL teachers of reading should teach the sounds of English. However, she maintains that teaching the sounds of the *letters* in the English alphabet is not useful because there is not a one-to-one correspondence between each letter and a single sound. She recommends teaching the sound-symbol correspondences of the *phonemes* (spelling of the sounds) of the English language. She states that the English phonemes should be directly taught with their common basic code spellings, rather than the International Phonetic Alphabet, which she believes can be confusing. So, for example, rather than teach the name and sound that the letter *b* stands for, teachers should teach the sound of the phoneme /b/ in a familiar word (*big*) and its usual spelling. (See also Szabo, 2010.) The following chart gives examples.

EXAMPLES OF ENGLISH PHONEMES			
Phoneme:	/b/	/f/	/f/
Found in the word	"big"	"fish"	"phoneme"
Usual spelling:	b	f	ph

A chart of all the phonemes of English (McGuinness, 2005) appears on page 00 of the Appendix.

Reading is characterized by constant eye movement.

Research summarized by Rayner (1998) has provided intriguing information about eye movement and reading. Contrary to what good readers imagine that they experience when they read, the eyes fixate briefly on almost every word in a text, moving rapidly from word to word. For a fluent reader in English, a fixation lasts about 200 milliseconds (200 thousandths of a second). According to Rayner, "Whereas the majority of the words in a text are fixated during reading, many words are skipped so that foveal [fixated] processing of each word is not necessary" (p. 375). The tendency is to skip over short words such as function words, and the longer the word, the more likely it is to be fixated.

What follows is a rather detailed description of eye movements during reading, but it's important for teachers of reading to understand this process. Rayner described eye movement as follows: During a fixation, the eyes focus directly on about seven to eight letters and/or spaces. Several areas of the brain are immediately activated to begin to identify the word, its meaning in the present semantic and syntactic context, and its phonological features. Studies show, however, that the eyes do *not* process a word letter by letter during a fixation; instead the eyes process phonemes (distinctive sound segments that distinguish words) and either entire words or word parts.

Simultaneously, just outside the direct field of vision, the eyes also grasp the next twelve to fifteen letters and spaces. The size of this perceptual span depends on the writing system and the skill of the reader. (In English, this span would be primarily the letters and spaces directly to the right. In languages such as Hebrew, it would be primarily the letters and spaces directly to the left.) The brain uses the information grasped in this way to predict what is likely to appear in the next fixation, based on the patterns of letters, spaces, and word length that are perceived.

Then the eyes move very rapidly to the next fixation, about seven to nine letters/spaces ahead in the text. During this movement (called a saccade), the eyes do not focus, but the reader doesn't register a blur, partly because the brain is actively engaged in processing and fine-tuning the input so far. The saccade lasts for about 30 milliseconds (ms), or 30 thousandths of a second. Then the eyes are fixated on the next group of letters or word. Not all saccades are forward in direction; about 15 percent of saccades are regressions that are caused by the reader's need to ensure understanding of a word or sentence already read (Rayner, p. 375).

Implications for Teaching: Since the reader focuses on almost every word and the brain makes probabilistic predictions on what word comes next based on a glimpse outside of the focus, students clearly need strong vocabulary skills. As Wolf (p. 210) explains, the teacher needs to "give daily emphasis to each of the major linguistic and cognitive processes used by the brain to read" including semantic families of words, awareness of sounds within words, orthographic letter patterns, syntactic knowledge, and morphological knowledge. Another implication is that teachers need to help students develop reading fluency by having them practice with materials that require scanning and reading rate improvement.

All reading comprehension is ultimately based on decoding.

Rayner makes it clear that effective automatic decoding is so rapid that the fluent reader is not aware of the process. However, when the fluent reader confronts a word that is difficult to decode, the process slows down and the decoding process can be observed as various regions of the brain are activated. Wolf (p. 123) gives examples of words that will slow down an expert reader's decoding speed because of their lexical and conceptual complexity. Try reading these rapidly: *periventricular nodular heterotopia, fiduciary, micron spectroscopy, tintinnabulation,* and *synecdoche.* You probably noticed that you slowed down and segmented the words.

Implications for Teaching: This is another strong argument in favor of teaching word segmentation, word families, and vocabulary building, including such lexicon-enriching concepts as synonymy and polysemy (multiple meanings of the same word), and other decoding skills.

In order to comprehend, the reader makes connections between what is found in the text and prior knowledge or experience.

An important step in understanding the reading process was the development of a model of text comprehension (e.g., Kintsch & van Dijk, 1978; Rumelhart & Ortony, 1977; Winograd, 1977) that applied an information processing analogy to understand how people think, learn, and remember what they read. According to this model, when a person reads, two aspects of the so-called "human information processing system" continuously interact. When the reader focuses primarily on what he or she already knows about the topic in processing a text, this is called a concept-driven or "top-down" mode. In this case, the reader will try to grasp the meaning by skipping over unknown words and will interpret the text based on prior knowledge. On the other hand, if a reader relies primarily on textual features (single words and phrases) to comprehend, this is called a data-driven or "bottom-up" mode (Rumelhart, 1980). In this case, the reader uses single words or phrases to build meaning.

In practice, these two processing strategies are employed interactively and simultaneously as the reader tries to relate the new information in the text to what is already known. But the two modes are not applied equally. According to Stanovich's interactive compensatory model of reading, "a deficit in any knowledge source results in a heavier reliance on other knowledge sources, regardless of the level in the processing hierarchy" (1980, p. 63). In other words, a reader who is familiar with the topic will rely on knowledge of the topic in order to comprehend (top-down processing); conversely, a reader who has a mastery of much of the text's vocabulary but is unfamiliar with the topic will rely on word knowledge in order to comprehend a text (bottom-up processing). (See also Coady, 1979.) Figure 1.2 on page 10 summarizes the reading comprehension process.

The text (shown at the bottom of Figure 1.2) is a set of graphic clues to the author's intended meaning. The reader decodes and instantly interprets the text at many levels of language simultaneously: typographical features, phonemes, phonological patterns, word patterns, associated meanings, syntactic structure, discourse structure, genre, context, and more.

At a conscious level, second language readers, especially beginners, often rely heavily on textual features, especially on single words (Coady, 1979). Reading and translating word by word, they try to put the words together to make sense of the text. This is natural (Stanovich, 1980). Until readers have acquired what Grabe (1986) termed a "critical mass" of language knowledge, they will read by focusing on words.

But relying primarily on textual features (bottom-up processing) will not always result in a successful interpretation of the author's intended meaning, because the author has made assumptions about the background knowledge that a reader will bring to a text. For example, when you read the passage (about making a kite) at the beginning of this section, you had to supply the topic from your own background

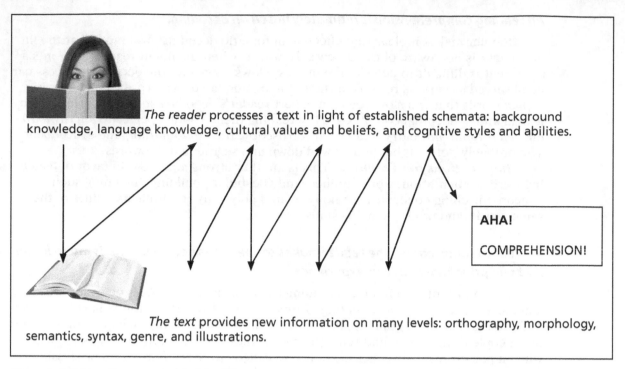

The reader processes a text in light of established schemata: background knowledge, language knowledge, cultural values and beliefs, and cognitive styles and abilities.

AHA!

COMPREHENSION!

The text provides new information on many levels: orthography, morphology, semantics, syntax, genre, and illustrations.

Figure 1.2 Reading as a Thinking Process

knowledge. There was no way that you could make sense of the passage on the word or sentence level.

The reader (shown at the top of Figure 1.2) possesses the cognitive and perceptual abilities needed to reason and form conceptual structures. In addition, the reader brings to the text all kinds of knowledge about the world. But the reader's mind should not be imagined as a storehouse of bits of randomly stored information. According to cognitive theory, the mind contains whole networks of interrelated mental structures, or schemata (Rumelhart and Ortony, 1977).

A schema is a mental network that is centered on a general idea about a set of similar or related concepts. For example, the schema you have for school consists of all the experiences you have ever had or learned about in connection with school. When you are confronted with a situation that you identify as a school (or something school-like), the connections in your school schema are activated, and you have an idea about what to expect and how to behave. (See Winograd, 1977; see also additional examples of schemata and a more detailed explanation in Appendix 00, p. 000.)

All readers have built up conceptual frameworks (schemata) of the sound-symbol correspondences, words, associated meanings, sentence structure, discourse structures and pragmatic aspects of their first language as well as some aspects of the new language they are learning. They have also built up other schemata, equally important, which are based on their knowledge and experience of the world, including cultural values, beliefs, and ways of talking and interacting that are learned along with their first language (Watson-Gegeo & Gegeo, 1986).

Goodman and goodman (1977), Smith (1973), and many others have argued that the concepts a reader brings to a text could be more important for comprehension than the words and ideas in the text. These concepts are applied when the reader activates the "top-down" processing strategies mentioned earlier. In terms of comprehension, the textual material itself is "gobbledy-gook unless the reader can breathe meaning into it" (McNeil, 1987; see also Kolers, 1973; Smith, 1977).

But when second language learners rely too heavily on top-down processing to comprehend a text, they can be misled if their interpretations are based on cultural schemata that do not match those the author had in mind. This was clearly shown in a study by Steffensen, Joag-dev, and Anderson (1979). They gave the same reading passage to two groups living in the United States, Indians from India and non-Indian Americans born in the United States.

Each group read two passages in English, one about a typical American wedding and one about a typical Indian wedding. Subjects read what for them was the native passage more rapidly, recalled a larger amount of information from the native passage, produced more culturally appropriate elaborations of the native passage, and produced more culturally based distortions of the foreign passage. Whether recalling the native or foreign passage, subjects remembered more text elements rated as important by other subjects with the same cultural heritage. These results show the pervasive influence of cultural schemata on comprehension and memory (Reynolds et al., 1982).

Clearly, cultural orientations and prior experiences influence interpretations. To test this notion, read the following passage and decide what the author is describing.

> At first you believe it is absolutely impossible to do, no matter how hard you concentrate. In fact, it always does take some time to get it right. Then, just when you get used to doing it competently, you hear of the alternate method. While the final choice is, of course, left to you, if you are mature and reasonable, you'll realize that there is one way which is superior. People sometimes need to do it in strange positions, so flexibility is definitely an asset. Taken seriously, this task should not result in injuries. One usually tries to avoid situations where one has to do it too often. (Zupnik, 1988)

This was written as a description of learning to tie your shoelaces. But many other interpretations have been put forth, including changing the oil in your car, learning a new dance, and tying a bowtie.

Implications for Teaching: As Figure 1.2 on page 10 demonstrates, it is important for teachers to recognize that the reader brings something essential to a text: previously acquired schemata—networks of prior interpretations (McNeill, 1987) that are the basis for comprehending. The meaning of a text is constructed by the reader, who makes connections between the text and the reader's established schemata, based on the individual's cultural values, beliefs, native language discourse processes, and consciousness of language. (See vanDijk & Kintsch, 1983, p. 56.)

Therefore, the *process* shown in Figure 1.2 may be universal, but *the resulting interpretation* is cultural (D'Andrade, 1981; van Dijk & Kintsch, 1983; Nespor, 1987; Stein, 1986). In order for students to comprehend texts in standard English, they need to develop new schemata of language, text, and interpretation, as well as schemata of alternative cultural practices and values. In other words, students need to learn to read, think, and interpret texts in new ways.

WHAT IS LITERACY?

A book on teaching ESL/EFL reading must include a discussion of literacy, since research has shown that the definitions and uses of literacy vary culturally, and the social contexts of literacy development are the basis for how reading and writing are acquired. Social contexts include the student's language and cultural background, prior knowledge, and language style, as well as the settings in which reading and writing are used and taught.

In the 1980s and 1990s, many exciting advances were made in our understanding of the nature and acquisition of literacy, thanks to groundbreaking work by such scholars as Besnier (1986), Scribner and Cole (1981), Cook-Gumperz (1986), deCastell, Luke, and Egan (1986), Gee (1996), Graff (1979), Heath (1984), Olson (1977), Ong (1982), Pattison (1982), Schieffelin and Ochs (1986), R. and S. Scollon (1981), Scribner and Cole (1981), Street (1984), Wagner (1987), and Watson-Gegeo (1986).

Research by these scholars revealed that literacy is not a universal technology that is defined the same way in every culture. In fact, the role and status of literacy and the practices and rules governing reading and writing are a part of a culture's ideology (Street, 1984). The concept of literacy is imbedded in local attitudes and beliefs about the uses of language and appropriate settings for reading and writing (literacy events). That is why the social context of literacy is basic to the acquisition of reading and writing skills. (See Gee, 1996; Heath, 1983, 1984.)

Since literacy is culturally defined, it is more than the technical process of decoding and encoding (Cook-Gumperz, 1986; Street, 1984). According to many scholars (e.g., Gee, 1986; Heath, 1983; Pattison, 1982; Scollon & Scollon, 1981; Watson-Gegeo & Gegeo, 1986), teachers need to consider a more accurate definition of literacy—one such as the following.

A DEFINITION OF LITERACY

Literacy, broadly defined, is a set of attitudes about written language that develops within a specific cultural context.

In every local culture, whether it is a village, an urban school, or a research lab at a famous university, reading and writing are used to express, expand, and support local cultural values and goals. In any society, the tasks to be accomplished that require reading and writing greatly influence how literacy is defined. What counts as literacy is determined by the dominant values and by what the dominant culture deems to be appropriate ways of reading and writing and talking about a text.

For many people, literacy means, quite simply, the ability to read and write, that is, to decode and encode a language, the ability to recognize and pronounce sound-symbol correspondences, and to produce the language in symbolic form. In the past, in fact, that was all that was required in order to be considered literate.

Among many teachers of English as a second or foreign language and in programs for adult basic education, the term *literacy* is still often understood that way. Teaching literacy often means introducing the concept of print to students who have no knowledge of printed language at all, or else it means teaching adults who, for some reason, have not developed basic reading and writing abilities.

Decoding and encoding are important skills for the further development of literacy, but literacy has a broader meaning: specifically, the ability to read and write in socially approved ways. Being literate in any culture means the acquisition of reading, thinking, and interpreting skills as well as the ability to write and speak in forms that are recognized locally as standard.

There is no argument with the necessity for teaching elementary literacy (decoding and encoding). The disagreement lies with certain common assumptions: (a) that elementary literacy is all there is to literacy, or (b) that such activities as learning the names and sounds of letters and words are disconnected from cultural values and beliefs. Even in learning the letters and sound-symbol correspondences in English, the student begins to develop a new schema of language. Elementary literacy —"learning your letters"—already contains cultural attitudes and values about language. For example, the type of orthography (ideographic or phonetic) a language employs is closely related to the way speakers of that language think. And not all language groups consider it natural to learn the letters of their "alphabet" as English-speakers do their ABC's. Certainly an ideographic language doesn't have an ABC song. It is important to remember that even teaching elementary literacy is teaching culture.

The meaning of literacy depends on the time and place. For example, in the United States, prior to World War I, anyone who could decode and encode could probably carry out most written language tasks. But today, much more complex uses of reading and writing are demanded, and consequently the definition of basic literacy has changed to meet those demands. And so, when people say that a recent high school graduate is functionally illiterate, they probably mean that the young person cannot accomplish with written language those tasks that our society regards as necessary today.

HOW ARE LANGUAGE, CULTURE, AND LITERACY CONNECTED?

The following points illustrate some of the deep connections between culture and literacy. While the information presented is based on research studies by scholars representing several disciplines, it should be noted that cultural anthropologists have contributed heavily to the present understanding of the importance of recognizing the cultural definitions of literacy. These scholars include Heath (1983), Michaels (1986), Scollon & Scollon (1981), Street (1984), and Watson-Gegeo & Gegeo (1986). Although their groundbreaking work was published back in the 1980s, their ideas reverberate today as teachers around the world face increasing numbers of students from diverse cultural backgrounds.

Attitudes toward reading and writing flow naturally out of the ways a local culture uses oral language.

Research in language socialization by Schieffelin and Ochs (1986), Heath (1982), and others showed how children learn culturally approved beliefs, practices, and attitudes concerning language in the process of socialization. Since oral language is the basis of reading and writing, these same cultural attitudes structure the norms concerning the uses of literacy. In fact, much of what we regard as literate behavior is learned before children ever go to school.

Heath, for instance, reported in *Ways with Words* (1983) about the relationship between oral language practices and literacy development among two small, culturally different working-class communities in North and South Carolina. She found that children in the two rural communities (one black, one white) "came to have different ways of communicating, because their communities had different social legacies and ways of behaving in face-to-face interactions" (p. 11). When they began school, Heath found that the children from both of these communities had difficulty in adjusting to school and learning to read. She stated that race was not a factor: the children's difficulties stemmed from the fact that in both rural communities the home language and literacy practices were not reflected in the way language was used at school. Children of middle-class townspeople, on the other hand, did not have these difficulties because they had been socialized from birth in the so-called mainstream language practices found in school.

Pattison (1982) described a historical example of the result of differences in attitude toward literacy. In ancient Greece, the Spartans and the Athenians both adopted writing and reading at about the same time. Yet these two cultures made very different uses of the printed word! These differences grew out of their already established values and beliefs and their consciousness of language.

> Once introduced into Athens, writing soon enhanced the already existing predisposition of Athenians to treat language with critical vigor and wit.　　　　(p. 52)

> But conditions were not right for the development of writing in all the Greek states. . . . The Spartan reticence about the use of writing results from their general approach to language. . . . Education for the Spartan was only secondarily about language; foremost it was training in the habits of good citizenship . . . . The Spartan ideal glorifies action and views language arts warily.　　　　(pp. 56–57)

The way ideas are organized in discourse varies across cultures.

Originally called to our attention by Kaplan (1966), this proposition continues to inspire contrastive research in several different languages. Ostler (1987) stated that the structure of expository writing in a language "reflects the rhetorical patterns esteemed in [people's] native cultures. . . . When individuals write other than their native language, they tend to use their native patterns in that discourse" (p. 171). This has been confirmed and clarified by recent research on learning and the brain mentioned earlier in this part of the book. (See also Wexler, 2006.)

Researchers have found that significant differences in text organization exist between English and Korean, German, Japanese (Eggington, 1987; Hinds, 1987), Arabic (Ostler, 1987), and Athabaskan Eskimo (Scollon & Scollon, 1981), to name a few. (See Connor & Kaplan, 1987, and also Connor, 1996, for more about the impact of such differences.)

Ostler (1987), for instance, reported that modern classical Arabic embodies the values of parallel structure, balance, rhythmical coordination, and symmetry found in the Qu'ran, which is based on oral language. In Arabic writing, all levels of language—from word choice to overall rhetorical pattern—exemplify these values. Arabic schools teach language and grammar through the Qu'ran, and this is done deliberately in order to maintain the sacred language.

In contrast, Ostler pointed out that English-speaking writers value "variety of sentence structure and the use of subordination [of ideas] and deletion [of redundancies]" (p. 172). So it is no wonder that speakers of Arabic often have difficulty learning to write and comprehend English texts. In addition, because of an underlying and perhaps unconscious belief that a text is "holy" and cannot be questioned or altered, Arabic students may find it difficult to learn to mark texts, skip words, or read critically.

It is logical to conclude from this that when individuals read a second or foreign language, they comprehend best what meets their beliefs and expectations about the rhetorical patterns of written language. To the extent that these patterns are different from those of their first language, the language learner is likely to have difficulty comprehending. (See Carrell, 1984.)

Cultures have different views of the role and responsibility of the reader and the writer.

As Hinds (1987) states, "In Japan, perhaps in Korea, and certainly in ancient China . . . it is the responsibility of the listener (or reader) to understand what it is that the speaker or author had intended to say" (p. 144). In contrast, "English speakers, by and large, charge the writer, or speaker, with the responsibility to make clear and well-organized statements" (p. 143). In terms of reading, this means that in Japanese, Korean, or Chinese, a careful, word-by-word reading of a text may be necessary in order to ferret out the author's intended meaning. People from these language groups may not be able to recognize, at first, that reading in English does not require such careful, text-bound interpretation.

Narrative structure is not the same for every culture.

A traditional narrative usually has three parts in English. Native English speakers take it for granted that there is "a beginning, a middle, and an ending." However, in some other languages, stories are structured in different ways: a story can be divided into four or five parts. (See Hymes, 1981, especially chaps. 3 & 4.)

Further, a narrative in standard English is expected to be topic-centered, that is, to have one controlling topic, one central idea. All parts of the narrative are subordinated to that topic. In contrast, speakers of languages based on oral traditions, including Black English (Gee, 1985) and Athabaskan Eskimo (Scollon & Scollon, 1981), form narratives that are topic-associated. That is, many related topics can be included in one narrative. The associations are not usually made explicit because the audience's awareness of their existence is assumed by the speaker or writer. Eggington (1987, p.166) summarized the implications of these ideas as follows:

> If reading is to be considered a "psycholinguistic guessing game," as Goodman (1970, p. 93) has posited, then readers and writers have certain built-in expectations about the ordering of ideas in any stretch of discourse. In an optimal condition, the reader shares the same expectations of what is to follow what as does the writer. Breakdowns in communication between writer and reader occur when these expectations are violated.

Implications for Teaching: Second language teachers often (consciously or subconsciously) expect students' reading skills in their first language to transfer to reading in the second language. The foregoing is important evidence for not expecting that to happen. Reading a language requires more than the mechanical decoding of print—it requires knowledge of particular ways of thinking and talking about print—not only recognizing words and sentences, but recognizing culturally based forms and making culturally favored interpretations. Because every culture has a somewhat different way of making sense of the world, learning to comprehend written text in a second or foreign language is a complex task. Anthropologists and linguists have shown what an important role culture plays in this enterprise.

If it is true that learning to read and comprehend a second language requires learning cultural interpretations, understanding cultural beliefs about language and discourse, and developing culture-specific formal and content schemata, then reading and comprehending a new language literally alters the learners' cognitive structures and value orientations. Teaching reading in Standard English to second language learners and other limited English proficient students, then, can be seen as teaching an alternative cultural literacy.

What this means for reading instruction is that English teachers cannot afford to ignore the social context in which reading is taught and learned. In the United States, in schools, reading is not a simple, value-free technology that teachers can pass on to their students. Reading well in English means being able to interpret a text in ways that are expected by mainstream culture.

Being literate in English means more than learning to decode.

Heath (1984) made an important distinction between literacy skills and literate skills. Literacy skills, she stated, are the decoding and encoding skills, while literate skills are the thinking processes about reading and writing that are influenced by the culture. In teaching reading, instructors need to be involved in helping language learners acquire the literate skills that will aid them in comprehending texts in Standard English.

Heath pointed out that in order to comprehend texts in English, the reader must learn to treat language as an object in and of itself, be comfortable with analyzing things (taking apart the ideas in a text), and make connections between the content of a text and external, objects, ideas, and people that are not present. Hoffman and Heath (1986) noted that facility with the academic language prevalent in schools, universities, and businesses in the United States requires a person to be able to use language to:

- talk about an ongoing sequence of events.
- compare one phenomenon or text with another.
- explain causes and effects.
- render near-verbatim retellings.
- tell topic-centered stories.
- realize that printed materials are a source of new information.
- examine ideas from multiple points of view.

Many children learn these literate skills before they even begin school, because they use similar language practices at home (Heath, 1983; Schieffelin & Cochran-Smith, 1984). These children are said to come from "mainstream" families, that is, families whose ways of talking to each other include the features listed previously. But students who do not grow up with this kind of language experience have difficulty with the language used at school and in fact may need to learn academic English as a "second language" even though they may speak English at home. This is true of non-mainstream native speakers of English as well as ESL/EFL students.

Heath (1984) argued that many ESL/EFL students have not been socialized into ways of talking and thinking that are the basis of academic language. "For most of our students," she wrote, "we have to make explicit the academic habits of using oral and written language which the school requires, and we have to provide social interactive meaningful occasions for repeating these habits again and again" (p. 25).

The type of literacy that exists in academic settings reflects specific learned attitudes about language. It is how people think and talk about a text that matters. That is the cultural part of reading that second language students must learn. It is the English teachers' job to teach their students the skills needed for effective reading by employing a methodology that focuses on the cognitive processes and language practices that are the basis of literate behavior in English. In fact, it is the teacher's responsibility to ensure that second language and other non-mainstream students learn these literate skills. As Gee (1989) has argued, "Short of radical social change, there is no access to power in the society without control over the discourse practices in thought, speech, and writing of essay-text [academic] literacy and its attendant world view" (p.60).

However, teachers should remember that what they are teaching is not an inherently better, value-free approach to comprehending text. It is teaching another way of thinking about language, an alternative way of interpreting text, a different consciousness, complete with values and attitudes that are likely to be at odds with the students' own. For example, students who have learned how to tell stories at home may have a different format for storytelling than what is found in literate texts (Michaels, 1986). We can teach the basic story forms found in English texts in ways that allow our students to retain their own cultural story forms. (See also Kintsch, 1977.)

In conclusion, teachers of English should be aware of the impact of culture on teaching reading. As Stein (1986) pointed out, "values are an inherent part of reading comprehension" (p.179). Teaching reading means teaching an alternative way of thinking and talking about text, a way required for academic success in English. But it is not the only correct way. It is important that students retain respect for their own cultural ways with words.

WHAT DO EDUCATIONAL RESEARCHERS RECOMMEND?

Here, very briefly, are the conclusions and recommendations of educational researchers.

- Cognitive psychologists have shown in their research that students learn new strategies or thinking processes most effectively when they are consciously aware of what they are doing (Brown, Armbruster, & Baker, 1986). Once students are conscious of the processes, they can monitor their comprehension and apply appropriate strategies as needed for comprehending a text (Brown, 1978).

- Interacting and talking about text in particular ways is essential (Casanave, 1988). Heath (1984), Vygotsky (1962), and others found that students develop literate skills when teachers encourage them to talk about written language, when teachers model comprehension strategies for them, and when students have opportunities to talk to each other about how they make sense of a text (Hoffman & Heath, 1986).

- A person's native language literacy is acquired from birth by being socialized into both the language and the local culture's ways of using language. Literate behaviors grow out of the spoken and written language practices of a local culture. Therefore, students best acquire a new literacy by serving as an apprentice to a "native." This means that teachers must provide models of literate behaviors and opportunities for students to practice new ways of talking and thinking about a text (Schiefelin & Ochs, 1986; Gee, 1996).

- Research also confirms that students must read faster and with more fluency if they wish to read effectively (Eskey, 1986; Anderson, 2010). Faster reading promotes reading in "thought units" and leads to improved comprehension. But according to Wolf (2007), "fluency is not simply a matter of speed; it is a matter of being able to utilize all the knowledge [a reader] has about a word" fast enough to think and comprehend (p. 130).

- Krashen (1985) posited that the best way to improve reading is by reading. In recent years, research and practice have validated that idea (Day & Bamford, 1998). The benefits of extensive reading include increased fluency, vocabulary acquisition, a greater awareness of grammar, models for writing, and an immersion in the culture of the second or foreign language.

- Vocabulary development is basic to reading improvement. Finding effective methods of promoting second language vocabulary acquisition seemed, for many years, to be an impossible goal. Thanks to groundbreaking work by Nation (2001), Coxhead (2000), Cobb (www.lextutor.ca), and others, word frequency lists are available that allow teachers to focus on the words that will be most useful for their students to master. Nation's approach combines direct instruction, extensive reading, and multiple exposures to the same words by any means necessary to promote learning.

- As summarized by Jensen (2005), research in cognitive neuroscience points out that establishing strong new neural pathways requires repetition and time. New learning establishes initially fragile neural connections. These connections will decay and disappear without repeated excitation. This underlines the importance of repetition and time in helping students learn new ways of reading and thinking.

WHAT DO ESL/EFL STUDENTS NEED?

In order to read well in English, then, students need to do the following:

1. Develop a schema of the reading process that includes the idea that reading is more than translating—reading is thinking.
2. Talk with their teachers and others about their reading and explain how they make sense of a text.
3. Develop reading fluency.
4. Read extensively for pleasure in English and discuss their reading with someone who can model the literate behaviors expected in an English-language context.
5. Read fast enough to allow the brain to process words as thought units instead of individual words and learn to vary their reading rate to suit their purpose in reading.
6. Employ top-down processing effectively by learning to make connections between what they already know and what they are reading.
7. Learn reading and thinking skills that fluent readers of English employ to strengthen both top-down and bottom-up processing abilities.

8. Enhance bottom-up processing by mastering the phonemes of English, acquiring the most useful vocabulary, and learning strategies for guessing word meaning in context.

9. Master the basic 2,000 words that constitute approximately 80 percent of all texts in English.

10. Acquire specific reading comprehension skills and learn to apply them strategically.

Putting this all together, it is clear that students will make the most progress in developing the ability to read effectively in English in a class that includes, on a regular basis, the following components:

- Substantial amounts of extensive reading for pleasure, with opportunities for talking about their books with people who can model the literate skills required in English-language contexts.

- Focused, interactive lessons on specific reading skills, with opportunities for students to explain their thinking and direct instruction on applying the skills strategically to a variety of texts.

- Decoding and vocabulary learning activities that include direct instruction in the phonemes of English and high frequency words, multiple opportunities for exposure to and manipulation of target words, and guidelines for individual vocabulary learning.

- Training and repeated practice in fluency development: skimming, scanning, previewing, and reading rate improvement.

PART II

EXTENSIVE READING

This part of the book contains a comprehensive discussion of extensive reading and its essential role in every reading class. It presents information about what, why, when, and where students should read extensively, as well as techniques for encouraging and evaluating such reading. Also included is a list of suggested books that have been evaluated for their accessibility to students who are not native speakers of English.

WHAT IS EXTENSIVE READING?

Extensive reading (also known as pleasure reading or free voluntary reading) is a highly individualized approach to reading improvement. It is introduced early in this book to make a point: in order to become fluent, competent readers in English, ESL/EFL students must develop the habit of reading massive amounts in English at linguistically accessible levels. Ongoing immersion in extensive reading is essential for developing and applying all of the reading skills (Eskey, 1986; see also Day & Bamford, 1998).

Extensive reading is, in many ways, the opposite of an activity known as *intensive reading*. In the latter activity, the teacher chooses a reading passage or story and leads the students in a close reading to study the language of the text, focusing on word meaning, applying reading, vocabulary, grammar, and other skills and strategies. While intensive reading lessons are an important component of a second or foreign language class, they are very different from extensive reading.

"An extensive reading approach aims to get students reading in the second language and liking it" (Day & Bamford, 1998). Students select their own books and read at their own pace. They read whole books—lots of them—and the emphasis is on the quantity of books that they read and their enjoyment of the books. The focus is on getting the meaning, not on ferreting out linguistic details.

WHY IS EXTENSIVE READING IMPORTANT?

Early research showed that vocabulary acquisition and writing ability are directly related to the quantity of reading students engage in (Krashen, 1985). Since then, further research has strongly supported the benefits of extensive reading for a number of reasons (Krashen, 1985; Nation, 1997; Day & Bamford, 1998; www.extensivereading.net).

Extensive reading has been shown to

- provide students with massive amounts of comprehensible input, the primary requisite for significant language acquisition.
- foster reading fluency.
- allow students to make gains in vocabulary and grammar knowledge.
- improve writing in the second or foreign language.
- foster the development of a positive attitude toward reading in the second or foreign language.
- motivate students to read more.

In addition, and importantly, extensive reading plays a vital role in improving academic performance.

Second language students in academic preparation programs must certainly master special skills for reading challenging academic texts. But unless they are also reading with fluency and confidence in the second language, they are unlikely to read broadly and deeply enough to achieve the mass of background knowledge on which speculative thinking depends. An extensive reading approach can make such reading possible for students. (Day & Bamford, 1998, p. 45)

WHAT SHOULD STUDENTS READ FOR EXTENSIVE READING?

In many classes, students are encouraged to read magazines, short stories, plays, and newspapers as part of their extensive reading. While all of those materials provide excellent practice, students benefit most from extensive reading when they read whole books that are written by one author. The students should select their own books, with guidance from the teacher to ensure that the books are easy enough for the students to understand and enjoy. Teachers should guide students to choose both fiction and nonfiction books.

Whole books written by single authors.

Students make the most progress when they read whole books. Reading a book written by one person allows a student to develop a print "relationship" with a single native speaker: the author. The vocabulary range is limited by the topic of the book and the author's finite lexicon, and once the student "gets into" a book, he or she will become familiar with the author's style, sentence structures, and viewpoint. As a result, the student's reading fluency will increase, and then he or she will be motivated to read more. In addition, for some students this will be the first time that they have read a whole book in English, and this experience can be very satisfying and boost the students' self-confidence. For these reasons, many successful extensive reading programs are based upon reading whole books (Helgesen, 1997; Edinburgh Extensive Reading Project: www.jalt-publications.org/tlt/files/97/may/choosing.html).

Self-selected books.

There are a number of pedagogical and psychological reasons for asking students to choose their own books. (See Krashen, 1985.) First, students tend to select books on subjects or in genres that are familiar to them, and this familiarity can enable students to read books that might otherwise be too difficult (linguistically). Students' language weaknesses can be balanced by background knowledge about the topics of the books they select. As students read about familiar topics, they often become aware that they are able to guess word meanings because of their prior knowledge of the subject.

Second, students' motivation increases when they read what they are interested in. This means that they will want to read more, and since reading improves with practice, reading self-selected books should consequently lead to improved reading.

Third, self-selected books are authentic reading materials. According to Edelsky (1986), an authentic reading activity must include the transfer of information through the medium of print. When students choose their own books, they are intrinsically interested in finding out what is in the book.

Finally, selecting their own books is an important aspect of literate behavior that may be new to some students. Students may need to discover that there is something special about selecting and reading a book of their own. This is a cultural attitude, and a very important one to develop, particularly if students are from cultures that foster very different attitudes about books. Approaching, discovering, handling, and examining books and comparing, choosing, and talking about books are all part of building literate behavior in English.

Sometimes teachers choose a book for the whole class to read and they call that "extensive reading." However, this practice usually turns a reading class into a literature class in which class discussions become *lessons about the book*. The teacher may use the discussion to practice specific aspects of language and literature: grammar, vocabulary, genre, reading strategies, sentence structure, cultural background, and so forth. Again, this is an important language and literature activity, but this practice does not yield the same benefits as true extensive reading, in which students select their own books.

Books that are linguistically and culturally accessible.

Students should be led to choose books that are at or near their reading skill level. Research has indicated (Sivell, 1987) that some students, when given a choice, select books that are much too easy for them. Such students should be encouraged to try more difficult books. Conversely, some students select very difficult books, perhaps because they do not understand that they are supposed to read for *pleasure*. These students may want to impress the teacher (and maybe themselves) by selecting books far beyond their ability to comprehend. Trying to read overly difficult texts usually discourages students and makes them not want to read at all. It is best if students are carefully led to books within their grasp.

For beginning and low intermediate students, many teachers use graded readers. Graded readers are written with controlled vocabulary, syntax, and content. At the lowest level, a graded reader usually contains about 200 different words (or fewer). Students should start out with a graded reader that is easy to read and gradually move up to books that are slightly more challenging, eventually reaching a stage (usually at about the level of a 1,200-word vocabulary) where they can begin to choose books intended for native speakers of English.

Graded readers in a series are available from a number of publishers, including Pearson Longman (Penguin Readers, Easy Starts), Oxford University Press (Oxford Bookworms), Macmillan (Macmillan Readers), Heinle Cengage (Thomson Graded Readers), and Cambridge University Press (Cambridge English Readers).

The Penguin Readers, for example, are produced in seven levels. The following list refers to "headwords." These are core words such as *talk, eat,* and *run.* When headwords are used in other forms (*talking, eating, running*), they are not counted as separate words in the books.

Easy Start	200 headwords
Level 1	300 headwords (Beginner)
Level 2	600 headwords (Elementary)
Level 3	1,200 headwords (Pre-intermediate)
Level 4	1,700 headwords (Intermediate)
Level 5	2,300 headwords (Upper Intermediate)
Level 6	3,000 headwords (Advanced)

Some graded readers are accompanied by CDs that allow students to read and listen at the same time. This valuable resource fosters reading fluency, listening comprehension, and a model of fluent oral reading. For a comprehensive list of these series for extensive reading, with details about each one, see David Hill's charts at www.extensivereading.net/materials or Hill's (2008) article in the *ELT Journal, 62*(2), 184–204.

As soon as students have achieved a fourth-grade reading level in the United States and/or a reading vocabulary of about 1,200 headwords, they can be introduced to books that were not especially written for limited English proficient students. One good source of such books is the "Young Adult" section of the library or bookstore.

These books are usually relatively easy to read and most students, even mature adults, can find books that appeal to them from the wide range available.

When helping a student to select a book, teachers should consider these criteria:

- Is the book interesting to read? Will it appeal to a student who is learning English as a second or foreign language?
- Is the language relatively straightforward and accessible? Is the book free of regional dialect; wordy, page-long paragraphs; and obscure, five-syllable words? (In other words, maybe we will have to put Mark Twain and Charles Dickens on hold for a while.)
- Is the theme of the book more or less universal? Does the book require only a minimum of cultural background knowledge to "get the story"?
- Is the book too easy or too difficult for the student? You can check this by having the student read the first page and see how many new words he or she encounters. If on one page the student encounters more than five unknown words that are key to understanding the passage, the book is likely to be too difficult. If, on the other hand, the student reads rapidly with complete understanding, perhaps the book is too easy.
- Is the topic of the book familiar to the student?

A NOTE ABOUT ADAPTED TEXTS

Many collections of graded readers include adapted, simplified versions of famous classics such as *Tom Sawyer* or *Billy Budd*. There is wide disagreement about allowing students to read adapted texts. Some teachers feel that by reading these adaptations, students have an opportunity at least to become familiar with famous authors and their stories. However, many others argue that the richness of these novels is lost in simplification because adapted readers tend to violate most notions of narrative and expository style and cohesion. Moreover, it is through the lengthy descriptions, etc., in non-adapted texts, that students become better readers. In fact, large numbers of graded readers written specifically for language learners and other simple non-adapted stories and short novels are available and should be considered better choices for extensive reading.

A balance of fiction and nonfiction titles.

Although students should be encouraged to read whatever interests them, the teacher should guide students to read both fiction and nonfiction. Studies have shown that young men, in particular, may prefer nonfiction books, while young women seem to prefer fiction. The teacher's challenge is to get students to strike a balance between the two.

That being said, it is the case that this book's Suggested Books list on pages 24–29 contains more fiction than nonfiction titles. There are numerous benefits of reading fiction in a second language. When they read fiction in English, students from non-English-speaking cultures can be immersed in the language that is used by native speakers of English in social situations, relationships, and events. Such language experiences can facilitate students' acquisition of English, broaden their understanding of English-speaking cultures and their often hidden values, and provide background knowledge necessary for understanding texts in English. In addition, fiction encourages readers to put themselves in others' positions and to experience vicariously a wide range of emotions and situations that may be well outside the readers' everyday experience. Also, there is something about a story that compels a reader to continue: the reader is eager to find out what will happen next. So fiction encourages a student to read more.

Teachers occasionally encounter a student who refuses to read fiction in

English because he or she does not consider it "serious reading." With a comprehensive list of titles, these students may be guided to select a book of fiction that will alter that preconception. The teacher might suggest a novel that centers on a field of interest to such students. For example, students with a background in the field of medicine have numerous mysteries to choose from (e.g., books by Robin Cook, Michael Crichton, and Patricia Cornwell).

On the other hand, students who usually read only fiction need to discover the pleasures they can find in reading nonfiction. In fact, many students' only experience with nonfiction often lies in their assigned textbooks for particular courses. For extensive reading, students can be encouraged to choose nonfiction books about topics that interest them. Students with a strong background in a particular field, for example, biology or politics, may find that they can read books at a more advanced level because of their background knowledge about the topic.

Titles from *Reading Power** List of Suggested Books

The following list can serve as a starting point for teachers and students (from *Reading Power 2, Fourth Edition*, 2009, pp. 23–28). The books on it are suitable for students who are about twelve years of age and up. Teachers are encouraged to make copies of this list available to their students.

The book list is divided into two sections: List A and List B. The former presents graded readers for English language learners; the latter contains titles of books written for native speakers of English. Each list is further divided into fiction and nonfiction, and List B includes books at two levels of difficulty. The number of pages given for certain books may vary slightly depending on the edition.

---

* *Reading Power* (Mikulecky & Jefferies) is a reading program published by Pearson Longman. It includes a series of student books, teacher's guides, and test booklets.

List A: Readers for English Language Learners (Examples at Level 2)

The readers on this list are all level 2 and are published by Penguin Longman. Other companies also have readers for English learners. The teacher should examine several levels in a series of readers before recommending a book because, in order to build confidence, students should begin with a level that is easy enough for them to comprehend. They can always move up to a higher level.

The books with a headphones symbol (🎧) also have an audio CD to allow students to listen while they read.

Readers: Fiction

🎧 *Anne of Green Gables.* Montgomery, L.M. A young girl from an orphanage wins the love of her new parents.

Babe – The Sheep-Pig. King-Smith, Dick. Farmer Hogget is a sheep farmer. When he wins a pig, he doesn't want it, and his wife wants to eat it, but Babe has other ideas.

Black Beauty. Sewall, Anna. A classic horse story about Black Beauty, who leaves the farm where he grew up and discovers the cruelty of humans.

🎧 *Christmas Carol, A.* Dickens, Charles. The famous tale about how cold, hard Scrooge learns that life is not all about money.

Dante's Peak. Gram, Dewey. A scientist who studies volcanoes goes to a small town where a volcano is about to explode.

Fly Away Home. Hermes, Patricia. Amy finds some goose eggs, but no mother, and so the baby geese think she is their mother. Can she teach them to fly south in the winter?

Freckles. Matthews, Andrew. Susie hates her freckles. Her best friend Donna doesn't have any. Then a new boy comes to school, and both Susie and Donna are interested.

Ghost of Genny Castle, The. Escott, John. Claire is staying near an old castle with a secret—accidents happen there: Animals and people die.

🎧 *Gulliver's Travels.* Swift, Jonathan. In this classic tale, Gulliver has adventures in a fantastic country of very small people.

🎧 *Jaws.* Benchley, Peter. At a quiet seaside town, a woman is killed in the water at night. The town policeman thinks it's a killer shark.

Jurassic Park III. Ciencin, Scott. Young Eric Kirby is in Jurassic Park with live, dangerous dinosaurs, and Dr. Alan Grant must save him.

🎧 *Kidnapped* Stevenson, Robert Louis. An adventure story about an orphan boy who is put on a ship to America by his evil uncle.

Lady in the Lake, The. Chandler, Raymond. When the body of a woman is found in a lake, Detective Philip Marlowe must discover who killed her.

Last of the Mohicans, The. Cooper, James Fenimore. A classic tale about Indians, British soldiers, and settlers in early America.

Lost in New York. Escott, John. On Nicky's first visit to New York, he finds himself in trouble, and soon the police are looking for him.

Men in Black. Gardner, J.J. In a strange future world, Kay and Jay are the Men in Black who must watch the aliens on Earth.

🎧 *Moby Dick.* Melville, Herman. In this famous story, a young sailor tells about Captain Ahab and his search for the great white whale.

Moonfleet. Falkner, J. Meade. Fifteen-year-old John accidentally finds out some dangerous secrets, and his life changes.

Mr. Bean in Town. Atkinson, Rowan; Clifford, Andrew; Curtis, Richard; Driscoll, Robin. More funny adventures for this man who can never do anything right.

Mummy Returns, The. Whitman, John. The people of Egypt are afraid of the Scorpion King, and someone must kill him.

Mysterious Island, The. Verne, Jules. Three men, a boy, and a dog are in a balloon that comes down over the Pacific.

Of Mice and Men. Steinbeck, John. George has to decide what to do when his friend Lennie gets into trouble.

Persuasion. Austen, Jane. When Anne meets Captain Wentworth again after many years, she still loves him, but she doesn't know if he feels anything for her.

🎧 *Pirates of the Caribbean: The Curse of the Black Pearl.* Trimble, Irene. On a Caribbean island, pirates arrive and show interest in young Elizabeth. Where are they from, and what do they want?

Prince and the Pauper, The. Twain, Mark. Two boys are born on the same day—one is a prince, and one is very poor. Then they change places in a game.

Project Omega. O'Reilly, Elaine. Julia wants to find her father, who has disappeared, but someone is trying to kill her.

🎧 *Robinson Crusoe.* Defoe, Daniel. The classic tale of a man who is shipwrecked on an island.

Scarlet Letter, The. Hawthorne, Nathaniel. Young Hester Prynne has a baby in seventeenth-century Boston, but she won't say who the father is.

Simply Suspense. Aumonier, Stacy; Burrage, Alfred; Stockton, Frank. Three exciting short stories about dangerous people and places.

Stranger than Fiction Urban Myths. Healey, Phil; Glanvill, Rick. A man falls from a very tall building, but he doesn't die. Why not? Read about this and other strange stories.

🎧 *Three Musketeers, The.* Dumas, Alexandre. D'Artagnan and his friends go to fight for the king and their country against the dangerous Cardinal.

Three Short Stories of Sherlock Holmes. Doyle, Arthur Conan. Three of the classic Sherlock Holmes detective stories.

Walkabout. Marshall, James V. The story of an Aboriginal boy and two American children in the Australian desert.

Wave, The. Rhue, Morton. Mr. Ross wants to teach his history class about the Nazis, so he starts an activity called "The Wave." At first, the students love it, but then it becomes dangerous.

Whistle and the Dead Men's Eyes, The. James, M.R. Two men are on vacation. Strange things happen in the hotel. People see things that aren't there, and there are noises in empty rooms.

White Fang. London, Jack. Half dog, half wolf, White Fang is taken from the mountains to the world of men, where he learns to fight and kill.

Readers: Nonfiction

Amazon Rainforest, The. Smith, Bernard. This forest is important for the world's weather and wildlife, but it is disappearing fast.

🎧 *Apollo* 13. Anastasio, Dina. The story of the excitement, difficulties, and glory of the first moonwalk in 1970.

Audrey Hepburn. Rice, Chris. Everyone loved this beautiful and successful actress, but her life was not always happy.

🎧 *Extreme Sports.* Dean, Michael. There are many new, exciting, and dangerous sports—what are they, and who does them?

Gandhi. Rolleson, Jane. Mahatma Gandhi worked for civil rights and led India to independence. In his time and today, many people follow his ideas.

🎧 *Nelson Mandela.* Degnan-Veness, Colleen. This is the story of a freedom fighter and one of the world's great leaders.

🎧 *Water for Life.* Smith, Bernard. We drink it, wash with it, cook with it. In some countries, people waste it; in other countries, they can't get enough.

List B: Books Written for Native Speakers of English

Easier Fiction

🎧 *Birchbark House.* Erdrich, Louise. The story of an Ojibwa (Native American Indian) girl in 1847 who lives through disease and difficulties. (256 pages)

🎧 *Children of the River.* Crew, Linda. A girl from Cambodia wants to fit in at her American high school, but she also doesn't want to go against her family. (213 pages).

Chocolate War, The. Cormier, Robert. A classic story of a high school student who becomes the hero of the school when he fights a secret society. (191 pages)

🎧 *Confessions of Charlotte Doyle, The.* Avi. Charlotte is accused of murder in this nineteenth-century tale of action on the high seas. (240 pages)

Esperanza Rising. Ryan, Pam Muñoz. Esperanza's life on a farm in Mexico is happy but suddenly she is forced to escape to the United States. (261 pages)

🎧 *Fallen Angels.* Myers, Walter Dean. A realistic and intense novel about a young African-American soldier in the Vietnam War in 1967. (309 pages)

Gentlehands. Kerr, M.E. A policeman's son falls in love with a rich girl, and they discover an ex-Nazi in her family. (326 pages)

🎧 *Giver, The.* Lowry, Lois. Jonas lives in a future society where there is no pain, crime, or unhappiness. But as Jonas learns, people pay a terrible price for all this. (192 pages)

Hatchet. Paulson, Gary. Brian is on the way to visit his father when his airplane crashes, and Brian finds himself alone in the Canadian wilderness. (195 pages)

Hattie Big Sky. Larsen, Kirby. In 1918, orphaned Hattie goes to Montana to make a life for herself and has to face the terrible prairie winter. (320 pages)

🎧 *Holes.* Sachar, Louis. A dramatic story in which Stanley is punished for a crime he didn't do and is sent to a detention camp for boys. (233 pages)

Homeless Bird. Whelan, Gloria. Married and widowed at the age of thirteen, Koly is caught between modern India and ancient Hindu culture. (192 pages)

How Tia Lola Came to Stay. Alvarez, Julia. At first Miguel and his sister are embarrassed by their aunt from the Dominican Republic, but then she helps them. (112 pages)

🎧 *Island of the Blue Dolphins, The.* O'Dell, Scott. This beautiful book tells the story of a Native American girl left alone for years on an island. (192 pages)

Julie of the Wolves. George, Jean Craig. Julie, an Eskimo girl, is married against her will at thirteen and runs away into the wilderness to live with the wolves. (176 pages)

🎧 *Last Shot: A Final Four Mystery.* Feinstein, John. Stevie and Susan discover that someone wants to fix the college basketball championships. (256 pages)

🎧 *Lion, the Witch, and the Wardrobe, The.* Lewis, C.S. The classic series about four children who travel through a wardrobe to another world. (206 pages)

No Turning Back. Naidoo, Beverly. A boy in South Africa runs away to the city and lives on the streets. (189 pages)

Pigman, The. Zindel, Paul. Funny and serious, moving and perceptive, this is a classic story about two young people's search for meaning in life. (192 pages)

🎧 *Princess Diaries, The.* Cabot, Meg. A high-school student in New York City, Mia, finds out that her father is really a European prince. (304 pages)

🎧 *Radiance Descending.* Fox, Paula. Having a younger brother with Down's Syndrome is not easy for Paul. (112 pages)

Roll of Thunder, Hear My Cry. Taylor, Mildred. An African-American family tries to keep their land and their dignity in 1930s Georgia. (288 pages)

SOS Titanic. Bunting, Eve. A young Irishman on the *Titanic* tries to rescue his friends as the ship sinks into the cold sea. (246 pages)

🎧 *Stormbreaker: An Alex Rider Adventure.* Horowitz, Anthony. In this spy thriller series, Alex finds out that his dead uncle was a spy. (192 pages)

Summer of My German Soldier, The. Greene, Bette. During World War II, an American Jewish girl falls in love with a German prisoner of war. (199 pages)

🎧 *Witch of Blackbird Pond, The.* Speare, Elizabeth George. In 1687, the Puritans in Connecticut think Kit is a witch when she moves there from the Caribbean. (256 pages)

🎧 *Wrinkle in Time, A.* L'Engle, Madeleine. Meg's father mysteriously disappears after experimenting with time travel. A classic. (217 pages)

Easier Nonfiction

Boy. Dahl, Roald. The funny and shocking childhood and school experiences of this famous English writer. (176 pages)

Chimpanzees I Love: Saving Their World and Ours, The. Goodall, Jane. The world-famous expert tells of her experiences with chimpanzees. (268 pages)

Escape: The Story of the Great Houdini. Fleischman, Sid. The rags-to-riches story of a poor Jewish boy who became a great magician and escape artist. (210 pages)

Go Ask Alice. Anonymous. The real diary of a fifteen-year-old girl who became addicted to drugs. (188 pages)

Helen Keller: From Tragedy to Triumph. Wilkie, Katherine E. Blind and deaf since she was a girl, Helen learned to communicate and became famous. (192 pages)

Immigrant Kids. Freedman, Russell. For immigrant children, America has meant freedom, but it has also meant hard work and horrible conditions. (80 pages)

It Happened to Nancy: By an Anonymous Teenager, A True Story From Her Diary. Sparks, Beatrice. The true story of a teenager who thought she had found love, but instead found AIDS. (238 pages)

J.R.R. Tolkien: The Man Who Created The Lord of the Rings. Coren, Michael. The fascinating and entertaining life of Tolkien. (125 pages)

Leonardo's Horse. Fritz, Jean. The life and times of Leonardo da Vinci and the story of a sculpture that he never made. (127 pages)

Pelé. Buckley, James. This is the story of the childhood and worldwide success of this famous Brazilian soccer player. (128 pages)

Promises to Keep: How Jackie Robinson Changed America. Robinson, Sharon. The author shares her memories of her father—the first African-American to become a famous baseball player. (64 pages)

Red Scarf Girl. Jiang, Ji-Li. This Chinese writer tells about her difficult childhood in China during the Cultural Revolution. (285 pages)

Rosa Parks: My Story. Parks, Rosa; Haskins, Jim. Rosa Parks tells of her life and her role in the civil rights movement in 1950s America. (188 pages)

🎧 *Sacagawea.* Bruchac, Joseph. This is the story of the young American Indian woman who helped Lewis and Clark find a way to the Pacific Ocean. (259 pages)

Team Moon: How 400,000 People Landed Apollo 11 on the Moon. Thimmesh, Catherine. A behind-the-scenes account of the people who made it possible to put a man on the moon. (80 pages)

Upstairs Room, The. Johanna Reiss. The story of two Jewish sisters who were hidden by a Dutch family for two years during World War II. (196 pages)

More Difficult Fiction

🎧 *Alfred Kropp.* Yancy, Rick. Young Alfred finds himself in a world of action and adventure in this thrilling and entertaining series. (368 pages)

Code Orange. Cooney, Caroline. When a New York teenager discovers a 100-year-old sample of smallpox, he and his friends are in danger. (208 pages)

🎧 *Code Talking.* Bruchac, Joseph. A novel about the Navaho Indians who joined the Marines during World War II and how they sent messages in their language to help America win the war. (240 pages)

🎧 *Countess Below Stairs, A.* Ibbotson, Eva. After the Russian Revolution, a beautiful young countess has to leave Russia and work as a servant in England. (400 pages)

Double Helix. Werlin, Nancy. A suspenseful novel about love and the genetic engineering experiments of Dr. Wyatt. (252 pages)

🎧 *Harry Potter and the Sorcerer's Stone (Original UK title: Harry Potter and the Philosopher's Stone).* Rowling, J.K. In these famous adventures, Harry discovers that he's a wizard. (312 pages)

Hitchhiker's Guide to the Galaxy, A. Adams, Douglas. This book is science fiction, fantasy, and lots of fun—a best-seller for many years. (224 pages)

House on Mango Street, The. Cisneros, Sandra. Young Esperanza learns to make a happy life in a poor Hispanic neighborhood in Chicago. (110 pages)

I Know What You Did Last Summer. Duncan, Lois. A horror story full of suspense about a group of young people and their secret. (198 pages)

🎧 *Kira-kira.* Kadohata, Cynthia. A Japanese-American family moves to Georgia in the 1950s, and young Katie has to deal with discrimination and death. (272 pages)

🎧 *Lavinia.* LeGuin, Ursula. This famous writer of science fiction has recreated the world before ancient Rome in a dramatic tale of passion and war. (299 pages)

Lord of the Flies. Golding, William. A classic. A group of English schoolboys find themselves alone on an island after their plane crashes into the sea. (208 pages)

Man from the Other Side, The. Orlev, Uri. In 1943 in Warsaw, Poland, a young man with anti-Jewish feelings discovers that his dead father was Jewish. (192 pages)

🎧 *Monster (Amistad).* Myers, Walter Dean. In this tense story, sixteen-year-old Steve tells about his trial for murder and his life until then. (288 pages)

Outsiders, The. Hinton, S.E. An intensely realistic and dark tale about youth gangs, written when the author was sixteen years old. A classic. (208 pages)

Perks of Being a Wallflower, The. Chbosky, Stephen. Brilliant but terribly shy, Charlie tells of his day-to-day life and dramas. (224 pages)

🎧 *Redheaded Princess, The.* Rinaldi, Anne. The dramatic story of the beautiful young princess who became Queen Elizabeth I. (224 pages)

🎧 *Silent to the Bone.* Konigsburg, E.L. Connor wants to find out what really happened to his best friend's sister and why his friend will no longer talk. (272 pages)

Single Shard, A. Parks, Linda Sue. An orphan boy grows up and overcomes great difficulties in twelfth-century Korea. (192 pages)

🎧 *Sisterhood of the Traveling Pants, The.* Brashares, Ann. Four teenage friends find a pair of magical jeans that they share over a summer. (336 pages)

Speak. Anderson, Laurie Halse. Why is Melinda no longer speaking to anyone? It's not because of the usual problems at home or at school. (208 pages)

Tamar: A Novel of Espionage, Passion, and Betrayal. Peet, Mal. A story of suspense and passion in Nazi-occupied Holland during World War II. (432 pages)

Uglies, The. Westerfield, Scott. This first book in a trilogy tells of a future world where everyone becomes beautiful at the age of sixteen. (432 pages)

🎧 *Whirligig.* Fleischman, Paul. Teenage Brent has to learn to live with the terrible consequences of his actions. (144 pages)

🎧 *Witness.* Hesse, Karen. When the Ku Klux Klan arrives in a small town in Vermont, the people in the town react in many different ways. (288 pages)

More Difficult Nonfiction

Alive: The Story of the Andes Survivors. Read, Piers Paul. The dramatic story of sixteen people who survived a plane crash in the Andes. (398 pages)

Diary of a Young Girl, The. Frank, Anne. This well-known book tells the true story of a Jewish girl hiding from the Nazis in World War II Holland. (368 pages)

🎧 *Legend of Bass Reeves, The.* Paulsen, Gary. The true story of an escaped slave who lived with Indians and then became a successful rancher. (160 pages)

Letters to a Young Brother: Manifest Your Destiny. Harper, Hill. A young black American writer tells his own story and answers letters from other young men. (192 pages)

Marley: A Dog Like No Other. Grogan, John. As a family dog, Marley is ninety pounds of trouble, fun, and love. (208 pages)

🎧 *Night.* Wiesel, Elie. Taken from his Hungarian village as a boy, the author survived the Nazi death camps. This book asks fundamental questions about life and faith. A masterpiece. (120 pages)

One Kingdom: Our Lives with Animals. Noyes, Deborah. The author looks at the ways animals and humans have connected throughout history. (144 pages)

Only the Names Remain: The Cherokees and the Trail of Tears. Bealer, Alex W. The sad history of the Cherokees from the sixteenth century to their removal from Georgia in 1837. (80 pages)

Perilous Journey of the Donner Party, The. Calabro, Marian. In 1846, ninety people travelling to California were trapped for the winter—only a few survived. (192 pages)

Phineas Gage: A Gruesome But True Story about Brain Science. Fleischman, John. After an iron rod went through his brain in 1848, Phineas Gage lived for eleven years. (96 pages)

Poet Slave of Cuba: A Biography of Juan Francisco Manzano, The. Engle, Margarita; Qialls, Sean. This biography tells of the suffering and the talent of a nineteenth-century Cuban poet. (192 pages)

Shipwreck at the Bottom of the World: The Extraordinary True Story of Shackleton and the Endurance. Armstrong, Jennifer. In 1914, the ship *Endurance* was trapped in the Antarctic ice. This is the story of the remarkable survival and rescue. (144 pages)

Something Out of Nothing: Marie Curie and Radium. McClafferty, Carla Killough. Curie's life and work as a scientist and as an independent woman. (144 pages)

Zlata's Diary: A Child's Life in Wartime Sarajevo. Filipovish, Zlata. Ten-year-old Zlata tells about the bombings and hardship of life in Sarajevo. (208 pages)

WHEN SHOULD STUDENTS READ EXTENSIVELY?

Teachers should encourage students to read their books every day in many different settings.

- **In Class.** Class time can be regularly scheduled for silent reading. Many students have never developed the habit of just sitting still and reading. When class time is set aside for extensive reading, students recognize that the teacher considers it a meaningful activity, and they begin to take it more seriously. Teachers should plan at least fifteen minutes for reading and should try to join in and read a book, too, especially early in the semester. This provides students with a role model for silent reading. In many schools, Sustained Silent Reading (SSR) is a long-established practice: teachers, students, custodians, office staff, and administrators all stop to read their own books for fifteen to twenty minutes every day. (See Krashen, 1985, for a summary of research on SSR.)
- **At Home.** Extensive reading should be a regular, ongoing homework assignment, and students should be instructed to read for at least thirty minutes every day.
- **Around Town.** Encourage students to take their books with them wherever they go. They can read everywhere: on the bus or train, waiting in lines, or waiting at the dentist's office.

HOW TO IMPLEMENT AN EXTENSIVE READING COMPONENT?

Starting an extensive reading component requires some effort at first, but the rewards more than make up for that. Here are some general guidelines for getting started.

"Sell" extensive reading.

Explain to the students what is meant by extensive reading. For example, use the following Sample Rationale:

SAMPLE RATIONALE

Extensive reading will help improve your reading and your English skills. Extensive reading means that you will:

- read many books.
- read books that you choose for yourself.
- read at your own pace.
- not have tests on the books.
- not write long book reports.
- enjoy your reading!

Explain that extensive reading is an important part of the course.

Convince students of the important status of extensive reading in the curriculum. Students need to see extensive reading as an "official" part of the course that is just as important as grammar or vocabulary. This can be accomplished by making extensive reading a part of the basis for grading. For example:

- Award points toward students' grades for the number of books or the number of pages that students read.

- Include extensive reading feedback from students as part of their grade. (Note: See page 32 for tips on how to evaluate extensive reading.)
- If a course has an oral component, give extra credit to students who give presentations about their extensive reading books.

Become a model reader.

Teachers need to show enthusiasm for their own extensive reading and should always bring to class the book(s) that they are currently reading. The teacher can demonstrate their enjoyment of their books by

- reading them in class during the time set aside for extensive reading.
- telling the class about the books, the authors, and the genres.
- giving a short presentation about a book when they have finished reading it. Chances are, one of the students will want to read it, too!

Make books available.

A successful extensive reading component is based on students' access to large numbers of books at many reading levels so that the teacher is able to help students select books at their level that they will like. At some schools, the school librarian may be willing to develop a section in the library for ESL/EFL books. In that case, the teacher should be prepared to help with the selection and arrangement of the books. Another possibility is to schedule periodic class trips to local bookshops and libraries. Such outings emphasize the importance of browsing, and they allow students to become acquainted with the wide variety of books available.

However, having a classroom library is even better. Establishing a print environment is essential (Krashen, 1985) because students become accustomed to seeing the books around them and picking them up during free moments. A classroom library makes it much easier for the teacher to guide each student to the appropriate book. The books can be arranged on shelves and labeled according to level of difficulty. Within the levels, the books can be arranged and labeled by genre: fiction (mystery, romance, science fiction, fantasy, intrigue), and nonfiction (by subject). This arrangement itself is a lesson: students learn about the categories of books as they browse among them. (See Bamford, 1984; Nuttall, 1982.)

It may be difficult to imagine starting a classroom library when not a single book is available. One way to begin is to ask friends, relatives, and other teachers to contribute books they no longer need. Students, too, can be encouraged to buy books and to donate them to the class library after they have finished reading them. In some cities, the public library has book sales that offer used paperbacks at a very reasonable price. A school budget might include a small amount for books. After a few semesters, the number of books in the classroom library grows rapidly.

Help students develop the habit of daily reading.

Like any other new habit, including reading in their daily lives may not be easy for many students, especially with the attractions of TV and computer games. Teachers can help, in the form of motivation and monitoring. The following monitoring techniques have been useful in many classes:

- Students can be given a chart on which they can keep a record of their reading: title of book, author, date, number of pages read, and length of time spent reading.
- Students can be required to bring their books and progress charts to class on a regular basis, and the teacher can determine students' progress. This takes just a couple of minutes if the students place their charts on their desks while the teacher walks around and glances at them, making appropriate comments as needed.

- About once a week, the teacher can ask if anyone in the class has completed a book. A few words of praise for those who have finished their books can be a powerful incentive to others. The teacher might ask these students a few gently posed questions such as: What is the title of your book? Who is the author? Did you like the book? Is it fiction or nonfiction? How many pages are in the book?

- Occasionally, without warning, the teacher can ask each student to report orally on the title of their book and the number of pages they have read so far. This practice helps ensure that students are keeping up with their reading, but it could embarrass some students. Therefore, the teacher's judgment is vital in deciding whether this is an appropriate technique for a particular class.

In addition to monitoring students' progress, teachers can motivate students with book-centered activities in class. These can include the following:

- At the beginning of the semester, instruct the students to write out their goal of how many books (or how many pages) they will try to complete. Then have the students keep a list of the books that they read, including the number of pages and the date completed. As their lists grow longer, the students feel a sense of accomplishment and this motivates them to read more.

- After a book conference or other evaluation activity, ask the student about what they plan to read next and be prepared to make one or two specific suggestions based on their previous reading and interests. This is when it is really helpful to have a classroom library because the teacher can show the student several books right then and there.

- Give "book talks." Read a book that is at the students' general level and present it to the class. In the book talk, show the book and give students information about the genre, author, and number of pages. Then summarize the beginning of the plot. Read one or two short passages that will entice students to consider reading the book.

- If possible, take students to the library and to local bookstores to find books from the Suggested Books list (on pages 24–29) or a book by an author they have already enjoyed reading. Teach students to preview possible extensive reading books by reading the front and back covers of the book, looking at the titles of chapters (if they have chapters) and reading the first page or two. Assign them the task of writing down the titles, authors, and brief notes about three books that they have previewed. Back in class, have students form small groups and tell each other about the books they noticed.

Evaluate extensive reading in a nonthreatening way.

Sometimes teachers are reluctant to allow students to read individually selected books because they think that it might be impossible to monitor and evaluate their students' reading. When all the students in the class read the same book, a teacher may feel a sense of control because she will also read the book and then it is quite a simple matter to test the students' understanding of the book. However, it is clear that selecting a book that every student can read easily and enjoy is probably impossible.

The evaluation of extensive reading needs to match its goal: students reading a lot for pleasure. This means that it is counterproductive to give tests or assign long, formal written book reports that lead a student to dread finishing a book. There are numerous ways to keep the students accountable for their reading and to reward their progress, including a combination of book conferences, peer book conferences, short reader response forms, book presentations, short dramatic readings of a few especially meaningful pages, illustrated "advertisements" for a book, and reading circles. These activities are described below.

Book Conferences

Book conferences are a pleasant and productive way to evaluate a student's extensive reading. A book conference is a one-on-one conversation about a book that the student has read and that the teacher may or may not have read. In school, the student is rarely the knowledgeable participant in an exchange of information with the teacher. A book conference offers an opportunity for the student to play that role. The student's and the teacher's awareness of this information gap in the book conference empowers the student, encourages the student to take risks, and keeps him or her talking! As Bamford has remarked, "These (yes, time-consuming) individual meetings with students to talk about their reading can be, at their best, a joyous thing. And they'll always help you better understand a student's attitude to reading" (www.extensivereading.net/discussion group Sept. 10, 2008).

Keep in mind that the students must *not* view book conferences as oral tests on their books. In fact, during the conference the teacher should refrain from taking notes that might appear to be an evaluation. The teacher should make sure that the student sees the teacher write his or her name, the title of the book, the author, and the date to ensure that the student recognizes that the book conference, even though informal, really "counts" as school work.

During a book conference, the teacher has an opportunity to model a native speaker's way of discussing books and to demonstrate cultural attitudes toward print that many native speakers of English take for granted as "natural." In fact, we are all socialized into cultural ways of discussing books, and the teacher can provide "scaffolding" for the student who is learning new ways of thinking and talking about a book. By carefully including a variety of elaborative questions such as those in the box on page 34, the teacher provides new avenues of thought that students can adopt and apply in reading their next books. It is important to remember that the questions are suggestions for the teacher; they should never be handed to the student as a quiz!

Obviously, the teacher does not ask all of these types of questions at every conference. The format of a book conference is conversational, and informality is essential. After two or three questions, the discussion usually takes on a life of its own, and the teacher may find that many of the elaborative questions arise naturally in the course of the conversation.

```
┌──────────────────────────────────────────────────────────────────────────┐
│                  TYPES OF QUESTIONS FOR BOOK CONFERENCES                    │
│                                                                            │
│   Expressive      Did you like the book? Why or why not?                    │
│                                                                            │
│   Factual         Who is/are the main character(s)? When does the story take│
│                   place?                                                    │
│                                                                            │
│   Experiential    Has anything like that ever happened to you?             │
│                                                                            │
│   Affective       How did that make you feel?                              │
│                                                                            │
│   Relational      Is something like this possible in your country (or       │
│                   neighborhood)?                                            │
│                                                                            │
│   Critical        Do you think that this could really happen?             │
│                                                                            │
│   Predictive      What do you think will happen next?                      │
│                                                                            │
│   Stylistic       Do the characters seem real?                             │
│                                                                            │
│   Sequential      What happened after that?                               │
│                                                                            │
│   Cause/Effect    What made a character decide to do something?           │
│                                                                            │
│   Summarizing     Can you retell the story (or important ideas) in just a few│
│                   sentences?                                                │
│                                                                            │
│   Inferential     Why do you think that the character did that?           │
└──────────────────────────────────────────────────────────────────────────┘
```

A practical objection to employing book conferences is the time factor. How can a teacher find the time to spend anywhere from ten to thirty minutes with each student several times during the term? This requires some juggling, and the solution will be local, depending on the type of program and the space available. Teachers have found a variety of ways to meet this challenge. For example, a student can be taken out of the class for a book conference while the rest of the students are engaged in extensive reading or are working on reading skills lessons in pairs or small groups. Another way is to make appointments just before or just after class, or during office hours, if that is a part of the program schedule. However, the benefits of book conferences far outweigh their logistical challenges. Besides the opportunity they provide for students to learn new ways of thinking about and discussing books, there are many other possible outcomes.

> ## SOME BENEFITS OF TEACHER-STUDENT BOOK CONFERENCES
>
> - The teacher and the student get to know each other better. Teachers have reported that their conferences with some of their quiet students caused them to revise their estimation of the students' abilities.
> - The teacher learns more about the student's attitude toward reading.
> - The student has the opportunity to relate school reading to his or her own life and past experience.
> - The teacher can suggest other books that the student might enjoy.
> - The student might suggest some other books that the teacher might enjoy!
> - The student speaks in English about something on which he or she is the expert, and for second language learners, that is highly motivating.
> - The conference gives the reading of books an important status and encourages students to read more.
> - Shy students who do not like to speak in front of the class have a chance to speak.
> - Students have an occasion to speak their mind. Quite often, the conversation strays off the actual topic of the book, and students are able to express feelings about important, sometimes personal, issues.
> - Students from cultures that do not encourage reading alone, but rather encourage group interpretation, will have the opportunity to display skills in interactive interpretation in which they may excel.
> - Students love these conferences.

Peer Conferences

If the goal is to give the students a maximum number of opportunities to talk in literate ways about their reading, two or three book conferences with the teacher are a good start. But certainly students can benefit from more practice. Besides, they should have an opportunity to play both roles in a book conference, not only responding to but also generating questions. Peer conferences can provide these opportunities. (Manning & Manning, 1984, cited in Krashen, 1985.)

It is important that students learn to ask elaborative questions when they participate in a peer conference. However, it would be inappropriate for the teacher to provide a list of written questions for peer work because the conference would not flow naturally and, in fact, it might feel like a test. Besides, one of the objectives of the peer conference is to give the students opportunities to learn how to formulate and to ask literate questions.

There are several ways to train students to make sure that peer conferences result in literate discussions of books.

1. Students can learn from a model book conference. Early in the semester, the teacher can present a tape recording or a video tape of a model book conference. Students can be instructed to take notes of the kinds of questions that come up during the model conference. The students can review the tape as many times as necessary in order to write down some of the questions they might want to use. (As part of a literacy project in a California elementary school, Heath produced a videotape called "Inside Learners" (Hoffman & Heath, 1986), which shows fifth-grade girls reading books to first-graders and asking elaborative questions.)

2. The students can tape-record, listen to, and analyze their own book conferences with the teacher, once again taking note of the questions that the teacher asked.

3. Students can tape-record their peer conferences and then analyze the discussion in order to find out what kinds of questions they asked and what they wish that they had included in the conference. (These tapes should be guaranteed "private and confidential.") Students can report the results of their analysis orally to you or to the whole class or they can write up a report. In every case, the language will be about the literate skills that they are developing, and this in turn leads to an enhancement of their metalinguistic awareness.

Book Response Forms

Students can fill in a book response form after they finish reading a book. The form on page 37 is taken from *Advanced Reading Power* (2007), page 24, and a version of this form has been used by teachers in many different ESL/EFL programs. Such forms, of course, should not be graded, nor should they be completed in conjunction with the book conference. The response forms are useful in several ways. Teachers can read them to look for ideas about which books to recommend to other students. In some programs, the completed forms are kept in a loose-leaf notebook that is available for all the students to use as a resource when they are looking for their next extensive reading book. Finally, filling in the form serves as an additional lesson for the students. As they fill it in, students learn to think objectively about their books, and this practice will help them to write book reviews when they are assigned in the future.

Book Presentations

Book presentations can be handled in several ways. One type of book presentation is a brief (about five minutes) informal oral report to the class about a book that the student has finished reading. Students will need careful directions to ensure that they are successful in making the presentation. They should be instructed to practice their talk ahead of time and to prepare several 3″ x 5″ note cards to guide them as they speak. On the cards, students should write:

1. Title, author, year first published, and some background facts about the author.
2. A brief summary of the plot in a book of fiction; a brief summary of the topic and main ideas in a nonfiction book.
3. The student's reaction to the book. Did he or she like the book? Why or why not?
4. Difficulty: What made the book difficult to read? Or easy to read?
5. One or two of the following topics:
   —An interesting part of the book or an interesting character
   —Personal experiences or thoughts that are related to the book
   —Larger issues that the book addresses (e.g., poverty, justice, love, or war)

Students who are listening to a book presentation also need coaching. This is a chance for them to practice forming elaborative questions such as those mentioned in the section on book conferences. After the presentation, several students should be called on to ask the presenter a question.

Another form of the book presentation is the rehearsed, dramatic reading of a short passage in the book that is especially meaningful to the student reader (two pages or so). If a student selects this form of presentation, he or she needs the teacher's help in deciding on a passage. The student should tape record his or her rehearsals and listen carefully in order to make improvements. Before beginning the reading, the student should provide the following information: author, title, genre, a brief summary of the plot or main points of the book, and a clear explanation about

Book Response Form

Book title: _____

Author: _____

Publisher: _____

Date published: _____ Number of pages: _____

Genre (Type of book)—Circle one:

    novel   mystery   science fiction   romance   biography

    history   science/technology   other: _____

Why did you decide to read this book?

_____

_____

_____

Were you glad that you decided to read it? Explain.

_____

_____

_____

What did you like best about this book?

_____

_____

_____

What did you like least?

_____

_____

_____

Would you recommend this book to a friend? Explain.

_____

_____

_____

How difficult was this book for you? (1 = easy, 10 = difficult) Why?

_____

_____

_____

why this was a meaningful passage to him or her. After the reading, the students who are listening should be prepared to ask questions.

A third form of book presentation is an illustrated advertisement for a book. Students who are gifted in art or in graphic design on the computer can choose to "sell" the book to his or her classmates. After completing the advertisement, the student presents it to the class along with an introduction that includes a brief summary of the plot or main points of the book and a clear explanation of why this is such a great book.

A reading circle is a small group of four to six students who meet regularly to talk about their extensive reading books and compare reading experiences. At the first meeting of the group, each student introduces his or her book to the group, providing details on title, author, genre, number of pages, predictions about the book, and why he or she chose to read it. These reports should be brief, five minutes or less, and one of the other students in the group should be assigned to time the reports. As one student speaks, the other group members should take notes, and each group member should be required to ask at least one question after the report is completed.

In subsequent, regularly scheduled meetings of the reading circle (about once a week), students give updates on their reading, including the number of pages they have read, their reaction to the book so far, what they especially liked about the book, and any difficulties or problems they had in reading the book. Each group member should read aloud to the group a very short passage (about half a page) that he or she finds surprising, interesting, or especially meaningful.

An alternative form of the reading circle is the reading club. In the reading club, all of the students choose to read the same book. At the first meeting, they talk about why they decided to read the book and share information about the author's background. Then they make predictions about the book and they decide how many pages they will all read before the next meeting. Before subsequent meetings all the club members are required to write several questions about the book to guide the discussion at the meeting. During meetings of the club, students talk about what they have read so far, address one another's questions, and decide how many pages they should read before the next meeting. When the book club has completed the book, they hand in their discussion questions and then prepare a group book presentation or enact a scene from a fiction book for their class.

WHY IS EXTENSIVE READING SO SUCCESSFUL?

Extensive reading for pleasure can transform a classroom into a book-centered, dynamic place. The students will read more, and they will acquire many of the cultural attitudes and values about books that are essential to developing literate skills. When extensive reading is the final item on the class agenda, it is not uncommon, at the end of the hour, for students to say, "I can't leave yet. . . . I just have a few more pages to read."[1]

---

[1] Teachers who would like to find out more about extensive reading should read *Extensive Reading in the Second Language Classroom* by R. Day and J. Bamford, Cambridge University Press, 1998; *The Reading Zone* by N. Atwell, Scholastic, 2007; and visit the Extensive Reading Web site: www.extensivereading.net.

This part of the book is divided into eight sections. Section A discusses reading skills and provides a rationale and suggested methodology for teaching reading comprehension by focusing on specific skills. Each of the remaining sections (B–H) focuses on reading skills that are grouped according to their primary role in reading development.

A | Rationale and Methodology

As explained in Part I, reading is a complex process that is affected by oral language, writing system, cultural literacy practices, learning environment, and individual habits and abilities. Yet, in order to teach reading, the process must be broken down into teachable parts. A commonsense approach is to ask, as McGuinness (2005, p. 216) has suggested, "What are the things a [person] has to be able to do to be a good reader?" The answer will provide guidelines for identifying specific reading skills.

WHAT ARE READING SKILLS?

Reading skills are the cognitive processes that a reader uses in making sense of a text. For good readers, most reading skills are usually employed unconsciously and automatically. For example, good readers subconsciously decode most words in a passage. But when they encounter a challenging text, they apply the necessary skills consciously and strategically in order to comprehend. Poor readers, on the other hand, are unable to monitor their comprehension because they have not developed a repertoire of reading skills. Consequently, they may resort to reading word by word, often failing to comprehend.

A person may be an excellent reader in his native language, but quite often that reading ability will not transfer automatically to English. As mentioned in Part I, every language requires a somewhat different set of reading skills, based on the writing system and structure of the language and the literacy customs and practices of the speakers of that language. Therefore, ESL/EFL teachers need to focus on teaching the skills that will enable their students to comprehend well in English.

In the excellent volume *Learning to Read Across Languages* (2008, p. 98), Koda breaks reading down into general subskills: decoding, orthographic processing, morphological processing, word identification, sentence processing, main idea detection, lexical inference, coherence building, and text-based inference. While these subskills are comprehensive, they are very general statements. In the list that follows, the skills are stated more specifically and this can be more helpful for teachers in making instructional plans.

The reading skills listed on page 40 foster the thinking processes that students need to develop in order to comprehend standard English effectively. Many are probably familiar to anyone who has taught reading (or writing). They are arranged, overall, in order of complexity. That is, in most cases each skill builds on the previous ones on the list. It is not an exhaustive list, and many of the skills overlap.

1. **Automatic decoding.** Being able to recognize a word at a glance.

2. **Previewing and predicting.** Giving a text a quick once-over to be able to guess what is to come.

3. **Specifying purpose.** Knowing why a text is being read.

4. **Identifying genre.** Knowing the nature of the text in order to predict its form and content.

5. **Questioning.** Asking questions about the text in an inner dialogue with the author.

6. **Scanning.** Looking through a text very rapidly for specific information.

7. **Recognizing topics.** Finding out what a text is about.

8. **Classification of ideas into main topics and details.** Categorizing words and ideas on the basis of their relationships; distinguishing general and specific.

9. **Locating topic sentences.** Identifying the general statement in a paragraph.

10. **Stating the main idea (or thesis).** Being able to state the main idea of a sentence, paragraph or passage. Knowing the author's general point about a topic.

11. **Recognizing patterns of relationships.** Identifying the relationships between ideas; recognizing the overall structure of a text.

12. **Identifying and using signal words.** Locating and employing words that signal the patterns of relationships between ideas. Being able to see connections between ideas by the use of words such as *first, then, later*.

13. **Inferring the main idea.** Using patterns and other clues to infer the author's main point about a topic.

14. **Understanding pronouns.** Recognizing and using pronouns, referents, and other lexical equivalents as clues to cohesion.

15. **Guessing the word meaning from context.** Using such clues as word parts, syntax, and relationship patterns to figure out the meaning of unknown words.

16. **Skimming.** Quickly getting the gist or overview of a passage or a book.

17. **Paraphrasing.** Restating the content of a text in the reader's own words in order to monitor comprehension.

18. **Summarizing.** Shortening material by retaining and restating main ideas and leaving out details.

19. **Drawing conclusions.** Putting together information from parts of a text and inducing new or additional ideas.

20. **Drawing inferences and using evidence.** Using evidence in a text to grasp facts or ideas that are unstated.

21. **Visualizing.** Picturing or actually drawing a picture or diagram of what is described in a text.

22. **Reading critically.** Judging the accuracy of a passage with respect to what the reader already knows; distinguishing fact from opinion.

23. **Reading faster.** Reading fast enough to allow the brain to process the input as ideas rather than single words.

24. **Adjusting reading rate according to materials and purpose.** Being able to choose the speed and strategies needed for the level of comprehension desired by the reader.

For instructional planning, it is useful to recognize that some skills implement the top-down processing mode, some activate the bottom-up mode, and others enhance the interaction of the two. (Refer to Part I (pages 9–11) for a discussion of these modes.) The sample exercises in this book have been grouped accordingly. In reality, a reader never totally employs only a single mode of processing.

Researchers have found that second language proficiency and background knowledge about the reading topic are two factors that influence which mode the reader relies on most heavily. As one would imagine, and as Coady's model (1979, p. 8) illustrates, the less linguistic ability a reader has, the more likely he or she is to be concerned with the elements of the text, such as words and phrases that might trigger some level of comprehension (bottom-up). On the other hand, readers who are fluent in a language can use much more of their processing time in making connections between the text and what they already know (top-down). (See also Stanovich, 1980.)

FOCUSING ON SPECIFIC SKILLS

The approach taken in this book is to present single skills as units of instruction, with each skill as the focus of a series of lessons. Students first need to learn and master a skill before they practice applying it (Alderson, 1984). Once students have mastered a skill, intensive reading lessons can be planned for practice in applying that skill and all previously learned skills. (Suggested Intensive Reading Lessons have been inserted in appropriate places throughout Sections B–H.)

There has been some disagreement among reading specialists about the value of breaking reading comprehension into subskills and working on the skills individually. Some reading professionals have argued that reading is a whole skill, impossible to break down (e.g., Thorndike, 1974). In response, one can imagine an analogy between reading and playing a sport, say tennis, for example. Tennis learners do not play game after game in order to learn: the tennis coach first teaches various ways of standing, holding the tennis racket, and serving or returning the ball. Interspersed with the lessons on specific tennis skills are practice games in which the tennis learner tries out the skills already learned. Similarly, research has shown that it is possible to divide reading into a series of subprocesses (Koda, 2008; Collins & Smith, 1980; Schank & Abelson, 1977) and that the language learner can develop the ability to apply the skills for comprehending a text (Palinscar & Brown, 1985).

Recent research on brain-based learning supports this approach. Thanks to advances in technology, there has been a tremendous expansion of knowledge about the brain and how it works during reading and learning. These advances have led to the notion of "brain-compatible learning" as described and explained in *Teaching with the Brain in Mind* (Jensen, 2005).

In order to base their teaching on how the brain actually works, Jensen (2005) believes that teachers need to become familiar with the brain's components and processes. He explains that the brain contains approximately 100 billion neuron cells—the brain cells that are activated by new information. Each neuron cell has a "tail-like extension called an axon and branch-like structures called dendrites" (Jensen, p. 17). These small extensions reach out to the dendrites of nearby neurons when learning is taking place. The point of contact between two neurons is called the synapse. According to Jensen and others, learning is a chemical and electrical process within the brain, and the networks of cells in the brain are built and altered by what is learned.

> When learning occurs, specific neurons connect and form a "junction box" at the synapse. When we say cells "connect" with other cells, we really mean that they are in such close proximity that the synapse is easily, almost effortlessly, "used" over and over again; the cells have changed their receptivity to messages based on previous stimulation and have "learned.". . . An individual cell may be connected, through synapses, to tens of thousands of other cells. At the simplest level, learning may seem microscopic, but each neuron plays its part in larger assemblies of cell networks. (Jensen, p. 18)

Jensen explains that each time the same information is sensed, the same network of neurons is activated. "Each future event requires less work to activate the same memory network" (Jensen, p. 16). In other words, the synapses are strengthened with each repetition, and eventually the network is so well established that the knowledge is automatically accessed by the learner. Knowing your name and knowing how to tie your shoes are examples of automatically accessed knowledge.

At the same time, it is important to remember that the physical connections (synapses) in the brain need timely repetition to develop and to continue to exist. When the brain receives input of the same information only sporadically or when the brain receives contradictory information, the synapses do not strengthen and learning does not occur. (For a complete, teacher friendly discussion, see Jensen, 2005.)

In light of this knowledge about how the brain works, it is clear that a series of lessons that focuses on a specific skill provides the brain with the repeated input necessary for building the strong connections required for learning to occur. Occasional practice in a skill does not provide the same opportunities for developing the neural networks.

Some may question whether training on specific skills transfers beyond the exercises used in the training. Research has shown that it does. In fact, as early as 1985, Palinscar and Brown showed that students can be trained in specific reading comprehension skills in a way that will enable them to transfer these skills to new reading situations. In discussing that research, Brown, Armbruster, and Baker (1986, p.72) pointed to some possible reasons for the success of the Palinscar and Brown studies:

- Training was extensive. Students received approximately 20 days of instruction.
- The trained activities were well specified theoretically and well established empirically as particular problems for poor readers.
- The training was tailored to the needs of these students (good decoders but passive comprehenders).
- The skills could be expected to be trans-situational (useful in many situations).
- A great deal of attention was paid to "metacognitive" variables: students were informed of the importance, generality, and utility of the activities.
- The reciprocal teaching mode permitted extensive [teacher] modeling in a reasonably natural setting and forced the students to participate so that teachers could evaluate current states and provide appropriate feedback and assistance.
- Every attempt was made to increase the students' sense of personal efficacy; they plotted success, planned strategies, monitored progress, and were shown to be competent and in control.

Although Palinscar and Brown were working with first language readers, their principles can be applied to reading in a second language as well. In fact, their approach is very similar to the one described throughout this book. As Hudson (1980) remarked, "It may be that the process of learning to read a second language is partially a matter of first experiencing skills and strategies as usable, and then abstracting principles for successful reading" (p. 20).

Reading Skills as the Basis of Lessons

Most educators would agree that what students do during a class is what they learn. So, for example, in ESL/EFL classes in which reading is taught using a strictly content-based approach, students work on texts that are followed by a variety of exercises that might include applying one or two relevant reading skills, vocabulary development, grammar use, writing, speaking, and listening. In such situations, reading skills are not the focus; the lessons focus on the content and the language of the passage. As asserted by Alderson and Urquart (1984), "Such a pedagogic practice—of focusing on the language of a text—may be justified as a language lesson, but it may very well be counterproductive as a reading lesson" (p. 246). When students read a passage or a story and then discuss its content or when they learn the vocabulary or grammatical structures found in a story, they may apply the reading skills they already know, but it is unlikely that they will learn new ones. After a reading class, students can say, "Today's lesson was about earthquakes (or fast-food restaurants, or dating practices of American teenagers)" or they can say, "Today we learned how to preview (or how to adjust our reading rate or how to identify the organization of an essay)."

While content is a familiar focus in a language class, reading processes and deliberate thinking about thinking processes are often new ideas for many students of English. They may not be accustomed to the concept of reading as thinking. In a study of reading processes that involved Russian university students reading in Russian and in English, the subjects remarked that one of the main things they learned from participating in the study was that "they think when they read!" (Mikulecky, 1991, p. 49). Furthermore, although the teacher may be conscious of both the content and the process involved in a lesson, it is not necessarily the case that the students will possess this awareness, unless it is made explicit.

Ironically, ESL/EFL teachers work very hard to design lessons that allow language learning to flow from the content of their lessons without the students' conscious awareness that they are actually doing, for example, a lesson on the present progressive tense. But for teaching reading/thinking skills, the opposite approach must be taken: the process of comprehending should be the explicit object of the lesson. Of course, the ultimate objective is for students to develop the ability to read and understand a text through automatic and/or strategic application of the skills. But skill instruction highlights the analytical thinking processes that the reader needs to use to understand a text in English.

Cognition and Metacognition

In the late 1970s, cognitive skills and metacognition were a major focus of research in cognitive psychology (Flavell & Wellman, 1977; Meyer, 1977). Cognitive skills are the thinking skills that the reader employs in making sense of a passage; reading skills are examples of cognitive skills. Research, mostly with first language speakers, has shown that students of all ages learn new skills and strategic thinking processes best when they are consciously aware of what they are doing and what their purpose is for doing it (Brown, Armbruster, & Baker, 1986, p. 74).

This means that reading skills lessons should not be taught as "recipes" or as rote exercises. Students should be made aware of the rationale for what they are learning and doing. According to Brown, Armbruster, and Baker (1986), "Providing the rationale for each component strategy leads to an understanding of the significance of those activities, and this awareness contributes to continued unprompted use" (p. 68). In other words, once they are conscious of the skills and how to use them, students can learn to monitor their own comprehension and apply appropriate skills strategically as needed in order to make sense of a text. And that is what is meant by metacognition: thinking about thinking.

According to McNeil (1987), "Metacognition transcends cognition by enabling individuals not just to use particular strategies, but to be aware of the importance of these strategies and how to appraise them. Metacognition emphasizes broad control processes rather than highly specific task strategies" (p. 91).

McNeil (1987, p. 68) describes three types of metacognitive processes:

- Self-knowledge—knowing one's own reading strengths and weaknesses.
- Task knowledge—knowing which strategies to use in a given situation.
- Self-monitoring—being aware of when one does not understand and knowing which strategies to use to deal with it (e.g., rereading or reading ahead).

When students work on reading skills lessons, they develop these three aspects of metacognition. As specific skills are mastered, intensive reading lessons (using selections from a reader, a newspaper, or a magazine) can provide additional practice in applying the reading skills strategically, monitoring comprehension, and deciding what to do when comprehension breaks down. Once students have learned to use specific skills, they can learn to decide which ones to apply to make sense of a passage.

TEACHING INTERACTIVE, SKILL-FOCUSED LESSONS

A list of reading skills is not going to make a difference in and of itself. It is in the approach to teaching the skills that the "magic" occurs: lessons in which students discuss and consciously work on the skills can promote the cognitive and metacognitive behavior necessary for the development of effective reading.

In designing skill-focused reading comprehension lessons, it is best to begin by deciding which reading skills would most benefit the students in the class. Often, the order in which the skills are listed on page 40 proves effective. Then, for each skill the teacher should select or design a sequence of exercises that begins with simple tasks and gradually increases in complexity (Tierney & Cunningham, 1984, p. 640). It is important to remember that when a reading/thinking skill is the focus of the lesson, that skill should be the only challenge. The inclusion of many new vocabulary items, unfamiliar concepts, or difficult grammatical structures in the same lesson usually clouds the issue and overloads the students.

A reading skill lesson should begin by providing opportunities for students to use the skill orally; students will be more able to read (or write) in new ways if they have first learned to speak in new ways (Hoffman & Heath, 1986). The more the students talk about making sense of a text, the more they will learn. Then they can apply these new ways of thinking and talking to their reading and writing. (These ideas are based on an understanding of learning developed by L. S. Vygotsky, whose work is cited in the bibliography; see also Toussaint, Clark, & Clark, 2008.) In fact, outrageous as this may seem, students at the beginning level of learning English could be allowed to use their own language as they work together on English reading skills exercises in order to facilitate the development of the desired cognitive processes.

In addition, students need opportunities to develop a consciousness of themselves as readers in English. This can be accomplished by teaching students to monitor their own progress, using a variety of record-keeping techniques, such as graphs, charts, and lists of books read. These devices also serve as motivating factors, and students usually gain a sense of satisfaction from looking back over the record of their efforts and accomplishments.

Teachers have found that students take a great deal of pride and interest in this approach to reading development. To maintain the focus on skills, it is useful to ask the students to volunteer to name the skills they have already worked on and ask them to give the class an explanation of the skill and a rationale for learning and using it in reading English. Quite often, it is the act of explaining that helps students consolidate their own understanding of a skill and its role in reading.

Working in Pairs and Small Groups

In order to become aware of their own reading/thinking processes, students should work in pairs or small groups on most of the reading skills exercises. Such peer interaction can add interest and enjoyment to their work as well as increase learning. (See Pica, Young, & Doughty 1987; Tierney & Cunningham 1984, p. 640.)

It is not always easy to convince students to work together. For some, it may seem a bit like cheating. For others, there is an assumption that all learning comes from the teacher and that listening to each other is a waste of time. Occasionally, students in a class may come from cultures or nations between which a long history of animosity has existed. It is a real challenge to figure out how to get such students to work together. In fact, the teacher's sensitivity to these factors is a key element in making such collaborative learning successful.

After students have worked together in pairs and small groups and have had a chance to talk about a new skill, they should have opportunities to practice and apply the skill on their own.

Planning Reading Skills Lessons

Recent research on brain-based learning, as discussed by Jensen (2005), has reinforced the approach just described. He recommends planning lessons with the following elements in order to foster skill learning (p. 116):

- Motivation to use the skill.
- Role modeling (a visible, tactile, or audible model).
- Direct instruction or simply an opportunity to acquire the skill.
- Time for trial and error, practice, and debriefing.
- Time to use and strengthen the skill in multiple contexts.

Keeping these features in mind, a general lesson plan that works well in conducting interactive classes on reading skills is included on page 46.

THE IMPORTANCE OF REPEATED PRACTICE

Students who are learning to read in a second or foreign language need more than a cursory introduction to these skills. Sometimes teachers introduce a skill just once and expect students to apply that skill in future reading; they forget that learning new thinking habits and reading skills means restructuring the brain. As explained in earlier parts of this book, students need to practice new skills repeatedly in order to build strong, new mental networks. This means that even though exercises and activities such as cloze exercises, scanning, and reading faster seem self-evident and automatic for the teacher, they must be repeated many times for students to benefit from the lessons and incorporate the new behaviors into their reading practice.

```
┌─────────────────────────────────────────────────────────────────┐
│                        GENERAL LESSON PLAN                        │
│  1. Focus on one reading/thinking skill at a time.               │
│  2. Explain the purpose for doing the exercises and how this     │
│     particular skill is important for effective reading.         │
│  3. Do a sample exercise with the whole class. Model aloud your  │
│     own thinking as you do the exercise.                         │
│  4. Put the students into pairs (whenever possible and           │
│     appropriate) and assign one practice exercise.               │
│  5. When the pairs have completed the exercise, discuss it with  │
│     the whole class. Ask how the students arrived at their       │
│     answers. Encourage friendly disagreement in pairs and in     │
│     the class as a whole. Ask, "What was your thinking as you    │
│     decided on that answer?" This means that if there is an      │
│     answer key, the students learn that they are not             │
│     necessarily "wrong" if they come up with an answer that is   │
│     different.                                                   │
│  6. In the same class and in the next few classes, assign        │
│     additional exercises that focus on the same skill,           │
│     increasing the complexity of the tasks. Make sure the        │
│     students work together whenever it is feasible.              │
│  7. Assign an exercise to be done by individuals, which they     │
│     will use to check their own ability and confidence in using  │
│     the skill.                                                   │
│  8. Assign further exercises as needed, based on your sense of   │
│     the students' mastery of the skill.                         │
│  9. Apply the new skill and practice previously mastered skills  │
│     in whole-class intensive reading lessons.                   │
│ 10. Interaction and a focus on thinking processes are the key    │
│     features of these activities!                               │
└─────────────────────────────────────────────────────────────────┘
```

The Teacher's Role in a Reading Class

No matter what methodology is chosen, the teacher's role is always very important. However, a lively, dynamic, interesting, and productive reading class requires even more of the teacher. According to Mahon (1986, pp. 98–99):

> Methodology aside, the teacher is the most important element in a reading class, for her attitude influences students and their performance. The teacher . . . should provide her students with:
>
> 1. An anxiety-free atmosphere so that they will feel free to experiment with a new reading style.
> 2. Practice so that they will master new strategies.
> 3. Pressure in the form of persuasion and timings.

The teacher also needs to be a model interpreter. Since making sense of a text is actually interpretation (Eskey, 1986, p. 9) and since so much interpretation is cultural (van Dijk & Kintsch, 1983; Heath, 1984), the teacher's modeling of native speaker-like comprehension is essential, in class and while working with individual students.

Finally, the reading teacher has to be a model thinker. Reading is like problem solving (see, e.g., Olshavsky, 1976), and the teacher can serve as a model by thinking aloud as she demonstrates the application of a reading skill.

APPLYING THE SKILLS IN INTENSIVE READING LESSONS

In addition to individual practice, the whole class should work collaboratively on applying the skills in intensive reading lessons. An intensive reading lesson is a whole-class activity during which students read a common text and practice applying the reading skills that the class has already worked on. Intensive reading lessons will be suggested at key points in the sections that follow. During these lessons, the teacher can encourage students to monitor their own comprehension and to discuss the skills that they have applied strategically in order to comprehend the passage. In the process, students develop their metacognitive abilities.

Selecting an appropriate passage for an intensive reading lesson is essential to its success. The teacher needs to take into account the interests, abilities, and goals of the students. Quite often, newspapers and magazines are good sources of interesting articles. Once students have learned to preview, they can be asked to preview three or four possible texts and then (as a class) select one to use for their intensive reading lesson.

NOTES ABOUT THE SAMPLE EXERCISES

Sections B–H of Part III feature sample exercises* that demonstrate a skill-focused approach to teaching reading. The skills have been grouped according to their primary role in reading development. The sample exercises are meant for students who have at least learned "elementary literacy" (i.e., are able to decode in English at at least a beginner level). It should be noted that the lessons usually involve as much speaking, writing, and listening as they do silent reading. A reading class that takes this approach involves metalinguistic activity; the students think and talk about English as an object. There is metacognitive activity, as well, as students learn to talk and to think about their own thinking. The overarching goal of every lesson is to encourage the students to be active, thinking readers.

Teachers are welcome to try out these sample exercises with their students, but first they should work through each exercise alone to get a sense of how it works. (An answer key for the sample exercises is located in Appendix V on pages 245–254.)

Teachers are encouraged to use these exercises as models for designing their own, based on their knowledge of their students' interests, abilities, and goals. It may take a few semesters of work to compile folders of exercises on each skill, but the payoff is the ability to tailor their lessons to their particular students. In some programs, reading teachers share their original lessons in common files, one folder for each reading skill, and that way they greatly expand the repertoire of every individual teacher.

Before introducing a new skill, the teacher should always begin with a rationale for learning that skill. Explain to the students what the skill is and how it can improve their reading ability in English. This helps the students put the skill in context and enhances conscious awareness of the skill as a strategy to use whenever it is required. A sample rationale is given for many of the skills in the sections that follow.

SCHEDULING ACTIVITIES IN YOUR READING CLASS

This might be a good point at which to discuss the scheduling of activities in a reading class. As mentioned in Part I, the most effective reading classes are those that include two or more of these four elements in every meeting of a reading class: Extensive Reading, Vocabulary Development, Skill Building, and Rate Building.

---

* Many of the sample exercises are taken from several editions of the *Reading Power* series.

First, the teacher needs to take into account the nature of the activities (individual, small group or pair work, or whole class).

Individual Activities
Extensive reading
Reading rate building
Developing bottom-up processes
Small Group and/or Pair Work
Reading skills exercises
Peer conferences, book clubs, reading circles
All-class Activities
Introductions to new skills
Intensive reading lessons
Rate-building training (e.g., pacing exercises)

Second, the teacher must tailor the scheduling of specific class activities based on the type of class, how often it meets, and other features of the curriculum.

- In an integrated skills class that meets for two to three hours per day, five days per week, allow about 30 minutes per day for reading activities. Here is a possible schedule.

Monday:	Exercises for rate building Extensive reading Vocabulary building
Tuesday:	Extensive reading and book conferences Reading skills exercises
Wednesday:	Exercises for rate building Reading skills exercises Vocabulary building
Thursday:	Reading skills exercises Extensive reading and book conferences
Friday:	Intensive reading lesson Extensive reading Vocabulary building
Homework:	Extensive reading

- In an integrated skills class that meets for three hours per week, use about one-third of class time for reading activities. In one week, students can complete the following:

    Four rate-building exercises

    Six pages of reading skills exercises

    One intensive reading lesson or extensive reading activity

    Homework: Extensive reading and practice on reading skills exercises

- In a reading class that meets two hours per week, students can work on these activities in every class:

    Reading skills exercises

    Rate-building exercises

    Individual practice

    Extensive reading and book conferences

    Intensive reading lesson

    Homework: Extensive reading

B | Activating Background Knowledge and Conceptual Frameworks

Previewing, predicting, and skimming are three reading skills that involve tapping prior knowledge, thus activating mental networks of information that will enable students to comprehend what they read. These skills also help develop reading fluency, so it is essential that students develop the habit of applying them automatically whenever they read.

As we noted earlier, dependence on bottom-up processing (text-centered, word-by-word reading) is natural when a person first reads a second or foreign language. This is caused by such factors as the reader's own "theory" of how to read, a lack of confidence, and a lack of knowledge of the target language.

Students can build confidence and success in reading a second language when they learn more about the reading process and become aware that reading is not the same thing as translating. They need to learn the importance of their prior knowledge in making sense of a text. In other words, they need to develop their top-down processing ability (Coady, 1979).

PREVIEWING

Previewing is a high-speed reading skill. It is a powerful skill because by previewing, the reader gains enough information from the text to begin hypothesizing about its contents and to engage many parts of the brain in the cognitive process of matching new information with what is already known.

We all preview in our daily lives. When we receive a letter, we check the return address, the postmark, the size and shape of the envelope, the style of the stationery, the handwriting, and other characteristics in a split second before we open it. When students sign up for a new course, they are encouraged to read the syllabus to find out what to expect during the semester. And before most people decide to read a book, they preview it by reading the front and back covers, the table of contents, and the author's name; they note the book's length and other features. However, students who may preview some things in their personal lives often neglect this important step when they are reading in a second or foreign language. It is especially helpful for students to learn about previewing at the beginning of the semester when they are likely to have several new textbooks that they can preview.

Benefits of Previewing

First, previewing allows the reader to establish the genre, context, topic, level of difficulty, and organization of the text to be read. Once aware of the topic, the student's activated background knowledge allows him or her to read for meaning, even if many of the words in the text are unfamiliar. The student realizes once again that it is not necessary to read every word in order to understand and gain information from a text. Training in previewing helps the student to develop the habit of giving texts a quick "once-over" before reading, the groundwork for learning to skim, which is a much more complicated task.

Once students have learned how to preview, they should be required to take a few minutes to preview whenever they are given a reading assignment. Here is a sample rationale for introducing students to the skill of previewing.

SAMPLE RATIONALE

Before you go on a trip, you probably look at a map or check the GPS in order to have a general idea about your route. You want to know what kind of roads you will drive on, which cities or towns you will pass through, how long it will take, and whether or not there are any interesting sights along the way. This helps you enjoy the trip and may keep you from getting lost.

Before you begin to read, you can find out about what you will read. When you look over (preview) a passage before you read it, you improve your ability to understand and remember what you read. When you preview, you find the answers to these questions:

- What kind of text is it? A newspaper article, a story, an advertisement, a textbook, a recipe, a letter—or what?
- What will you be reading about? What do you already know about this topic?
- How carefully should you read? Will you read to remember every word?
- Will you just look for one or two pieces of information? Will you read for pleasure, with no need to remember all the details?

Students often do not have a systematic approach to previewing, so although the following steps in previewing may be obvious to the teacher, it is important to point them out before the class begins to work on the previewing exercises.

STEPS IN PREVIEWING

1. Read the title.
2. Look at any pictures.
3. Notice if the text is divided into parts.
4. Read the first sentence of each paragraph.
5. Read the last paragraph or at least the last sentence.
6. Notice names, numbers, dates, and words that stand out.

Demonstrating the Effectiveness of Previewing

In order to make sure that students realize how helpful previewing is, the teacher can begin with an exercise that allows students to experience the power of previewing and begin to recognize the importance of background knowledge. This can be done by having students preview a passage and then answer several multiple-choice questions about the passage without having a chance to actually read the passage. The ideal passage for this activity would be at the students' reading level and would be followed by eight to ten multiple-choice questions. The passage in Sample Exercise B.1 on page 52 is an example of the type of text that works well.

Before assigning this exercise, the teacher should prepare students in the following way:

1. Explain the steps in previewing (listed on page 50).
2. Tell the students that they will have two minutes to preview the passage. Explain that at the end of the two minutes, they will turn the page and answer the comprehension questions *without looking back at the passage.* Tell them to guess if they are not sure of an answer.

After the students have completed answering the questions, hand out the answers and ask them to check their work. (See page 245 of the Answer Key.) Students can usually answer several of the questions correctly, which surprises them. Ask students to explain how they got their answers. Point out that they applied prior knowledge in answering the questions, and that is what good readers always do. Students gain confidence from this demonstration of the importance of background knowledge.

On the other hand, some students may not agree that guessing is "really reading," and they may say that they think guessing is "cheating." It is important to discuss this issue with the class because, in fact, accessing background knowledge and guessing make it possible to be an effective reader. The teacher should point out that the students understand and remember what they read because of their prior knowledge and because of their ability to guess.

After this discussion, direct the students to read the passage, looking for further information that supports or contradicts what they learned in their preview.

Directions: A. Preview this passage. You will have two minutes.

SUCCESSFUL LANGUAGE LEARNING

What does it take to be a successful language learner? Gilberto is a good example. He learned Spanish from his family, and he learned English when he started school. He had some classes in Spanish and some in English, so he learned to read and write in both languages. He found that he liked learning languages, and he was good at it. What made Gilberto a successful language learner?

First of all, Gilberto learned English as a second language when he was a child. Children who learn a second language learn important facts about languages. For example, they learn that they can say the same thing in two ways. They also find out that every language has different sounds. In addition, they know how to switch from one language to another. With family, they speak their home language and at school, the second language.

Second, Gilberto found out that knowing two languages could help him. When he went to the store, he could use English to buy things. And because he knew English, he could succeed at school. On the other hand, when Gilberto visited his grandparents, he could use Spanish. He could also use Spanish with other friends and relatives from Central and South America.

Third, Gilberto was always a very friendly type of person. He liked meeting new people and talking with them. He was also not afraid of trying to speak a new language. He didn't feel bad if he made a few mistakes. He really just wanted to communicate. He wanted to learn about different places around the world and the way people live in other places.

Fourth, Gilberto was a good student. He studied hard and he loved to figure out the rules of a language. In class, he took part in all the activities. At home, he listened to music and watched videos in the new language. When he spoke, he tried to sound like a native speaker of the language.

Being a successful language learner helped Gilberto a lot. In college, he studied Russian and Serbo-Croatian. After college, he was able to find a good job. He went to Russia to teach English in a Russian university. After a few years, he moved back to the United States and worked for the U.S. government at the Language Institute. He taught the Serbo-Croatian language to government workers. Today, Gilberto is a professor of Russian and Serbo-Croatian at Dean University in California.

Now turn the page and answer the questions. Do not look back at the passage.

B. *Based on your previewing, circle the best answer.*

1. This passage is about
   a. how Gilberto got a good job in the United States.
   b. how Gilberto learned English at school.
   c. why Gilberto traveled to Russia to teach English.
   d. why Gilberto became a successful language learner.

2. At school, Gilberto used
   a. English in all of his classes.
   b. Spanish in all of his classes.
   c. Both English and Spanish.
   d. English only for speaking.

3. Children who learn two languages
   a. speak English at school.
   b. can't learn English easily.
   c. can't speak Spanish anymore.
   d. learn a lot about languages.

4. It's important to know that
   a. different languages have different sounds.
   b. some languages are too difficult to learn.
   c. all languages have the same sounds.
   d. some languages are only spoken in school.

5. Children who speak two languages can
   a. learn to read at a young age.
   b. switch between languages.
   c. speak English only in school.
   d. never speak any language well.

6. Gilberto could succeed in school because he
   a. had good teachers.
   b. was good at math.
   c. knew Spanish.
   d. knew English.

7. When Gilberto made mistakes, he
   a. felt very bad.
   b. asked his teacher.
   c. didn't feel bad.
   d. stopped speaking.

8. Gilberto got a good job after college because he
   a. could read and write in Spanish.
   b. was a good language learner.
   c. wanted to live in Russia.
   d. was interested in other places.

(From Reading Power, Third Edition, *2005, pp. 261–262)*

Previewing Articles and Essays

Students should be taught to preview before they begin to read any assignment. Sample Exercise B.2 gives students practice in previewing a newspaper article. This exercise works well with students at every level of reading ability. From a newspaper, the teacher should select a news article that reports on an event and is accompanied by a photograph. Each student should receive a copy.

SAMPLE EXERCISE B.2. PREVIEWING A NEWSPAPER ARTICLE

Directions: Review the steps in previewing. Then preview this newspaper article. You will have one minute. Work with a partner and answer these questions without looking back at the story. Compare your answers with those of another pair of students. Then reread the article to check your answers.

1. What is the article about?
2. What kind of story is it? Is it true or made up?
3. What do you already know about this?
4. Is the story difficult for you?
5. What are some of the names, dates, numbers, or other important words you noticed?
6. Did you learn anything new? What?

Previewing Textbooks

Previewing is especially relevant if students are using textbooks in their classes. It is best to teach textbook previewing hands-on with a textbook they are currently using or one of several that the teacher brings to class. If the students have an opportunity to preview textbooks from several different subject areas, they can discover how textbooks from different fields vary in organization and even in appearance. Begin by handing out the directions for how to preview a textbook (see the box that follows), and then demonstrate with one of the textbooks so that students will understand how much information they can obtain from a brief preview.

The following sample exercises are useful for teaching previewing a textbook for a general overview of the book and for previewing a textbook chapter in preparation for reading and study.

HOW TO PREVIEW A TEXTBOOK

1. Read the title page and the copyright page. Find the author's name(s) and the date of publication. This information is important because the reader can decide if the book contains the most up-to-date information.
2. Read the table of contents. Check the organization of the book, the number of sections, and the number of chapters.
3. Scan the first chapter. Look for illustrations, charts, tables; read the headings; check to see if there is an end-of-chapter summary or a set of discussion questions. It is not "cheating" to read the end of the chapter first.
4. Look at the first page of each chapter and/or part of the book.
5. Look quickly through the final chapter because it sometimes contains a conclusion that the author uses to tie together the main points of a book.
6. Look at the materials at the back of the book to see if there is an index, a glossary (definitions of key words), bibliography, charts and tables, or other aids.

SAMPLE EXERCISE B.3. **PREVIEWING A TEXTBOOK**

Directions: Preview one of your textbooks. Then fill in the information below. Working with another student, compare your textbooks. Afterwards, tell the class what you have found out.

1. Title _____

2. Author (s) _____

3. Date of publication _____

4. Number of pages _____

5. Check (✓) the features. Does your textbook contain

_____ a table of contents?

_____ an index?

_____ a glossary?

_____ a bibliography?

_____ end-of-chapter questions?

_____ illustrations?

_____ charts and graphs?

SAMPLE EXERCISE B.4. **PREVIEWING A TEXTBOOK CHAPTER**

Directions: Form a group of three or four students. In your own textbook or one that your teacher gives you, each student should choose a chapter, preview it, and answer the questions below. Then compare your chapter with those of the other students in your group.

1. What is the title of the chapter?
2. How many illustrations are found in the chapter? Are they photographs, charts, graphs, maps, or other types of illustrations?
3. Is the chapter divided into parts? If so, how many?
4. Read the first and last paragraphs of the chapter. What did you learn about the chapter?
5. Is there a summary or are there discussion questions at the end of the chapter?

Previewing Books for Extensive Reading

Extensive reading of self-selected books may be a new experience for some students, and they may need instruction in how to preview books for personal reading. To introduce this kind of previewing, the teacher should bring a big bag of paperback books to class and assign Sample Exercise B.5 on page 56. Explain each item on the checklist and why it is important. Students may not realize, for example, that very small print will make their eyes tired and discourage them from reading. (Remember to give the students *a very strict time limit* when they preview.)

Directions: Choose a book. Preview the book and fill in the checklist below. Then compare your work with another student's. You will have five minutes to preview.

Checklist of key features:

_____ Title _____

_____ Author _____

_____ Type of book _____ Fiction _____ Nonfiction

_____ What is it about? _____

_____

_____ Date of publication _____

_____ Number of pages in the book _____

_____ Print easy to read? _____ Yes _____ No

_____ Front and back cover gives what type of information? _____

_____ Would you like to read this book? Why? _____

PREDICTING

In some ways, predicting is difficult to separate from previewing. When a reader notices something in a text while previewing it, relevant mental networks are activated, and on the basis of these associated networks, the reader develops expectations about the contents of the text. However, while previewing primarily focuses on identifying text features, predicting focuses on the possible content of a text. And while previewing is a pre-reading skill, predicting needs to occur both before and during reading.

Training Students to Make Predictions

In practice, we know that predicting is usually subconscious, but for the purpose of highlighting the *thinking processes* underlying predicting, it is necessary to assign exercises that will allow students to focus on the act of predicting. Students should learn to predict whenever they read, and predicting should be an explicit part of whole-class intensive reading lessons.

As with every skill, an introduction to predicting should begin with a sample rationale that will enable students to recognize the purpose of working on the predicting exercises.

Sample Exercises B.6–B.8 (on pages 57–59) may be used with students of
every reading level, but they are especially useful for students at beginning levels.
In Sample Exercise B.6, the teacher could also use a large illustration from *National
Geographic, Time,* or another popular magazine. When they compare their predictions, students are sometimes surprised by the differences. Notice that in Sample
Exercise B.8, students can learn that predicting is not just a pre-reading activity:
they should predict all the time when they are reading.

SAMPLE EXERCISE **B.6.** PREDICTING FROM A PICTURE

*Directions: Here is a picture of the place you have decided to go on your vaca-
tion. Answer the questions to make predictions about your vacation. Then talk to
another student about your answers.*

1. What will you do during the day?
2. What will you do in the evening?
3. What will you eat?
4. What will you wear?
5. What will you buy?
6. How will you feel when you return home after your vacation?

SAMPLE EXERCISE B.7.   PREDICTING FROM A TITLE

Directions: Do you think you will find these ideas in a magazine article with this title: "Boston: A Good Place to Live"? Write Yes or No after each sentence. Then talk to another student about your answers. Are they the same?

Boston: A Good Place to Live

1. There are many poor people in Boston. _____
2. The spring flowers are beautiful in Boston. _____
3. There are many universities in Boston. _____
4. Jobs are hard to find in the Boston area. _____
5. Winters in Boston are cold and snowy. _____
6. Boston City Hall is very beautiful. _____
7. There are many famous old buildings in downtown Boston. _____
8. People are not very friendly in Boston. _____
9. The Charles River flows by the city. People like to walk along the river in the parks. _____
10. Apartments are very expensive and hard to find. _____

SAMPLE EXERCISE B.8.   PREDICTING WHAT WILL COME NEXT

Directions: Circle the letter of the sentence that could come next. Then talk about your answers with another student. Do you agree?

Example: Yesterday, there was a big snowstorm in Detroit. Many schools were closed, and people had to stay home from work.
   a. It was a warm, sunny day, and the beaches were crowded.
   b. It was very cold, but the snow on the trees looked beautiful.
   c. Only one inch of snow fell in the downtown area.

The correct choice is *b*. Choice *a* is not correct. People don't go to beaches when there is snow! Choice *c* is not correct. In a big snowstorm, many inches of snow fall.

1. There were many good shows on TV last night. The Smith family stayed home.
   a. They turned off the TV and went to bed early.
   b. The only interesting show was about traveling by bicycle.
   c. They saw a play, a music show, and the news.

2. John and Alice Babson are not happy with the school in their town.
   a. Their children love to go to school.
   b. The classrooms are too crowded.
   c. It is a beautiful building.

3. Many young people move to New York City after college.
   a. New York is a dangerous city.
   b. It's difficult to find jobs in New York.
   c. There are lots of interesting things to do in New York.

4. Fly Happy Time Airlines! Take an exciting trip to Holiday Island!
   a. This trip is very expensive.
   b. Holiday Island has warm, sunny weather.
   c. Happy Time Airlines is never on time.

5. Alex had trouble falling asleep last night. He was awake until 3:00 a.m.
   a. This morning, he feels tired.
   b. This morning, he feels rested and ready to work.
   c. This morning, he is hungry.

6. The roads were covered with ice and were dangerous today.
   a. Sam drove home quickly.
   b. Sam took a long time to drive home.
   c. Sam enjoyed driving home.

(From Reading Power, Third Edition, *2005, p. 32)*

Sample Exercises B.9 and B.10 (on pages 60–61) are designed for more advanced students, although the same activity could be used with content suitable for lower level students, The table of contents in Exercise B.9 is from *Nisa: The Life and Words of a !Kung Woman,* by Marjorie Shostak.

This book is the life story of Nisa, a woman in her fifties who lives in the Kalahari desert in southern Africa. She is a member of the !Kung tribe of hunters and gatherers. In any culture, Nisa would be considered a remarkable woman: as a small child she saved her newborn brother from being killed; at the age of twelve she was married to a man she did not want. She was separated, divorced, remarried, and widowed. She had four children, but none of them survived. Nisa was independent; she took care of herself and foraged for food in one of the world's most hostile environments. This book tells her story in her own words as recorded by anthropologist Marjorie Shostak. Together, Nisa and Shostak broke through the immense barriers of language and culture to produce a fascinating account.

Directions: A. Read this table of contents. Work in small groups of three or four students. Answer the questions that follow. Then make at least five predictions about what you think you would find in the book. Each group will report its predictions to the class and explain its reasons for making them.

Contents

(From Nisa: the life and words of a !Kung woman. *New York: Vintage Books, 1983.)*
(Used by permission of the estate of Marjorie Shostak)

Questions:

1. Is this a book of fiction or nonfiction?
2. What is it about?

Predictions: _____

_____

_____

B. *Talk with your group about your predictions. Then have one member report your group's predictions to the class and explain your reasons.*

SAMPLE EXERCISE B.10. PREVIEWING A TEXTBOOK CHAPTER OUTLINE

Directions: Many textbooks begin each chapter with an outline. You can learn a lot about the chapter by previewing a chapter outline because then you will know what to expect as you read. Read the outline for Chapter 3 of Society: The Basics, *and answer the questions that follow. Then compare your answers with another student's. If you disagree, look back at the outline to check your work.*

CHAPTER 3 - SOCIALIZATION

The Importance of Social Experience
  Human Development: Nature and Nurture
  Social Isolation

Understanding Socialization
  Sigmund Freud: The Elements of Personality
  Jean Piaget: Cognitive Development
  Lawrence Kohlberg: Moral Development
  Carol Gilligan: The Gender Factor
  George Herbert Mead: The Social Self

Agents of Socialization
  The Family
  The School
  The Peer Group
  The Mass Media

Socialization and the Life Course
  Childhood
  Adolescence
  Adulthood
  Old Age
  Death and Dying
  The Life Course: An Overview

Resocialization: Total Institutions

Summary

Key Concepts

Critical Thinking Questions

(From J. J. Macionis, Society: The Basics, *Fourth Edition,* Upper Saddle River, NJ: Prentice Hall, 1998)

1. What is the title of Chapter 3?
2. Which topics are familiar to you?
3. Which topics do you think would be most interesting to read about?
4. Are there many unfamiliar words or names in this outline? List some of them.
5. Would this chapter be difficult for you to read? If so, why?
6. What study aids are included at the end of Chapter 3?

Using Strip Stories for Teaching Predicting

Strip stories work well for teaching students how to predict what will come next in a story. While students work on ordering the events in a story and suggest which part of the story they think should come next, they have to explain their reasons to the other students in their group. Articulating their reasons reinforces their awareness of the role of predicting in reading. This type of exercise also gives the students an opportunity to read aloud in an authentic fashion as each group reads and rereads its strips in order to put them in the correct sequence.

These directions for using strip stories to teach predicting are adapted from Grellet's book, *Developing Reading Skills* (1981). Select a short story with a fairly clear sequence of events. The story can be a simple folktale, fairy tale, or children's story that might not otherwise find its way into the classroom. (Grellet used "The Unicorn in the Garden" by James Thurber.) Type the story in separate strips, and cut the strips so that the students can physically reassemble the story. Put students in small groups and give each group a complete set of strips. Read aloud to the class the strip that states the opening of the story. The students' task is to put the story together in its original order. After the groups have finished working, a student from each group should write the group's answers on the chalkboard. The class should compare the answers from each group, and if they are not all the same, each group should explain why they think their answers are correct.

For beginning level ESL/EFL students, the teacher should be sure that the story is a very simple one. This activity is more difficult than it appears to be.

SAMPLE EXERCISE B.11. USING A STRIP STORY TO PREDICT

Directions: These strips are parts of a story. Your group has to decide on the best order for the strips. Read your own strip silently. The teacher will read the first part of the story to you (Strip d). Then each student will read a strip aloud to the others, and the group will decide the correct order of the strips.

Write the best order for the strips:

1. _d_ 2. ____ 3. ____ 4. ____ 5. ____ 6. ____ 7. ____

Story in strips:

The Stolen Car

a. Greg called the police and went with them in a search of the area around the airport.
b. Greg Winter, the father of the child, left the car for just a minute. He ran into the terminal building to bring a lunch to his wife, Susan.
c. When he came out of the terminal, he was frantic—his car was gone!
d. A car thief at Boston's Logan Airport got more than he expected last week. The car he decided to steal was not empty.
e. The thief, apparently recognizing his mistake, had abandoned the car in East Boston.
f. The car (with child and dogs still safe inside) was found in less than two hours.
g. A two-year-old girl and two poodles were asleep in the back seat.

Making Semantic Associations for Predicting

PreP (Pre-reading Preparatory Instruction—Langer, 1981) is another way to help students to activate concepts and background knowledge before they read, and it provides a systematic way to apply the skills of previewing and predicting. PreP is a "pre-reading plan intended to make readers aware of what they already know about a topic to be read about and to activate their memory and expectations," (Schulz, 1983). It is a form of brainstorming. Students can learn to follow the PreP steps before they read independently, and PreP can be included in the pre-reading activity before an all-class intensive reading lesson.

PreP consists of three phases. The procedure requires almost no teacher preparation, and it can be used with any text at every language proficiency level. PreP also provides the teacher with reliable feedback for estimating the students' conceptual and linguistic background knowledge about a topic. As usual, the teacher should begin with a rationale for working on this activity.

- **Phase One.** From a text that the class will read, select a key word, phrase, or picture that will stimulate group discussion. (This is not the same as pre-teaching important words from a text. The key word does not even have to appear in the text.) Ask the students to make associations with this word, phrase, or picture. List all of their associations on the chalkboard without commenting on them.
- **Phase Two.** The students tell the reasons for the associations they have made. This reflecting step activates a network of additional associations. As they discuss their initial associations, students will be reminded of other related ideas (Schulz, 1983).
- **Phase Three.** Ask the students for additional associations that have come to mind during the discussion and write these on the chalkboard as well.

According to Langer (1981), who introduced this procedure, "the three levels of response elicited by the PreP not only help the students to comprehend a text, but greatly facilitate the student's ability to recall the text after reading."

Students should understand why the PreP procedure is useful and what they gain from doing it. In order to stress this, the teacher should ask the students to evaluate the procedure after they have done it several times. Point out the ways PreP helps students to think and predict before they read and how such thinking assists in comprehending and remembering.

Students can also do PreP in pairs, using a PreP worksheet devised by the teacher. Using the title, an accompanying illustration, or the first sentence of the passage as a catalyst, two or three students can perform the steps of associating, reflecting, and further associating together.

Some students may have little or no experience with free association. Sample Exercise B.12 (below) is an activity that gives students a sense of how to free-associate. It can be adapted by using stimulus words that might be more appropriate for a particular group of students. Before they begin to work on the exercise, the teacher should provide an example by writing the word *school* or another general word on the board and then write all of the students' associations on the board without commenting. Once they get the hang of it, students enjoy this activity.

SAMPLE EXERCISE B.12. MAKING ASSOCIATIONS

Directions: On the worksheet, you will find ten words. On the line next to each word, write the first thing you think of. Then compare your associations with a partner's. Are they the same? Tell the class about how they are similar and how they are different.

1. doctor _____

2. ice cream _____

3. television _____

4. war _____

5. book _____

6. New York _____

7. zoo _____

8. hungry _____

9. music _____

10. job _____

SAMPLE EXERCISE B.13. FREE ASSOCIATING ON A TOPIC

Directions: Work in a small group with two other students. Each student should make associations about this topic: Being Afraid in the Dark.

1. Write a list of all of your associations. Write every idea that you think of.
2. Read your lists to each other. Explain why you thought of your associations. Are all of the lists alike?
3. Then think again, and write any new associations you have thought of.
4. Talk about your new associations and explain why you thought of them.

Applying Previewing, Predicting, and PreP

The following activity applies previewing and predicting in a reading lesson that allows even beginning level students to get something out of a passage that might ordinarily be too difficult for them. This lesson plan is also valuable for preparing to discuss a passage that is a prompt for a writing assignment.

A MODEL PreP READING LESSON

1. Select a one- or two-page passage that is appropriate to the general reading level of the students in the class. It is important that the passage be interesting and attractive. Prepare eight to ten True/False questions about the passage.

2. Have the students preview the passage for about two or three minutes.

3. Then tell the students to put the passages aside and ask them to tell what they remember from the preview. Write all of their ideas on the board, and discuss them following the PreP phases outlined previously, on page 63.

4. Next, tell the students to predict what else they might find when they read the passage, based on what they have collectively seen in the preview. Students give reasons for their predictions. These are, in effect, the further associations of PreP.

5. Then distribute the True/False questions and have students answer them without looking at the passage.

6. After they have written their answers to the True/False questions, direct the students to read the entire article, looking for confirmation of their predictions and for verification of their answers to the questions.

7. Give the whole class a chance to discuss the extent to which their predictions proved to be accurate, and why or why not. Then continue with the class discussion of the passage.

8. *(Optional)* Devise a writing assignment based on the passage. Or give an Internet research assignment on the topic of the passage.

Many types of passages can be used in PreP lessons. Often there are interesting selections in readers that already have True/False questions accompanying them. Other good sources are *Parade Magazine, People,* newspapers, some of the popular special interest magazines, and news magazines. (Of course, for those articles, the teacher will have to write the True/False questions.)

This procedure could be included in every intensive reading lesson because student interaction and student/teacher interaction are essential in such lessons. When they explain their thinking processes, students have an opportunity to discover new ways of thinking about a text. As they work together, predicting and making associations about a text, they practice the thinking processes involved in relating the text to what they already know. Once they have practiced talking this way together, it is possible for them to internalize these processes and apply them when they read alone.

INTENSIVE READING LESSON

After students have a clear sense of what it means to preview and predict, the teacher should plan an intensive reading lesson to apply these skills. An intensive reading lesson is an activity in which the whole class works on a story or article that will be the basis of a class discussion and/or a writing assignment. Using a text selected for its interest to the class, the teacher should begin the intensive reading lesson with the PreP steps.

SKIMMING

Skimming, like previewing, is very fast-paced reading. However, it has a very different purpose. The reader *previews* to get a glimpse of the contents of a text before reading in order to get a general sense of the genre, topic, and length of a passage. But the reader *skims* to obtain an overview of the form and contents of a text, including such information as the writer's main point, style, focus, point of view, the overall organization of the material, and how the text relates to the needs, background knowledge, and interests of the reader. Armed with such information, the reader can decide how much more thoroughly a text should be read.

Skimming is also different from scanning, another fast-paced reading skill that will be discussed in Section C (pages 72–89). Scanning is useful for finding specific pieces of information in a text, for example, a phone number in a directory, a word in the dictionary, or a birthdate in a biographical description. On the other hand, skimming is more comprehensive: effective skimming requires knowledge of textual organization, awareness of lexical clues to point of view, the ability to infer main ideas, and *many* other advanced reading skills.

In fact, skimming may be all that is necessary to obtain the information the reader wants (as in skimming a newspaper or magazine article). And sometimes the reader skims in order to decide whether or not to read a text thoroughly or to review a text already read.

Effective skimming requires the reader to process a text rapidly at many levels in order to get an overall picture of it. About 800 words per minute is considered a good skimming rate (Fry, 1978). In order to skim, the reader has to be capable of quickly seeing the "skeleton" that underlies the text. It is easier to do that if the reader is aware of how texts are organized—for example, that in English, the main point is usually stated at the beginning of a paragraph, section, or chapter. The reader should also be familiar with the important clues that are represented by differences in size and style of type in the text, as well as the lexical items used for signaling relationships between ideas and the vocabulary of textual cohesion (e.g., *first, second, last; on the other hand*). This is knowledge that most second language learners need to acquire before they can skim effectively. Therefore, it is a good idea to delay a focus on the skimming skill until second language readers and other limited English proficient students have developed the ability to apply many of the other reading skills presented later in this book.

As with the teaching of any of the skills, the teacher should make students aware of the practical reasons for skimming. A discussion of questions such as those in the sample rationale on page 67 will help students understand why they need to learn to skim.

Teaching Students How to Skim Effectively

Once students have discussed the reasons for skimming, they need to learn how to skim. The most direct way to accomplish this is to have students read a passage that has been set up to show which parts should be read during skimming. In Sample Exercise B.14, parts of the text have been x-ed out for this purpose.

SAMPLE EXERCISE B.14.   SKIMMING A TEXT WITH SHADED-OUT PARTS

Directions: A. When you skim, move your eyes very quickly over a text, and read only the parts that will help you find the information you need. The passage you are going to read has missing, or x-ed out, parts. Use the parts that are left to figure out the writer's ideas or opinions. You will have one minute to skim the passage. Then write the answers to the skimming questions. Afterwards, read the whole passage to check your answers.

Questions for Skimming:

1. What is this passage about?
2. What does Tomiko like about New York?
3. What are some of the things Tomiko likes to do in New York?
4. How does Tomiko feel about her life in New York?

A BUSY STUDENT

Tomiko is happy to be a student in New York. She is studying English at Columbia University. She plans to finish her English course in June. Then she will work on her master's degree at New York University.

Tomiko likes the many beautiful buildings in New York. xxxxxxxxxxxxxxxxxxx xxxxxxxxxxxxxxxxxxxxxxxxxxxxxxxxxxxxxxxxxxxxxxxxxxxxx

Tomiko also likes the people in New York City. xxxxxxxxxxxxxxxxxxxxxxxxxxx xxxxxxxxxxxxxxxxxxxxxxxxxxxxxxxxxxxxxxxxxxxxxxxxxxxxxxxxxxxxxx xxxxxxxxxxxxxxxxxxxxxxxxxxxxxxxxxxxxxxxxxxxxxxxxxxxxxxxxxxxxxx xxxxxxxxxxxxx

Best of all, Tomiko loves the theaters in New York. xxxxxxxxxxxxxxxxx xxxx xxxxxxxxxxxxxxxxxxxxxxxxxxxxxxxxxxxxxxxxxxxxxxxxxxxxxxxx xxxxx xxxxxxxxxxxxxxxxxxxxxxxxxxxxxxxxxxxxxxxx

Tomiko is far from her home in Japan. But she is not sad. xxxxxxxxxxxxxx xxxxxxxxxxxxxxxxxxxxxxxxxxxxxxxxxxxxxxxxxxxxxxxxxxxxxxxxxxxxxxxxxxx xxxxxxxx She is very busy and happy in New York.

B. Stop here and answer the skimming questions. Then read the whole passage below:

A BUSY STUDENT

Tomiko is happy to be a student in New York. She is studying English at Columbia University. She plans to finish her English course in June. Then she will work on her master's degree at New York University.

Tomiko likes the many beautiful buildings in New York. In fact, she plans to become an architect. Then she can build great buildings, too.

Tomiko also likes the people in New York City. There are many different kinds of people. They speak many languages. Tomiko has made new friends from other countries.

Best of all, Tomiko loves the theaters in New York. She goes to plays almost every week. Sometimes the plays are in theaters on Broadway. Sometimes the plays are in small theaters in other parts of the city.

Tomiko is far from her home in Japan. But she is not sad. She goes to classes every day. She visits her friends. She goes to see new places. And she attends many plays. She is very busy and happy in New York.

C. Check your answers to the questions. How many did you answer correctly?

Applying the Skill of Skimming

Sample Exercises B.15–B.17 (on pages 69–71) give students practice in applying the skimming skill on several different types of reading material: a book review, magazine article, and Web site. Teaching students how to skim book reviews serves the added purpose of encouraging them to look for books to read for extensive reading.

SAMPLE EXERCISE **B.15.**   **SKIMMING A BOOK REVIEW**

Directions: Book reviews are published in print and online newspapers and magazines. In a review, the writer usually tells something about the subject of the book and gives an opinion. By skimming a book review, you can quickly find out if the book would be interesting or useful for you. Here is a review of the book Go Ask Alice. *Read these questions and then skim the review for the answers. Work as quickly as you can—no more than one minute for the skimming. Compare your answers with another student's.*

1. Is this book serious or funny?
2. Is it a good book to give to a fourteen-year-old girl? Why or why not?
3. Would you like to read this book? Why or why not?

GO ASK ALICE: A REAL DIARY

Author Anonymous—185 pp. New York: Simon & Schuster Inc.

In this diary, the reader enters a girl's life at about the time of her fifteenth birthday. It seems a very ordinary life in many ways. She argues with her parents and doesn't enjoy schoolwork. She worries about what others think of her, and at times she feels she is ugly, fat, and unappreciated. But on the other hand, she loves her family and they care a great deal about her. She is bright and can do well in school when she wants to, and she has friends whom she enjoys being with. And then her father's job changes, the family moves to another part of the country, and her life falls apart.

How her life falls apart and how she struggles to put it back together again is the story we follow in this anonymous diary. We never learn the name of the author, but after just a few pages we feel we know her well. Indeed, we probably all do know someone like her: an unhappy, insecure teenager who suffers tremendously for the real or imagined slights of her parents and her peers.

For this girl and for all too many like her, this adolescent lack of self-esteem is accompanied by a desperate need for approval and gratification. When she changes schools, she is faced with the ordeal of being the friendless new student in school. The humiliation she suffers at the hands of her uncaring and sometimes cruel fellow students further destroys her self-image.

Then, over the summer, new friends play a trick on her, adding LSD to her Coke. After that experience, she tries LSD again, and begins to experiment with other kinds of drugs. Before long, she is an addict, and drugs have taken over her life, alienating her from family, friends, and school. Eventually, she runs away from home, lives for a time as a prostitute, and ends up on the streets, filthy, hungry, and ill. There are moments of hope when she manages, with the help of her family, to break out of the drug habit. Several times she attempts a new start, only to be betrayed by her own insecurity or by the terrible pressure of her drug-taking friends.

Through all this, she writes faithfully in her diary, and so we follow every twist and turn of events, every high and low of her emotions. Though the language is that of a teenager, it is so alive and vivid that we are drawn in to her life, participating in her anguish, her alternating lucidity and recklessness, her love for her family and their desperate love for her. As a diary, it does not offer any solutions or any general truths about the teenage drug problem, but it does help us understand one person's choices and the consequences for her.

(From More Reading Power, *Second Edition, 2004, p. 44)*

Directions: Read the skimming questions below and then skim this magazine article. Remember, you need to read only a few sentences and words. Then, working with another student, write the answers to the skimming questions. You will have one minute for the skimming.

1. What is this article about?
2. What is the problem that is discussed in this article?
3. What is the new plan for forest fires?

Burning Trees to Save a Forest

By Liz Westfield

Burning trees to save a forest! Strange as it sounds, that is the United States Forest Service's new idea for saving America's forests.

For more than a hundred years, Americans were taught that fires in a forest were always bad. When trees burned in the forest, it was a disaster which would ruin the forest. The Forest Service promoted this idea in many ways. They even invented a character named Smokey the Bear, who always said, "Remember, only <u>you</u> can prevent forest fires."

In the past, whenever there was a fire in the forest, the rangers immediately put it out. No fires were allowed to burn, even in places where many of the trees were dead or diseased. This did not help the forests, however. In fact, with so many dead and diseased trees, the forest fires in the western United States have been far worse in recent years.

The new chief of the U.S. Forest Service recently explained that there is a new and better way to save our forests. He said, "Small, limited fires are part of nature. That is the way that old, dead, and diseased trees are cleared away to make room for new trees."

Now the Forest Service has new plans. They will start small fires in forests, but they will control the fires. The fires will be started in parts of the forest which are old and full of diseased trees. The rangers plan to burn about 30,000 acres a year for the next twenty years.

As the chief said, it took many years for the forests to become old and diseased, and so it will take more than twenty years to correct the problem by using controlled fires.

(From Reading Power, *Third Edition, 2005, p. 146)*

Directions: Skimming is also helpful when reading articles on the Internet. Read the skimming questions and then skim this article. You will have two minutes for skimming. Then, working with another student, write the answers to the skimming questions. Go back and read the article to check your answers.

1. What is this article about?
2. What does the company want to do?
3. What is the effect on the employees?
4. Why is this an important problem?

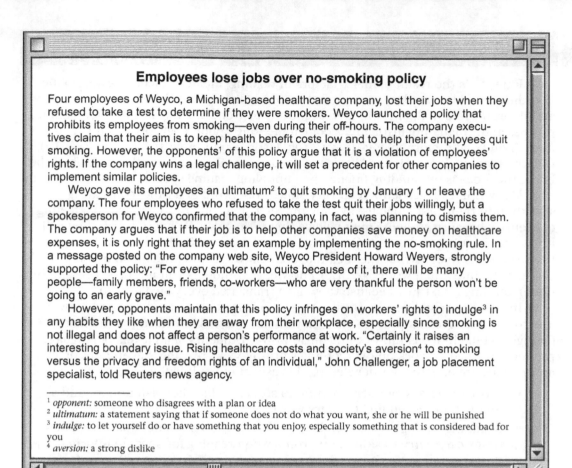

Employees lose jobs over no-smoking policy

Four employees of Weyco, a Michigan-based healthcare company, lost their jobs when they refused to take a test to determine if they were smokers. Weyco launched a policy that prohibits its employees from smoking—even during their off-hours. The company executives claim that their aim is to keep health benefit costs low and to help their employees quit smoking. However, the opponents[1] of this policy argue that it is a violation of employees' rights. If the company wins a legal challenge, it will set a precedent for other companies to implement similar policies.

Weyco gave its employees an ultimatum[2] to quit smoking by January 1 or leave the company. The four employees who refused to take the test quit their jobs willingly, but a spokesperson for Weyco confirmed that the company, in fact, was planning to dismiss them. The company argues that if their job is to help other companies save money on healthcare expenses, it is only right that they set an example by implementing the no-smoking rule. In a message posted on the company web site, Weyco President Howard Weyers, strongly supported the policy: "For every smoker who quits because of it, there will be many people—family members, friends, co-workers—who are very thankful the person won't be going to an early grave."

However, opponents maintain that this policy infringes on workers' rights to indulge[3] in any habits they like when they are away from their workplace, especially since smoking is not illegal and does not affect a person's performance at work. "Certainly it raises an interesting boundary issue. Rising healthcare costs and society's aversion[4] to smoking versus the privacy and freedom rights of an individual," John Challenger, a job placement specialist, told Reuters news agency.

---

[1] *opponent:* someone who disagrees with a plan or idea
[2] *ultimatum:* a statement saying that if someone does not do what you want, she or he will be punished
[3] *indulge:* to let yourself do or have something that you enjoy, especially something that is considered bad for you
[4] *aversion:* a strong dislike

(From Advanced Reading Power, *2007, p. 229)*

INTENSIVE READING LESSON

The teacher can plan an intensive reading lesson that includes practice in the skills taught so far. Hand out an article on a subject that could be controversial, such as the one in Sample Exercise B.17. Ask students to preview it, make predictions about the contents, and read the article to discover the author's opinion. Then hand out another article on the same topic. Students should be given two minutes to skim the second article to determine whether or not there is new information about the topic and to determine the author's opinion. Students should then form groups and compare their answers. A follow-up lesson could include an assignment to search the Internet for one or more additional articles on the same topic.

Fluency is the result of many factors in reading, including accurate automatic decoding, word knowledge, good prosody, and reading speed. Other factors also play an important role in fluency. In fact, according to Wolf, "fluency is a developmental process and...many linguistic areas contribute to it...phonology, orthography, vocabulary, syntax, and morphology" (www2.scholastic.com/browse/article.jsp?id=4470). Clearly, reading fluency is the "bridge to good comprehension." In this section of the book, the focus is on building fluency by improving reading speed.

Many ESL/EFL students read very slowly, one word at a time, translating silently into their first language as they proceed. This practice can lead to a feeling of security because students may believe that if they decode every word, they will know the meaning of the text. Of course, that is not necessarily the case because the reader has to construct the meaning of a text by relating the *ideas* in a text, not just the individual words, to prior knowledge. Students will not be successful in understanding a text just because they have translated every single word.

In order to read fluently, students need to learn to stop reading word by word and to guess or even skip words that they do not know. They need to read fast enough to take in ideas rather than single words. Students of all levels of language proficiency need to work on overcoming word-by-word reading. Several direct approaches are effective for developing this aspect of reading fluency.

- Cloze exercises can demonstrate to students that they can understand a text without attending to every word.
- Scanning—a high-speed reading skill—can show students that it is sometimes *necessary* to skip many words when reading for specific information.
- Training in reading faster can make it physically impossible for students to read every word. Pressure to speed up forces the reader to read for ideas, to look for key words and groups of words (collocations), and to skip over parts of the text. In fact, studies have shown that "Word recognition became more efficient, not attenuated, as fluency was acquired" (Levy, Nichols, & Kohen, 1993, quoted in McGuinness, 2004, p. 207).

CLOZE EXERCISES

Cloze passages are familiar to many teachers. In a cloze passage, the first sentence is left intact, and then words are systematically deleted (e.g., every fifth word or every seventh word). Cloze exercises can be used to determine text readability (the original use by Taylor, in 1953), and to teach many aspects of language, including grammar and vocabulary. (For further discussion of the cloze procedure, see the Appendix I, page 227.)

Cloze passages can also be used to demonstrate the fact that in English, it is possible to grasp the meaning of a passage without reading every word. Even with 18 percent or more of the words missing, students will discover that they can understand and even answer comprehension questions about a passage. (If the topic is a very familiar one, probably 90 percent of a text could be eliminated, and still the students could "read" it.)

However, it should be kept in mind, as Eskey (1973) pointed out, that when students are required to write words in the blank spaces, the cloze exercise is actually a vocabulary or grammar task. Therefore, in using cloze as we do here, the students need to be reminded that what matters is *not* providing the missing words but understanding the text *in spite of* the missing words.

Students can learn to risk skipping over unknown words and unimportant parts of texts, and they learn best when they experience the effect of skipping over words.

As always, the teacher should begin with a rationale for doing the exercises. In order to raise the issue of word-by-word reading, teachers can ask their students to respond to the following questionnaire:

READING QUESTIONNAIRE

True or False?

1. It is important to read every word if you want to understand.
2. You will learn more if you stop and look up every new word in the dictionary.
3. You should be able to say every word as you read.
4. If you read fast, you will not understand.
5. You should write the words in your own language above the English words when you read.

All of the statements are false, but students often argue that many of them are true. A class discussion of this questionnaire will provide an opportunity for the teacher to explain the reasons for not reading every word.

Cloze exercises such as the samples that follow will help students to realize that they do not have to read every word in order to comprehend a text. The teacher should select passages that are simple for students to understand. They should have no trouble answering a few questions about the passages. The teacher should start with a passage from which every tenth word is deleted. Then assign passages from which every seventh word and then every fifth word are deleted.

Many different materials can be used for cloze reading exercises. Grellet (1981) suggested using examples from everyday life: postcards that have gotten smudged in the mail, with half the words illegible; titles on very old copies of books, with many of the letters in the titles missing. Horoscopes, instructions for completing a process, descriptions of places, or narratives are also useful. The teacher's goal is to convince students that they can discover the meaning of a text even if they do not read every word. The exercises on pages 74–77 will demonstrate to students that they do not have to read every word in order to comprehend a passage.

SAMPLE EXERCISE C.1. CLOZE ACTIVITY WITH EVERY TENTH WORD DELETED

Directions: Read the passage. Do not write the missing words. Answer the questions. Then talk to another student about your answers. Do you agree?

Dennis and Linda Wilson are married. They have three children _____

school. Dennis works as a full-time teacher and Linda _____ a part-time

job in the town library. She is _____ in the afternoon to take care of the

children _____ to clean the house and cook their meals. Now _____

Wilson family needs more money for clothes and food. _____ wants to get

a second job on Saturdays and _____ wants to work full time at the library.

But _____ will take care of the children?

Questions:

1. Do Dennis and Linda both have full-time jobs? _____
2. Why does the family have a problem about money? _____
3. Who cleans the house? _____
4. Who earns the money? _____
5. What is another problem for the Wilson family? _____

SAMPLE EXERCISE C.2. CLOZE ACTIVITY WITH EVERY SEVENTH WORD DELETED

Directions: Read the passage. Answer the questions. Do not write the missing words. Then talk to another student and explain your answers.

Internet Shopping

Shopping on the Internet is popular around the world. People shop at home

and do _____ use their cars, so they save money _____ gasoline. They

save time because they don't _____ to drive to stores, and they _____

more time to relax. And often people _____ money, too. Some things cost

less on _____ Internet than they do in shops.

True or False?
1. Everyone shops on the Internet.
2. Shopping on the Internet always costs more.
3. Most Internet shopping is done from home.

SAMPLE EXERCISE C.3.   CLOZE ACTIVITY WITH EVERY FIFTH WORD DELETED

Directions: Read the passage. Answer the questions. Do not write the missing words. Then talk to another student and explain your answers.

Barbara Gomez doesn't need to own a car. She is forty years _____, single, and she works _____ a cook in a small _____. She doesn't earn much _____, but she likes to _____ a lot. She often _____ car on the weekends _____ the prices are lower. _____ also rents a car _____ several weeks during the _____ because she likes to _____ to the lake in _____ warm weather.

True or False?
1. Barbara Gomez is married.
2. Barbara likes to travel.
3. Barbara often rents a car.
4. Barbara never takes a vacation.

Longer passages with the comprehension questions already written (e.g., passages from readers) can easily be adapted for cloze reading exercises. One such passage, shown in the sample exercise that follows, is from *Reading Power, Third Edition* (2005), page 251.

SAMPLE EXERCISE C.4.   LONGER PASSAGE WITH EVERY FIFTH WORD DELETED

Directions: A. Read the passage. Do not write the missing words. Then answer the questions that follow the passage.

Time to Dance

Are you the kind of person who likes to move with the music? It's a natural thing _____ do. Even little children _____ jumping up and down _____ they hear music. In _____, people have always danced _____ important moments in their _____. It's part of the _____ experience, like music or _____.

Scientists say that _____ dance, too, but their _____ is different. The "dances" _____ animals send messages to _____ animals. These messages are about _____ physical needs, such as _____, or danger. But when _____ dance, they express feelings _____ life and love, or about _____ and sadness. From early _____, dancing has been a _____ to show feelings about _____ very human experiences.

Dances _____ also an important part _____ every culture. In the
_____, each culture had its _____ dances. In Scotland, for _____,
everyone learned Scottish dancing. _____ days, the situation is _____
different. In the past _____ hundred years, many people _____ the world
have moved _____ other countries. When they _____, they brought along
their _____ and their dances. This _____ that today you can learn many
_____ kinds of dances. You _____ learn Greek, Scottish, Egyptian,
_____ Indonesian dances. You can _____ the Viennese waltz, the
Argentine _____, or American swing dancing.

_____ kinds of dances are _____ for you in the _____ ways. For
one thing, _____ is good for your _____. It makes your heart _____, it
makes you breathe _____, and it makes you _____ your arms and your
legs. _____ you go dancing often, _____ can keep physically fit. _____
also is an enjoyable _____ to try to lose weight.

_____ may feel very tired _____ dancing, but you'll probably
_____ feel relaxed and happy. _____ is the other important _____
about dancing. It gives _____ a chance to express _____ feelings and feel
better _____ yourself. If you are angry _____ upset about something,
dancing _____ those feelings go away. _____ you are afraid or _____,
dancing helps you forget _____ fear. When you're dancing, _____ can
forget yourself completely _____ feel like another person.

_____ finally, there is another _____ point about dancing. It's
_____ social activity. Some dances _____ for couples and some _____
for groups. But all _____ of dances give you _____ chance to meet new
_____ or to do something _____ with friends.

B. *Circle the best answer. Do not look back! Then compare your answers with
    another student's. If the two of you do not agree, look back at the passage and
    explain your answers.*

1. This passage is about
   a. different kinds of dances.
   b. reasons for dancing.
   c. how animals dance.
   d. learning to dance.

2. Animals dance
   a. to express feelings to other animals.
   b. because they hear music.
   c. for the same reasons as people.
   d. to send messages to other animals.
3. For people, dancing is a way to
   a. express feelings.
   b. warn other people.
   c. become a child.
   d. become American.
4. In the past, each culture had
   a. Viennese waltzes.
   b. the same dances.
   c. its own dances.
   d. new dances.
5. Today you can learn
   a. many kinds of dances.
   b. how animals dance.
   c. few kinds of dances.
   d. only modern dances.
6. Dancing is
   a. bad for your heart.
   b. not good for your legs.
   c. bad for your body.
   d. good for your body.
7. After dancing, you feel
   a. better about yourself.
   b. angry with everyone.
   c. tired and unhappy.
   d. afraid of other people.
8. One important point about dancing is that you
   a. can become famous.
   b. do it with other people.
   c. can do it only in groups.
   d. don't have to pay much.

SCANNING

Scanning is a high-speed reading skill that is used for locating specific information. Scanning is not the same as skimming, which was discussed in Section B. Skimming is a much more complicated skill than scanning. Skimming requires the rapid reading of an article to extract the main ideas and some supporting details.

Scanning is important and useful for all readers because it is another skill that helps students develop reading fluency. When students practice scanning, they learn that they can obtain information from a text without reading every word. In addition, they develop the ability to visualize words in English as they scan for them. And they discover that they can use scanning as a strategy for speeding up their sampling of any text, even a text that they cannot fully comprehend.

Scanning cannot be learned in a single lesson. Students need repeated practice in order to improve their ability to move their eyes rapidly and feel comfortable in skipping over large amounts of text. Students must understand that scanning is an *extremely* high speed reading activity and that they should *not try to read* an entire passage carefully. The teacher should impose strict time limits for completing a scanning exercise in order to keep students working at top speed.

Some teachers have found that if they make scanning exercises into competitions, either between two groups of students or between everyone in the class, the students are more willing to risk skipping over many words in the text to find the information required. The success of this use of competition will depend, of course, on the background of the students and their familiarity with (and acceptance of) competitive activities.

Scanning Exercises Based on Realia

The most exciting and productive scanning exercises are those that the teacher designs, because the activities can be geared to the ages, proficiencies, and interests of the students in the class. Successful scanning lessons can be based on restaurant menus, TV program schedules, articles from *Time* and *Newsweek,* restaurant reviews, movie listings, and most popular of all, classified ads.

A scanning lesson can include many different kinds of questions. The best questions are those that are written with a specific class in mind. For instance, a scanning exercise can serve simultaneously as a review of *wh-* questions. In addition, by varying the difficulty of the questions, the same material can be used for students with widely differing proficiencies in English. (For example, two levels of questions are presented in Sample Exercise C.5.) As always, the teacher should introduce this skill with a rationale such as the following.

SAMPLE RATIONALE

If you need to find someone's telephone number, you do not read the whole telephone directory! You read only what you need. This is called scanning.

Can you think of any other materials that you can scan? (Students will probably mention schedules, indexes, ads, and dictionaries.)

Scanning is a very high-speed reading skill that will help you to improve your reading in English. When you need information from a newspaper or a book, you do not need to read every word—you can scan.

In most exercises, students read a question and then scan for the information. In that case, they will have a visual cue to guide them as they scan. However, it is also possible to for the teacher to pose the questions aloud. This is more challenging, since students must listen for the cues and then visualize them as they scan.

Sample Exercise C.5 is based on a typical breakfast menu. For regular classroom use, it would be more interesting for the students if the teacher used menus from local restaurants.. The two sets of scanning questions demonstrate how to adapt this exercise to the English proficiency level of a specific class.

SAMPLE EXERCISE C.5.   SCANNING A MENU

Directions: Read each question and scan the menu to find the answer. Work fast! Then talk about your answers with another student. Do you agree?

Scanning Questions (for beginning and low intermediate level students)

1. What is the price for one egg?
2. How many kinds of bread are on the menu?
3. What is the price of a cup of coffee?
4. Can you order a boiled egg?
5. What kinds of fruit juice can you order?

CITYSIDE BREAKFAST RESTAURANT

BREAD SELECTIONS
CISSEL, MARBLE RYE, PUMPERNICKEL, CHALLAH, WHEAT, SOURDOUGH

BAGEL SELECTIONS
PLAIN, SALT, ONION, POPPY, SESAME, MARBLE, EGG, CINNAMON RAISIN, THE WORKS, AND WHOLE WHEAT

FARM FRESH EGGS with your choice of bread or bagel
YOUR WAY: POACHED, SCRAMBLED, SOFT BOILED, HARD BOILED OR SUNNYSIDE UP
ONE $3.95   TWO $4.95   THREE $5.95

BREAKFAST SANDWICH
FRIED EGGS, HAM, MUENSTER, TOMATO & ENGLISH MUFFIN $6:95
FRIED EGG B.L.T. OPEN FACED CHALLAH, SMOKED BACON, LETTUCE, TOMATO $6.95
FRIED MATZO WITH CINNAMON SUGAR $7.95
CORNED BEEF HASH & EGGS $9.95
LOX, ONIONS & SCRAMBLED EGGS $11.50
BEEF SALAMI & SCRAMBLED EGGS $8.95

CUSTOMIZED OMELETTE $6.95 with your choice of bread or bagel
CHOOSE FROM: SMOKED BACON, HAM, SAUSAGE, ROASTED PEPPERS, ONION, MUSHROOMS, OLIVES, SPINACH, TOMATO, BROCCOLI, SWISS, CHEDDAR, MUENSTER, AMERICAN, PROVOLONE, FETA, SALSA, CHIVES, GOAT CHEESE, FIRE-ROASTED TOMATOES $1 EACH

BREAKFAST BEVERAGES
DARK ROAST COFFEE (BOTTOMLESS)..$2.50
POT OF TEA (BOTTOMLESS)..$2.50
MILK $1.50
   SKIM, PLAIN, COFFEE OR CHOCOLATE
ICED TEA..$1.95
ICED COFFEE $2.25
HOT CHOCOLATE $1.95
FRESH SQUEEZED ORANGE JUICE..$1.95
   LARGE $2.95
FRESH SQUEEZED GRAPEFRUIT JUICE $1.95
   LARGE $2.95
FRUIT JUICES $1.50
   V-8, APPLE, CRANBERRY, PINEAPPLE
   LARGE $2.50

Note: The following questions for higher level students are based on the same menu.

Scanning Questions (for higher level students)

1. How many ways can you order eggs?
2. What is the price of a large orange juice?
3. In a customized omelette, how much would it cost to add 3 items?
4. What is in a fried egg B.L.T.?
5. How many different kinds of bagels are on the menu?

The following sample exercise is taken from a newspaper article. Once again, teachers are encouraged to use current newspaper articles to add interest to the exercise. It is not necessary to edit newspaper articles because students do not need to be able to understand every word in order to scan.

SAMPLE EXERCISE C.6.   SCANNING A NEWS ARTICLE

Directions: A. Scan the news article to find the answers to these questions. Work fast!

1. How many stores were damaged in the fire?
2. In which store did the fire (blaze) start?
3. What time did the fire start?
4. Where is the shopping center?

---

12 Newton Stores Damaged by Fire

Special to *The Boston Daily News*

NEWTON, Nov. 12-A five alarm fire damaged 12 stores today in the Mill Valley Mall, the largest shopping center in Georgetown County.

Fire investigators said the blaze apparently started in an electric service box in the basement of a clothing store and spread through a utilities duct below the 11 other stores. The fire started at 5:40 P.M. and was not controlled until 8:15 PM. The center is on the Mill Valley Parkway at the Lincoln Thruway.

Four firefighters were treated at the scene for minor burns. Capt. Alan Solomon of the Newton Arson Squad said the cause of the fire was under investigation.

B. *Write two more questions about this news article and ask a partner to scan for the answers.*

1. _____

2. _____

Using Textbook Passages for Scanning Exercises

Teachers can find exercises for scanning in many published materials. For example, most of the volumes in the *Reading Power* series (Mikulecky & Jeffries) include a section that focuses on scanning. In addition, *Skimming and Scanning* (Fry, 2000) is a workbook that includes a nice introduction to the scanning process and many exercises that use materials from daily life. It is important to note that when students work on such exercises on their own, they almost always slow down and read the entire passage carefully, thus defeating the purpose. Therefore, scanning exercises from these books are best used for whole-class activities, with the teacher reading the questions aloud. Alternatively, students can be paired and can take turns reading the questions aloud and timing each other. Another option is to allow the students to work independently, but under *strictly timed conditions*.

Building up the skill of scanning should begin at a simple level. The following sample exercise is from *Reading Power 2, Fourth Edition*, 2009, p. 118.

SAMPLE EXERCISE C.7. SCANNING FOR KEY WORDS

Directions: Look for the key word and circle it every time you see it. You will have 60 seconds.

Key Words

1. way	wag	warp	way	way	why
2. fast	fast	fail	fast	fist	fact
3. right	rigid	rigor	right	rite	right
4. with	white	with	wink	with	witch
5. best	best	best	beet	beat	bent
6. every	early	evenly	every	envy	every
7. read	rend	read	reed	real	read
8. save	save	sane	serve	salve	save
9. down	dawn	down	done	down	dove
10. good	goof	goad	good	good	goal
11. were	wire	were	were	ware	where
12. have	hare	hair	have	harm	have
13. back	bake	back	bark	bask	back
14. think	think	thick	thing	thank	think
15. people	pepper	people	popular	period	people
16. there	there	their	three	there	theme
17. thought	through	thorough	thought	thought	though
18. with	white	with	wish	wife	wilt

Another source of material for scanning practice is the *Rate Builder* kit, a set of reading cards published by Science Research Associates (SRA). The main purpose of the cards is to practice reading rate improvement, but their format can easily be adapted for scanning practice.

Each *Rate Builder* card consists of a short passage followed by several comprehension questions. Because many of the questions are literal, students can readily locate the answers *without* reading the passage. Students should be instructed to read the questions first and then scan the *Rate Builder* card very rapidly for the answers. Since each card is different, students will have to work independently, but if the teacher imposes a very short time limit (two minutes maximum), the students will not have time to read every word in the passage.

The sample exercise on page 82 is based on a *Rate Builder* card.

Directions: Do not read the passage. Read each question at the bottom of the card and then scan the passage for the answer. Work fast! You will have one minute to answer all the questions. Then talk to another student about your answers. If you do not agree, read the passage to check your work.

A hermit crab that has found an empty shell for its new home may share its dwelling. It chooses a sea anemone to settle on top of the shell. This flower-like animal's usual home is on a rock.

The sea anemone gains by the partnership. As it rides on the shell, it has a better chance of getting food. Pieces of food torn by the crab as it dines may also reach the anemone's mouth.

The crab profits in its turn. Its enemies find the crab harder to see and to attack. Around the anemone's mouth are tiny arms called tentacles. These shoot out threads that poison and even kill.

A hermit crab sometimes becomes a "two-gun" wanderer. It carries an anemone on each claw of its first pair of legs.

1. The crab in this partnership is the
   - **a.** spider crab
   - **b.** fiddler crab
   - **c.** hermit crab
   - **d.** sponge crab

2. Its partner is described as
   - **a.** a sea plant
   - **b.** an animallike flower
   - **c.** sea flower
   - **d.** a flowerlike animal

3. The crab's partner lives
   - **a.** inside the shell
   - **b.** on a nearby rock
   - **c.** on top of the shell
   - **d.** none of the above

4. The sea anemone gains because it has a better
   - **a.** supply of food
   - **b.** place to hide
   - **c.** both a and b
   - **d.** neither a nor b

5. The crab gains because it is
   - **a.** better hidden from its enemies
   - **b.** protected by its partner's tentacles
   - **c.** both a and b
   - **d.** neither a nor b

(D. Parker, Reading Laboratory Kit 3a, 1973. Reproduced with permission of The McGraw-Hill Companies.)

READING FASTER

Some teachers may be surprised when they hear that they should teach their ESL/EFL students to read faster. However, there are both pedagogical and practical reasons for including reading rate improvement in the ESL/EFL reading class.

First, reading faster leads to greater reading fluency and this, in turn, leads to increased comprehension. Faster reading aids comprehension by encouraging students to read in "chunks" instead of one word at a time. (For more information about "chunking," see Nation, 2001, p. 337.) "According to 'Research-Based Principles for Adult Basic Education Reading Instruction' (National Fluency Government Partnership for Reading, 2007), students who are not fluent readers will spend more time on decoding than they do on understanding the meaning of the text" (Brady & Kritsonis, 2008). (See also N. Andersen, 1999.)

Second, working on increasing their reading rate reinforces for students the idea that it is possible to understand a passage without necessarily reading every word, one word at a time. That is a very difficult habit to break, and many students balk at skipping words. They often say, "That's not *really reading*." It is important to remember that reading word by word may be more than just a habit. It often reflects a student's cultural understanding about the nature and purpose of reading, and it may be essential to read word by word (or character by character) in the student's first language.

Third, in academic settings that require reading in English, one of the most difficult challenges students face is the large number of reading assignments. ESL/EFL students who do not learn to read faster can spend three to four times longer than their native English-speaking classmates on completing the reading for a course. Then they have little time left for thinking over and synthesizing the ideas they have learned from their reading. In fact, an inability to keep up with the reading is often one of the main reasons some ESL/EFL students drop out of college.

Most importantly, reading rate affects comprehension. Research shows that the short-term memory will not hold information for more than a few seconds. The reader needs to take in enough of the text at one time to allow the brain to make sense of it. The brain cannot do its work effectively unless students learn to read at a rate of about 200 words per minute (Smith, 1986). Therefore, improved comprehension will result from learning to read faster.

Students make the most progress in reading faster when they have the opportunity to practice reading rate improvement several times a week in class and, if possible, have additional practice in a reading lab or at home. Students should read materials at their English language proficiency level "against the clock" and then answer comprehension check questions. Once they get into the routine, students enjoy using a graph or chart to keep a record of their rate and comprehension.

When reading rate improvement exercises become a regular part of the reading class, even at the beginning level, students *do learn to read faster*, and they also learn to vary their reading rate, depending on what they already know about the topic of the passage and their purpose for reading it.

Materials for Practicing Reading Rate Improvement

Materials for reading rate improvement should not be too difficult for the student. In most classes, this means that the students will not all work on the same materials. Furthermore, students usually have a wide range of reading rates. It makes sense, then, to individualize reading rate practice, assigning appropriate materials to each student to work on at his or her own pace.

It is important to use rate-building materials strictly for that purpose and not, for example, for testing comprehension, vocabulary, or grammar. Students should feel free to risk experimenting with rate-building strategies as they work on the practice materials. When students believe that they will "be held accountable" in a serious way for what they are reading for reading rate practice (more than privately checking their own comprehension), they usually slow down, and their reading rate will not improve.

Some of the materials for reading rate improvement described in the following paragraphs were not designed especially for ESL/EFL or other limited English-proficient students. These materials often lack illustrations that can help the reader establish context, and they often assume the cultural background knowledge that native speakers of English usually possess. However, these materials do provide interesting practice passages at multiple proficiency levels, and they are conveniently packaged with answer keys, making them suitable for independent, individualized use by the students.

Teachers with little experience in working with students on reading rate improvement will appreciate the Jamestown *Timed Readings* series by Spargo and Williston (1989) because at the front of each student book they will find thirteen pages of helpful instructions and guidelines for the teacher. This widely used and highly respected series consists of books at ten reading ability levels, ranging from grade four to college level in the United States. The fifty 400-word passages in each book are followed by ten questions, five literal and five interpretative.

Another set of materials is the *Rate Builder* kit from SRA mentioned earlier. These materials have been popular in school and college reading labs for many years. An example of a typical *Rate Builder* card was shown on page 82 in the section on scanning. The kit contains 150 such reading cards at ten reading levels. This makes it possible for the teacher to individualize reading rate practice and assign each student to his or her own reading level. Each card, including comprehension questions, is designed to be completed in the same amount of time, with the entire class timed simultaneously by the teacher. The notion is that students will gradually increase their reading rate and advance at their own pace to higher levels with longer passages with more questions.

The SRA cards, while useful, have some limitations. The practice of giving a set time limit for the reading is not always popular with students and, hence, not always motivating. Students often prefer to be actively engaged in reading against the clock and independently calculate their reading rate in words per minute, rather than having the instructor time them. In addition, many of the *Rate Builder* cards assume prior cultural knowledge that may not be familiar to ESL/EFL and other "non-mainstream" students. Furthermore, the passages on the *Rate Builder* cards are often very short, and research has shown that longer passages are more helpful in achieving higher reading rates.

The *Reading Power* series emphasizes faster reading. Each volume in the series, except for *Basic Reading Power (Book 1)*, contains a section on reading faster, with a sufficient number of passages (with comprehension questions) to provide a full semester of rate improvement practice. The *Reading Power* books offer guidelines for the teacher, progress charts, and other motivating techniques for teaching students how to read faster. Sample Exercise C.4 (a cloze exercise on pages 75–77) showed an example of a typical timed reading passage in *Reading Power*, Third Edition (2005).

Another way to promote reading rate improvement is to teach students to use their own individual extensive reading books for reading against the clock. If they keep a record of their reading rate, they almost always show an increase. (This is partly because of the student's adaptation to the style and lexicon of the author of the book and the buildup of contextual knowledge as the students get into the book.) Students can use the Extensive Reading Rate Finder and the Extensive Reading Progress Chart on pages 85–86 to compute words per minute and keep a daily record of their reading rate.

FIGURE OUT YOUR READING RATE FOR YOUR OWN BOOK

You can use your own book to learn to read faster. About once a week, use the Extensive Reading Rate Finder below to check your reading rate. Just remember to time yourself when you read.

Extensive Reading Rate Finder

Book Title: _____

1. Find a full page in your book. Count the number of words in three

   lines: _____ words.

2. Divide that number by three to get the average number of words in

   one line: _____ words.

3. Count the lines on one page: _____ lines.

4. Find out how many words there are on the page. Multiply the average number of words in one line by the number of lines on the page.

   _____ × _____ = _____
    (words in one line)   (lines on one page)   (words on one page)

   Now that you know how many words there are on one page in your book, you can figure out your reading rate (words per minute).

5. Open your book and mark the page you are on.

   Before you start to read, write the starting time: _____ min. _____ sec.

   When you stop reading, write the finishing time: _____ min. _____ sec.

6. How many minutes did you read? Finishing time minus starting time equals

   reading time: _____ min. _____ sec.

7. How many pages did you read? _____

8. How many words did you read? _____

   _____ × _____ = _____
    (pages)   (words on one page)   (number of words you read)

9. To find your reading rate, divide the number of words you read by the number of minutes.

   _____ ÷ _____ = _____
    (words)   (minutes)   (words per minute)

   Write the title and author of your book, today's date, and your reading rate on your Extensive Reading Progress Chart (on page 86).

Extensive Reading Progress Chart

Book Title _____   Book Title _____

Author _____   Author _____

RATE (words per minute—WPM)

480											
460											
440											
420											
400											
380											
360											
340											
320											
300											
280											
260											
240											
220											
200											
180											
160											
140											
120											
100											
80											
60											
40											
20											

Date

Guidelines for Teaching Reading Rate Improvement

Over the years, a number of different techniques have been developed for teaching students to increase their reading rate. Three of these techniques will be described on pages 88–89. However, no matter which technique a teacher decides to use, some basic guidelines should be followed. As usual, the introduction of a new skill requires a rationale for the students.

SAMPLE RATIONALE

Reading faster is important, even in a second language. Research shows that you will not understand if you read slowly. Your brain needs to receive ideas very quickly to make sense of what you are reading. Reading faster is a skill that you can learn, just like running faster. It takes practice and some training from the "coach." We will work on reading faster in our class. Most students will be able to read twice as fast by the end of the semester.

Select materials at appropriate levels.

Students must be able to easily understand their rate-building materials. If a student is assigned to a level that is too difficult (unable to score above 60 percent on subsequent comprehension check questions), that individual should be assigned to a lower level. But obviously, for self-esteem purposes, it is always better to estimate low and then have to *raise* a student to a *higher* level rather than vice versa.

The SRA *Rate Builder* kit is accompanied by a placement test that makes it easy to assign the students at the proper level. The Jamestown *Timed Readings* include no such placement test, but the levels can be assigned informally. For example, cloze tests can be devised from several passages from the Level 5 *Timed Readings* book, the middle of the series. Students should select the cloze passage they wish to read so that topic interest is not a major factor in their scores. Students who read a cloze version of a Book 5 passage at a passing level (33–38 percent correct, exact word scoring) can be assigned to that book. Other levels can be extrapolated from there.

The passages for faster reading in the *Reading Power series* were written at the proficiency level of each book's target audience. Therefore, the passages will be at the appropriate level for the students who are using other parts of the book. The *Reading Power* books provide comprehensive instructions in the teacher's guide for teaching faster reading. The passages in each book are introduced carefully to the students. Unlike the other materials mentioned above, the passages in the *Reading Power* series are topically related to each other, rather than passages with topics that are discrete and randomly selected. Charts and graphs for recording progress are also included.

Make reading rate lessons whole-class activities.

The suggested procedures outlined here are based on using either the Jamestown *Timed Readings* or the *Reading Power* series. In this approach, the teacher acts as a coach in helping students develop the skill of reading faster.

Take a base rate.

Before any instruction takes place, students should measure their initial reading rate. They should do more than a single "base reading rate" in words per minute to allow them to learn the procedures for accurate timing and recording their own progress on charts and graphs. (Record keeping is an important motivator, and students should do this for themselves.)

For the initial training, the teacher will have all the students begin reading at the same time, but they will finish reading at different times. They need to be able to record exactly what time they finish reading a passage, so the teacher should have a large clock (digital or face clock) on which the seconds are clearly visible to the class. *The questions are not timed.*

As a part of this initial timing, the teacher should reinforce the skill of previewing. Students should be taught to preview a passage for five to ten seconds before reading it. Please refer to Part III, Section B (pages 49–50) for directions and a rationale for teaching the previewing skill.

Set goals.

All students can improve their reading rate. In one semester, it is not unusual for many to double their reading speed. The class should discuss this after they have found their initial rates. Then they can set realistic goals for the semester.

Record progress.

Recording progress is a real motivator. Although there is much to be said in favor of a graph for recording reading rate progress, (e.g., the graph shown on page 86), teachers might want to consider using a Reading Rate Progress Chart instead like the one below; this chart is effective because in addition to quantitative information, students can record the titles of the passages and their comments about their own performance. They can give reasons for their reading rate and comprehension scores (e.g., unfamiliar/familiar topic; noise in classroom; feeling good today; interesting/uninteresting topic). Such record keeping builds motivation because it provides concrete evidence of progress.

Reading Rate Progress Chart

Name _____

Date	Title of Passage	Rate	Comprehension	Comments

Whatever record keeping system is used, the teacher should circulate around the classroom while the students are recording their scores, briefly discuss the results with each student, and ask for reasons for variations in rate.

Three Popular Techniques for Structuring Reading Rate Practice

There are a variety of ways to structure reading rate practice. The teacher should choose one of the following techniques and make sure that students are trained in using it.

Technique A: This is the simplest and probably the most commonly employed method.

Step 1. Student previews and then times his or her reading of a passage, recording the starting time and finishing time for reading the passage, not including the questions.

Step 2. Student answers comprehension check questions without looking back at the passage and then checks his answers for accuracy.

Step 3. Student records the results.

Step 4. Student goes on to the next passage and repeats Steps 1, 2, and 3.

Technique B: This is the same as Technique A for Steps 1, 2, and 3.

Step 4. Student reads the passage a second time and has a second chance to answer the comprehension check questions. He or she adds a second comprehension score to the progress chart.

Technique C: Called rereading, this approach has been used for over 100 years, starting in 1908 by the famous reading expert E.H. Huey. Recent rereading research began in the 1970s, and controlled studies in the 1980s confirmed the effectiveness of this technique (Herman, 1985; Roshotte & Torgeson, 1985; Dowhowerm 1987, all cited in McGuinness, 2004). With this technique, students set a modest reading rate goal and reread the same passage many times until they have reached the goal. However, some recent research has shown that for high school-age students, rereading does not seem to be more effective than reading other passages, as in Technique A (Wexler, Jade et al., 2008).

Step 1. Student sets a modest goal based upon (and only slightly higher than) his or her initial reading rate score.

Step 2. Student previews and then times his or her reading of a passage, recording the starting time and finishing time for reading the passage, not including the questions.

Step 3. Student answers comprehension check questions and then checks the answers for accuracy.

Step 4. Student records the results.

Step 5. If the reading rate goal was not reached, the student does a timed rereading of the *same passage,*

Step 6. Student continues this timed rereading of the same passage until the reading rate goal is achieved.

Step 7. A new modest goal is set, and the process begins again with a new passage.

When reading rate improvement exercises become a regular part of the reading class, even at the beginning level, students *do learn to read faster,* and they also learn to vary their reading rate, depending on what they already know about the topic of the passage and their purpose for reading it.

Effective top-down and bottom-up processing are essential and indivisible components of the reading comprehension process. As we noted in the diagram of the reading process in Part I, (Figure 1.2, page 10), the reader begins to make sense of a text by engaging in bottom-up processes, noticing the genre, the orthography, sound–symbol correspondences, morphophonemic structures, word forms and word meanings, and grammatical cues to meaning. The diagram also shows that these concrete, bottom-up processes allow a reader to make connections between the text and what he or she already knows.

Many students, especially ESL/EFL students, rely excessively on bottom-up processing, mostly word-by-word reading, translating as they move through a text. This is partly because when students read a second language, they will compensate for a lack of topic information or language knowledge by relying on word-level clues to meaning (Stanovich, 1981). In addition, they may have been taught that reading is a process of translating words. However, relying only on bottom-up processing may lead second language readers to unconsciously and mistakenly notice textual features that might function as clues to meaning in their native language, but not in English (Cziko, 1978; Birch, 2002).

ESL/EFL reading teachers, faced with some students' overreliance on word-by-word reading, often decide to stress strategies for activating the top-down processes at the expense of teaching bottom-up strategies. However, the success of top-down processing depends on accurate bottom-up processing. So in order to promote the development of fluent, effective reading, teachers need to include instruction on bottom-up processes (Birch, 2002). There are several ways to improve bottom-up processing at the letter, syllable, and word level. These include training in (1) recognizing English letters and words, (2) automatic decoding of high frequency words, and (3) recognizing the role of spelling, grammar, and phonological awareness in bottom-up processing. In Section D, the following aspects of bottom-up processing skills will be addressed:

- Perceptual skills: recognizing English letters and words.
- Automatic decoding.
- Linguistic features and bottom-up processing.
- Lexical items that signal textual cohesion.

PERCEPTUAL SKILLS: RECOGNIZING ENGLISH LETTERS AND WORDS

Birch (2002), Koda (2004), Wolf (2007) and many others have pointed out that the differences in writing systems lead to differences in the cognitive mechanisms required for reading. As Koda has stated, "Collectively, these findings provide solid empirical reinforcement for the postulation that reading a particular writing system entails a command of the cognitive mechanisms specifically designed for dealing with its structural and representational properties" (p. 37).

In other words, children learn to read and write in their native language by concentrating on the important features of that writing system. This establishes mental habits of processing that are unique for reading that language. In acquiring the Japanese writing system, for instance, children from an early age learn to process the characters by paying careful attention to the details of the characters. Especially in reading *kanji* (a Japanese writing system that uses pictorial characters), they must focus on the visual and spatial features of chunks and segments of each character in order to read it accurately. In contrast, the formation of the letters used in writing English is relatively unimportant. English letters can be shaped in a variety of ways, but a word still means the same thing. What is most important in decoding English is processing the sound–symbol correspondence of the English phonemes (the smallest meaningful units of speech that people can hear). Hence, when Japanese students are learning to read in English, they have to learn to ignore some of the mental processes that they developed in learning to read in Japanese. They need to develop new mental habits for processing or decoding the words in an English text.

The same can be said of any student whose native writing system differs from the Roman alphabet. Such students (at all levels of English proficiency) can benefit from working on exercises in letter, cluster, word recognition, and segmenting words into smaller parts and syllables. The more automatically they are able to recognize letters, word parts, and their phonemic correspondences, the less conscious attention they have to pay to decoding, and the more attention they can give to comprehending the text.

Research has shown that good readers unconsciously perceive and recognize such aspects of text as letter shapes and common words (Haber & Haber, 1981). Stoller (1986), Birch (2002), and others argue that visual discrimination training is essential for ESL/EFL readers. According to Stoller:

> The word and phrase recognition exercises are intended to help students develop their so-called "bottom-up" skills. That is, students learn to react rapidly and accurately to the appearance of English words and then English phrases as a whole. From these activities, students develop a sense of the visual image of key words and phrases. (p. 56)

The exercises for perceptual training included in this part of the book (modeled after Stoller, 1986; Harris, 1966; and especially Miller & Steeber de Orozco, 1990) are intended for visual discrimination practice. Meaning and pronunciation of the lexical items are temporarily ignored. The goal is to train students in rapid visual discrimination and identification of words and phrases. Students will improve their reading in English if they have an opportunity to work on such exercises regularly over several weeks. That is how they will develop strong new mental networks. As with every skill, teachers should provide a rationale, such as the following, for doing the perception exercises on pages 92–93.

SAMPLE RATIONALE

Your eyes and your brain know the letters, words, and phrases of your native language automatically. You can recognize them without even thinking, and that helps you to read fluently in your native language. But English is new to you. If you want to read and think in English, your eyes and brain need to learn to recognize English letters, words, and phrases automatically, too. These exercises will help you train your eyes to recognize the size and shape of letters and words in English.

The following exercises proceed from simple to complex. In order to prevent students from pronouncing the words, teachers should give the students a very short time limit for doing each exercise.

SAMPLE EXERCISE D.1. NOTICING WORDS THAT BEGIN WITH THE SAME LETTER

Directions: Read each row of words. Do not try to pronounce them. Circle the words that begin with the same letter as the key word. Work fast!

Key word

1. down	do	bow	dance	bone	done	town
2. tell	tie	two	time	bell	tea	fell
3. four	fast	tour	fair	face	tear	fan
4. hand	land	hard	hall	had	lad	have
5. jump	jam	bump	just	jail	lump	gone
6. went	were	mint	want	vent	won	wet
7. lime	love	last	long	time	line	fine
8. pass	past	pan	post	bass	fast	piano

SAMPLE EXERCISE D.2. NOTICING WORDS THAT BEGIN WITH THE SAME LETTERS

Directions: Read each row of words. Circle the words that begin with the same letters as the key word. Work fast!

Key word

1. flower	floor	flag	four	flat	blower	flight
2. prefer	poor	practice	predict	plastic	pray	present
3. cream	scream	crust	crack	clean	crash	cross
4. glad	glass	gold	globe	goose	glove	glitter
5. train	rain	track	try	tame	trust	trouble
6. those	toes	then	whose	thousand	these	their
7. spoke	smoke	speak	sport	speed	special	soak
8. drop	drink	door	dream	drag	down	dress

SAMPLE EXERCISE D.3. NOTICING WORDS THAT END WITH THE SAME LETTER OR LETTERS

Directions: Read each row of words. Circle the words that end with the same letter or letters as the key word. Work fast!

Key word

1. right	mat	sight	sign	rent	cannot	bought
2. bread	bed	read	break	said	led	instead
3. brown	when	men	blow	clown	farm	happen
4. far	star	fat	year	over	fat	father
5. happy	daily	silly	easy	east	pretty	salty
6. stop	tap	stay	pop	hop	still	step
7. tell	smell	tall	hotel	pill	still	dial
8. sing	sign	wing	thing	big	ring	king

SAMPLE EXERCISE D.4. NOTICING THE WORD THAT IS DIFFERENT FROM THE OTHERS

Directions: Scan each line of words and cross out the word that is different from the others. Work very fast!

Example: our ~~own~~ our our our

1. new	new	new	now	new
2. is	in	is	is	is
3. my	my	by	my	my
4. me	me	me	we	me
5. one	out	one	one	one
6. him	him	him	him	his
7. had	had	did	had	had
8. may	may	my	may	may
9. there	these	there	there	there
10. when	then	when	when	when

SAMPLE EXERCISE D.5. NOTICING THE KEY PHRASE

Directions: Read the key phrase. Then underline the key phrase every time you see it. Work at top speed.

1. Key phrase: **after class**

after math after class   under class   after class   other class   mother's class
after closing   math class   after class   other math   after class   master class

2. Key phrase: **rent a movie**

sent a movie   rent a car   sent a note   rent a movie   rent a tape   sent a movie
make a movie   rest a while   rent a van   rent a movie   read a novel   sent a van

3. Key phrase: **across the street**

across the road   across the aisle   under the street   across the street   across the screen
across the bridge   acorns in trees   across the street   after the treat   across the street

Perception exercises can also be devised using words or phrases that a teacher would like to review. For example, a class has just read a story that included the key words in Sample Exercise D.6.

SAMPLE EXERCISE D.6. NOTICING THE KEY WORD

Directions: Scan each line of words and underline the key word. Work very fast!

Key word

backaches	bookmarks	backpacks	backyards	backaches
doctors	doctors	directors	doctors	dentists
soaked	socked	soaked	soaks	sealed
small	snail	small	small	smell
being	buying	boring	being	betting
needle	noodle	needle	normal	needle
pain	pane	pine	paint	pain
specialist	sportsman	specialist	spicier	special
decade	decide	decorate	denied	decade

Word visualization and recognition ability can also be enhanced by using word search puzzles. Such puzzles reinforce the language learners' perception of letters and words in English. They can also be used to reinforce the spelling of specific words and the spelling rules of English when false "almost" words are included in the puzzle. Inexpensive software for devising word search puzzles is available online. (See, for example, www.WordSearchMaker.com.) A word search puzzle can also reinforce students' knowledge of semantic categories. In Sample Exercise D.7, all of the words that students must find are in one category: family members.

SAMPLE EXERCISE D.7. FINDING HIDDEN WORDS

Directions: Find and circle the hidden words. Some are hidden across, some are up and down, and some are at an angle from top to bottom or from bottom to top.

Hidden words: father, grandson, uncle, aunt, daughter, mother

```
d  f  n  o  c  w  d  y  a  e  l  k
i  a  a  o  l  d  n  a  l  r  m  t
s  t  u  f  e  m  n  c  v  c  x  z
i  h  n  g  r  a  n  d  s  o  n  v
w  e  t  r  h  u  j  l  m  i  b  B
p  r  a  t  h  t  r  c  r  i  n  Z
r  e  h  p  o  q  e  r  t  l  c  W
m  o  t  h  e  r  h  r  m  c  v  X
```

Word search puzzles can be customized by the teacher in several ways. For example, they can be assigned with no word list provided, giving simply the category and the number of words that are hidden. In addition, the hidden words can be selected according to the vocabulary knowledge of the students. Teachers can also devise word search puzzles for reviewing vocabulary or for introducing new words within a category.

Another exercise for training students in word perception in a meaningful context is shown in Sample Exercise D.8 (which is modeled after Haber & Haber, 1981). The upper half of every word is missing. The students are asked to read the passage and mentally supply the missing halves of the letters. Teachers can adapt any short text to create similar exercises.

SAMPLE EXERCISE D.8. READING A PASSAGE WITH THE LETTERS CUT IN HALF

Directions: As you read this passage, you will find that you can understand the story and answer questions about it even though only half of each letter is printed. Your brain makes up the other half! After reading the story, mark each statement True or False.

Swimming, bicycling, and running are three very popular
sports. Some people like to do all three sports in one race, called a
triathlon, which means "three sports." In a triathlon, people swim
for a mile and ride a bicycle for about 10 miles. Then they have
to run for 3 miles. Only the strongest athletes can win a triathlon.

True or False?

1. _____ A triathlon is a swimming race.
2. _____ No one can win a triathlon.
3. _____ The running part of a triathlon is the longest.

AUTOMATIC DECODING

Decoding— recognizing and identifying words— is one of the processes that good readers employ automatically with large portions of a text (Haber & Haber, 1981). Listed here are 100 words that make up about 50 percent of a typical page of an English language text. This list is from the *American Heritage Word Frequency Book* (1971), and it is very similar to other lists such as the first 100 words of the Brown corpus list (found at http://www.edict.com.hk/default.htm).

Automatic recognition of these 100 words makes comprehension of a text easier because it allows the reader to use more of the limited capacity of the eye-brain information processing system for attending to other aspects of the text and for making connections with prior knowledge (Stanovich, 1980). Teachers should make copies of this list available to their students.

100 MOST FREQUENTLY USED WORDS IN ENGLISH			
a	from	next	these
about	had	no	they
after	has	not	this
all	have	now	through
also	he	of	time
an	her	on	to
and	here	one	two
any	him	only	up
are	I	or	was
as	if	other	way
at	in	our	we
back	into	out	well
be	is	over	were
been	it	said	what
before	its	she	when
but	like	so	where
by	many	some	which
can	may	such	who
could	me	than	will
did	more	that	with
do	most	the	would
down	much	their	years
even	must	them	yes
first	my	then	you
for	new	there	your

(from Basic Reading Power, Second Edition, *2004, p. 129)*

In the following sample exercises (on pages 96–98), students practice rapid identification of these important words. As always, teachers should give students a rationale such as the following before they work on the exercises.

SAMPLE RATIONALE

The key words in this exercise are from the list of the 100 most frequently used words in English. They are small but important. On every page that you read in English, about half of the words are the words on the list.

SAMPLE EXERCISE D.9.   NOTICING THE KEY WORD

Directions: Work at top speed. Read the key word and then scan the line. Circle the key word every time you see it.

Key word

1. into	onto	unto	until	into	intra	into
2. been	been	bean	born	been	bane	been
3. back	black	bark	back	back	book	both
4. must	much	must	mist	must	mash	muse
5. then	them	then	thin	then	their	then
6. way	way	why	wax	way	way	wry
7. out	our	cut	oust	out	our	out
8. all	all	ail	aim	all	owe	aim
9. with	witch	with	wish	sill	with	wilt
10. over	ever	over	aver	our	out	over
11. they	thy	they	then	thirty	them	they
12. what	what	which	what	when	what	white
13. down	dawn	darn	done	down	dean	down
14. may	may	my	many	way	may	marry
15. time	turn	town	time	twine	time	tine
16. would	want	would	could	should	would	world
17. you	you	yes	yon	you	your	yore
18. also	alas	alto	also	alter	also	ails
19. much	must	mast	must	much	munch	mulch
20. after	alter	altar	afar	after	otter	after

Exercises such as Sample Exercise D.10 can raise students' awareness of the spelling of the 100 most frequently used words in English. In this exercise, the students are required to spell a word and also to write it.

SAMPLE EXERCISE D.10.   LEARNING TO SPELL THE 100 WORDS

Directions: Learn to spell the 100 most frequently used words in English. Find the words on the list and fill in the missing letters. Then write each word on the line. Look at the list of 100 words to check your work.

1. d _o_ _do_ _____

2. w __ s _____

3. b __ t _____

4. t h __ _____

5. w i l __ _____

6. y o __ _____

7. w __ y _____

8. o __ t _____

9. w __ _____

10. s __ __ e _____

11. s u __ h _____

12. w __ t h _____

13. l i k __ _____

14. o n l __ _____

15. m __ n y _____

16. b __ e n _____

17. u __ _____

18. b a __ k _____

19. y o __ r _____

20. a b __ u t _____

21. w o u l __ _____

22. a __ t e r _____

23. w h e __ e _____

24. b e __ o r e _____

A word search puzzle, such as the one in Sample Exercise D.11 (on page 98), can also be used to reinforce automatic recognition of the words.

SAMPLE EXERCISE D.11. FINDING THE HIDDEN WORDS

Directions: Find and circle the hidden words. Some are hidden across, some are up and down, and some are at an angle from top to bottom or from bottom to top.

Hidden words:

after	Are	did	had	me	of	they
all	before	down	he	most	or	to
also	But	even	him	my	our	up
and	By	for	in	new	some	way
any	Can	from	may	no	then	your

```
N  A  F  T  E  R  F  R  O  M
E  L  Z  O  H  A  D  B  U  T
W  S  R  N  I  N  A  L  L  H
D  O  W  N  M  A  Y  A  R  E
I  M  O  S  T  N  O  C  A  N
D  E  V  E  N  D  U  O  F  A
B  E  F  O  R  E  R  X  T  N
L  Z  O  U  R  S  T  H  E  Y
W  L  R  P  H  A  I  M  O  O
A  N  E  R  E  L  N  E  B  Y
Y  T  O  M  Y  S  O  O  R  C
```

Cloze-type exercises such as Sample Exercise D.12 can also help students to develop automatic identification. In such exercises, outlines of the words are shown, but not the actual letters. Such exercises can be aided (hidden words given in a list) or unaided (hidden words not given), depending on the needs of the students.

SAMPLE EXERCISE D.12. IDENTIFYING WORDS BY THEIR SHAPE

Directions: Read the story and use the shapes to guess the hidden words. Write the passage on a separate sheet of paper and fill in the missing words. Work with another student. You may use a word more than once.

Missing words:

a	was	and	about	But	about	could	not
of	She	this	to	This	the	she	

Helen Keller

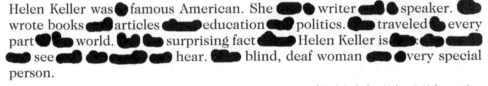

Helen Keller was ⬤ famous American. She ⬤⬤ writer ⬤⬤ speaker. ⬤ wrote books ⬤ articles ⬤⬤ education ⬤ politics. ⬤ traveled ⬤ every part ⬤⬤ world. ⬤⬤ surprising fact ⬤⬤ Helen Keller is ⬤:⬤⬤ ⬤ see ⬤⬤ ⬤⬤⬤ hear. ⬤⬤ blind, deaf woman ⬤⬤ ⬤very special person.

(Modeled after Haber & Haber, 1981, p. 173)

LINGUISTIC FEATURES AND BOTTOM-UP PROCESSING

Knowledge of many linguistic features affects reading ability. The lessons in this section are examples of meaning-based practice for helping students develop a greater awareness of some of the lexical and grammatical features that are especially useful for improving reading. The more textual clues to meaning that the reader can take note of, the more rapid, accurate, and fluent the reading will be. Sample Exercises D.13–D.15 (on pages 99–101) touch briefly on spelling, grammar, punctuation, and phonology.

Spelling

In the following sample exercise from *Basic Reading Power, Second edition* (Mikulecky & Jeffries, 2004), the spelling of some of the 100 most frequently used English words is practiced in context.

SAMPLE EXERCISE D.13.   PRACTICE WITH SOME OF THE 100 WORDS

Directions: Some of the most frequently used 100 English words are in these sentences. Write the missing letters of those words. Then read the dialogue aloud with another student.

1. Allen: W o u l d yo__ lik__ so__e milk w____h y__u__ coffee?

   Lynne: N__, thanks. I l__k__ black coffee.

2. Suha: Wh__t __s yo__r name?

   Yuki: M__ name i__ Yuki.

   Suha: I__ th__t a Japanese name?

   Yuki: Ye__, i__ __s.

3. Pat: Whe__e a__e yo__ fr____?

   Stan: I'm fr____ Texas.

   Pat: D__ yo__ li____ t__ ride horses?

   Stan: N__, no__ al__ Texans li__e t__ ride horses!

4. Stefan: D__ yo__ li____ to read love stories?

   Milly: N__, I don't. I l____e to read ab_____ science an__ computers. Th__y're m____h m__r__ interesting.

5. Craig: Wh__n di__ y____ call yo__r mother?

   Ivan: I called h____ be_____ lunch.

   Craig: W__s sh__ a__ home?

6. Ivan: No, s____ w__s still __t work.

   Craig: Wh____e does s____ work?

   Ivan: A____ bank i__ New York.

   Craig: Does s____ come b__ck home f____ lunch?

   Ivan: N__, s____ eats lunch a__ work.

A cloze activity that also reinforces spelling skills is the C-test, developed by Raatz and Klein-Braley (1984). In this activity, every second word is deleted. In order to make it possible to find the correct word, the first half of the deleted word is left standing. Only entirely correct words are counted as right. This develops bottom-up skills because students focus on the words in the text and use the first half of the missing words to help them choose the correct word. In Sample Exercise D.14, the English C-test, Senior Version, is excerpted from Raatz and Klein-Braley (1984).

SAMPLE EXERCISE D.14.   FILLING IN THE MISSING PARTS OF WORDS

Directions: In this story, parts of many words are missing. Using the story to help you, write the missing parts on the lines. Then read the story aloud to another student.

The evening of October 3, 1938, was just like any other quiet Sunday night

to most of the people of America. Many fami __ __ __ __ were a__ home

rea__ __ __ __ the pap __ __ or listening t __ the rad__ __ . There we__ __

two prog__ __ __ __ that nig__ __ which attr__ __ __ __ __ large

audi __ __ __ __ __. One w__ __ the pl__ __ produced b__ Orson Welles.

T__ __ listeners prep__ __ __ __ themselves f__ __ an ho__ __ of

enjo __ __ __ __ __ excitement, b__ __ after th__ opening

announ__ __ __ __ __ __, the pl__ __ didn'__ start. Instead there was

dance music.

Grammar

Cloze exercises are an effective way to make students aware of how grammar knowledge facilitates reading. Deletions of grammatical categories can heighten the learners' awareness of the importance of grammatical knowledge for skilled reading. For example, given a text that has all of the prepositions deleted, the students will learn the importance of using the correct preposition in English. Sets of directions or recipes work especially well for this kind of exercise.

A classic example is the recipe for "How to Make a Peanut Butter Sandwich" with all of the prepositions removed and listed on the bottom of the page. Working in a small group, students first read the recipe and write in the blanks what they think are the correct prepositions. Then they exchange recipes with another group of students who—supplied with bread, peanut butter, and knives—attempt to follow the directions to the letter. A mistake may mean spreading the peanut butter *under* the bread.

Punctuation

In order to call attention to the importance of punctuation as clues to meaning and to develop the language learner's awareness of syntax, a passage with all the punctuation removed is effective (Grellet, 1981). As students work together on such a passage, they predict where sentences are likely to stop, based on the meaning of the passage. The following example (Sample Exercise D.15 on page 101) would work best for students with higher levels of English proficiency. When they work on this exercise, students may have differing ideas about the correct placement of the punctuation. When they compare their work, such differences can lead to fruitful and interesting discussions.

SAMPLE EXERCISE D.15. **MARKING THE PUNCTUATION IN A STORY**

Directions: Read this fable and then, working in pairs, decide where the punctuation should go. Compare your results with those of another pair of students. If you disagree, explain the reasons for your punctuation.

THE LION AND THE MOUSE

One day a mouse ran over the tail of a lion that was sleeping in the middle of the path the lion awoke with a start and became very angry at being awakened he caught the mouse with his great paws and put the mouse in his mouth the mouse shouted oh please do not eat me if you let me go maybe i can help you some day oh please mr lion let me go and the mouse cried and cried the lion laughed loud to hear the tiny mouse say he could help him some day but he let him go because he was so amused one day a few weeks later the mouse found a lion caught in a great rope net the lion was roaring fiercely and trying to get out but he was trapped in the net the more he struggled the more he was caught the little mouse peered into the net and saw that it was his old friend the lion he remembered the lion's kindness he gnawed the net he worked all afternoon finally there was a hole for the lion to crawl through the lion said even little friends can be big friends

---

Phonology

Birch (2002) and others agree that reading comprehension depends to some extent on phonological processing. This means that as we read, we subconsciously hear the sounds of the words, and the sounds assist us in processing the words' meanings. We become conscious of our dependence on phonological processing when we have to slow down to process a long word or a name that is unpronounceable. Think for a moment about the time it would take to process Russian names in a novel by Dostoyevsky (e.g., Andrey Semyonovich Lebezyatnikov).

Students need to learn that written English stands for the sounds of English. McGuinness (2004) has argued that traditional phonics lessons in which students learn to "sound out" a word by giving a sound to each letter may not be the best approach. McGuinness maintains that students should *not* learn sound-letter correspondences because English is a very opaque language. That is, the letters in many words do not correspond directly in a one-to-only-one fashion to the phonemes in English words. Other languages are much more transparent. Every letter in a word in Italian, for example, corresponds directly to a single sound. But how can you use the letters in English to sound out the word *laugh*? In fact, *spoken words* are not made up of letters, but of phonemes.

According to McGuinness (and others, including Szabo, 2010), effective reading depends on students learning to recognize English phonemes and their spellings. She developed a chart of English phonemes (2004), from which the following portion is extracted. (For the complete chart, see Appendix II, page 232.) Notice that this chart is not based on the International Phonetic Alphabet (IPA), but on the basic code spellings in English. The seventeen phonemes in the portion of McGuinness's list on page 102 are the ones that are actually transparent in English; therefore, they are the easiest for students to master and should be taught first.

17 ENGLISH PHONEMES AND THEIR BASIC CODE SPELLINGS		
Consonants		
Sound*	As in _____	Basic Code Spelling
/b/	big	b
/d/	dog	d
/f/	fun	f
/g/	got	g
/h/	hot	h
/j/	job	l
/k/	kid	k
/l/	log	L
/m/	man	m
/n/	not	n
/p/	pig	p
/r/	red	r
/s/	sat	s
/t/	top	t
/v/	van	y
/w/	win	w
/z/	zip	z

*Sounds are indicated by letters within slash marks.

(From Diane McGuinness. *Language Development and Learning to Read: The Scientific Study of How Language Development Affects Reading Skill*. Table, pages ix-x: English Phonemes and Their Basic Code Spellings, © copyright 2005 Massachusetts Institute of Technology, by permission of The MIT Press)

Afterwards, students should be introduced to the spelling of more difficult English phonemes. For example, how many additional spellings are there for the English sound /f/? (*gh*, *ff*) or the English sound /sh/? When students encounter a word that includes the suffix -*tion*, they should be able to recognize that this includes a spelling of the phoneme /sh/.

According to McGuinness, lessons for sounding out words should be based upon the phonemes in words and the spellings of the phonemes. For ESL/EFL students, this means that a lot of the work on phonological processing should involve listening activities. In fact, according to some researchers, lessons in listening comprehension (and not pronunciation) can enable students to hear separate words and syllables, as well as correct phrasing in fluent English.

Listening comprehension can be part of the reading class. However, in order to make the transfer from listening to reading, students should read along when they are working on listening comprehension. For example:

- Teachers can read aloud while students follow along.
- Students can listen to recordings of materials as they read them.
- Teacher and students can do paired readings, taking turns in reading a text.
- Teachers can give dictation exercises for practicing the correct spellings of phonemes.
- Students can play rhyming games, recite poetry, and sing songs.

LEXICAL ITEMS THAT SIGNAL TEXTUAL COHESION

For enhancing students' bottom-up processing and comprehension, teachers should provide exercises in the vocabulary items that serve as cohesion devices, tying the text together and signaling the relationships between concepts and ideas (Cooper, 1984). These words are an essential component of vocabulary development for skilled reading, and this section will focus on pronouns, synonyms, hyponyms, and summary words These lexical items are best learned in context, as shown in the sample exercises on pages 104–111. Transition words—words that signal relationships between ideas in a text (also known as signal words)—will be examined in Section G (on pages 163–194).

Pronouns

Pronouns present a double problem for second language students: local meaning within a sentence and text-level meaning as signals of connections between parts of a text. Lessons on the use of pronouns for reading improvement may represent a new way of thinking about pronouns for some teachers whose usual practice is to teach pronouns from a strictly grammatical point of view. Activities such as Sample Exercises D.16–D.18 (on pages 104–106) can be effective ways to teach the pronouns and their functions as devices of textual cohesion within a meaningful context. Before working on these exercises, students should be given a rationale such as the following for learning pronouns as textual cohesion devices.

SAMPLE RATIONALE

Do you ever find that you understand most of the words you are reading, but you cannot understand what the writer means? Sometimes this happens when you do not pay attention to the connecting words. These words are often small, but they are important.

Pronouns are an example of these small, important words. Writers use pronouns instead of repeating the same word or name many times. Pronouns can be singular or plural. That is, a pronoun can refer to a single name or thing or to a group. In order to understand what you read, it is important to know what a pronoun refers to. That is called the referent. Here are some pronouns and an example how they are used.

Pronouns: *he, she it, we, you, they, who*
me, him, her, us, them
my, your, his, her, our, their, its
myself, yourself, herself, himself, itself
this, these, those, that, there

Example:

Mary Simms lives in New York City. <u>She</u> has an apartment near Central Park, and <u>she</u> goes running <u>there</u> three times a week. Mary says that running is good for your health for a few reasons. <u>It</u> is especially good for your heart, and if you do <u>it</u> a few days a week, your heart will be stronger. <u>It</u> is also good for your legs, and many people believe <u>it</u> is also good for your mind.

<u>She</u> and <u>she</u> refer to *Mary Simms*, the referent.
<u>there</u> refers to *Central Park*, the referent.
<u>It</u>, <u>it</u>, <u>It</u>, and <u>it</u> all refer to *running*, the referent.

SAMPLE EXERCISE D.16. IDENTIFYING REFERENTS OF PRONOUNS
(FOR BEGINNING LEVEL STUDENTS)

Directions: In these sentences, the pronouns are underlined. Circle the referents. Then compare your work with another student's. Do you agree? The first one is done for you.

1. (Running) is not a new sport. People were doing <u>it</u> hundreds of years ago.
2. Runners know that a good diet is important. <u>They</u> eat very healthy foods, especially before a race.
3. Every year, many long races take place around the world. Sports fans watch <u>them</u> on television.
4. The Boston race is called the Boston Marathon. <u>This</u> is one of the oldest races in the United States.
5. In some races, the winners get large amounts of money. But for almost 100 years, <u>they</u> got no money at all in the Boston race.

SAMPLE EXERCISE D.17. **IDENTIFYING REFERENTS OF PRONOUNS**
(FOR INTERMEDIATE LEVEL STUDENTS)

Directions: In each paragraph, the pronouns are underlined. Write the referent for each pronoun on the lines below. Then compare your work with another student's.

Pedicabs

1. A pedicab is a small cab that is pulled by a bicycle. This human-powered transportation has been popular in Asian countries for many years. Two years ago, a local businessman decided to introduce (1) it in Denver, Colorado. So far, (2) he has four of (3) them on the road. He explained that (4) they do not take the place of taxis, because people use (5) them for short rides. The passengers are often people who don't want to walk because (6) they are dressed in evening clothes.

(1) it _____   (4) they _____

(2) he _____   (5) them _____

(3) them _____   (6) they _____

2. The drivers of pedicabs are usually young students with strong legs and friendly personalities. (1) They pay the owner $15 to $25 to rent a pedicab for a night. (2) He expects (3) them to keep the cabs in good condition. A typical driver earns about as much as (4) he would by working as a waiter. (5) He can keep all the money that passengers pay (6) him. One pedicab driver said that (7) he feels like a businessman. (8) He can earn a good wage and be (9) his own boss.

(1) They _____   (6) him _____

(2) He _____   (7) he _____

(3) them _____   (8) He _____

(4) he _____   (9) his _____

(5) He _____

(from More Reading Power, Second Edition, 2004, p.61)

SAMPLE EXERCISE D.18. **IDENTIFYING REFERENTS OF PRONOUNS**
(FOR ADVANCED LEVEL STUDENTS)

Directions: Some of the pronouns in this passage are underlined. As you read the passage, draw an arrow from each of these pronouns to its referent. Work with another student.

THE ENSEMBLE

The best plays are created by a "tight ensemble." <u>This</u> means that the actors know each other well and that <u>they</u> trust each other. <u>They</u> seek advice from one another and ask for feedback. <u>They</u> do not fear making "mistakes" in rehearsals. <u>That</u> is what rehearsals are for. The same situation is beneficial to a group of language learners. <u>They</u> should feel free to criticize one another in a constructive manner, and <u>they</u> should learn to enjoy experimenting with the new language in front of their peers.

Language teachers can foster this feeling by minimizing the inhibitions of <u>their</u> students. The most obvious approach is to avoid making students' inhibitions any worse than <u>they</u> already are. The language class, like the rehearsal, should have an atmosphere conducive to open experimentation with the second language. It is much easier to be open and relaxed in front of friends than strangers.

(Adapted from S. Smith, The Theater Arts and the Teaching of Second Language. *Addison Wesley Publishing Co., 1984)*

Synonyms

Students with a limited vocabulary may mistakenly infer that two different things are mentioned in a text when, in fact, two words or phrases refer to the same thing. A series of exercises that focus on synonyms will bring this to the students' attention. Synonyms are more complex than teachers may realize. There are hyponyms (synonyms at different levels of specificity) and summary words (general words that replace a group of words). After students have had some practice in recognizing the functions of synonyms in a text, they can use their knowledge as a strategy for sorting out passages that do not make sense to them. Student should be given a rationale such as the following for learning how to recognize synonyms before they practice the skill.

SAMPLE RATIONALE

Writers make their writing more interesting and enjoyable to read by *not* repeating the same words over and over. They may use different words to name the same thing. You can learn to read better if you learn to recognize how synonyms are used in English.

SAMPLE EXERCISE D.19. **IDENTIFYING SYNONYMS** *(FOR ADVANCED LEVEL STUDENTS)*

Directions: Read the following sentences. Draw an arrow from the italicized word to the word or words that have the same (or almost the same) meaning as the italicized word. Notice that sometimes you have to draw an arrow to a group of words. Also, notice that the meaning of a word may be repeated with words that have a different form (e.g., an adjective may be re-expressed in a noun form).

Example:

Weyco, a medical benefits provider based in Okemos, Michigan, this year banned *employees* from smoking on their own time. Workers must submit to random tests that detect if someone has smoked.

1. More *companies* are taking action against employees who smoke off duty, and in an extreme trend that some call troubling, some businesses are now firing or banning the hiring of workers who light up even on their own time. (1 synonym)
2. The *outright bans* raise new questions about how far companies can go in regulating workers' behavior when they are off the clock. The crackdown is coming in part as a way to curb soaring health care costs, but critics say companies are violating workers' privacy rights. The zero-tolerance policies are coming as more companies adopt smoke-free workplaces. (3 synonyms)

(Adapted from "Trend: You Smoke? You're Fired!" by Stephanie Armour: *USA TODAY*, May 11, 2005)

Hyponyms

Hyponyms are synonyms that name members of the same category but at different levels of specificity. The hyponyms in the following passage are underlined.

Jane was rereading page 9, as the teacher had suggested. The page was very difficult for her. In fact, the whole chapter was almost impossible to understand. She took a break, sighed, and went back to her book. She wished that the teacher would assign easier reading materials.

Notice that there is a pattern in the use of hyponyms: Each succeeding hyponym is more general than the one preceding it. This is often found in English. Students can learn how to use such knowledge about hyponyms to improve their reading comprehension. As always, it is a good idea to encourage students to discover patterns such as the one for hyponyms rather than giving them a rule at the outset. Sample Exercises D.20 and D.21 (on pages 107–108) will give students practice in recognizing hyponyms.

SAMPLE EXERCISE D.20.   **ORDERING SYNONYMS FROM SPECIFIC TO GENERAL**

Directions: All of the items in each group refer to the same thing, but some are more general than others. Rewrite the list in order, beginning with the most specific and ending with the most general. Work with a partner. In the example, the synonyms are listed from most specific to most general.

Example:
Boston Red Sox baseball team
Major league baseball team
American sports team
Sports team

1. Mount McKinley
   Alaskan mountain
   mountain
   snow-capped mountain
2. Mr. Kim's house on Beacon Street
   house on Beacon Street
   house
   house in Boston

3. Los Angeles
   city on planet earth
   city in the United States
   city in California
4. evergreen tree
   tree
   tall pine tree
   Mrs. Brown's tall pine tree

Directions: A word is underlined in the first sentence of each passage. Circle the word or words in the next sentence that mean almost the same thing as the underlined word. Work with another student.

1. Liz moved to <u>Paris</u> last month. She likes the city very much.
2. Hiroko plays the <u>violin</u> in the Tokyo Symphony Orchestra. The sound of this stringed instrument is sweet and pure.
3. The <u>president of the city council</u> gave a long speech. As the leader, she has to plan many new projects.
4. The <u>hurricane</u> hit a small town in Texas. The storm swept down the main street three times, and the terrible winds destroyed most of the town.
5. <u>Lemons, oranges, and limes</u> are all very good to eat. These citrus fruits are also very healthy for you because they are a good source of vitamin C.

Write the hyponyms for each passage in order, from specific to general. The first one is done for you.

1. <u>Paris, city</u>

2. _____

3. _____

4. _____

5. _____

Many ESL/EFL and other English textbooks include one or two exercises similar to Sample Exercises D.20 and D.21, and it may be possible to find enough such exercises from several sources to be able to develop a sequence of lessons. But it is usually more effective when a teacher designs and writes the exercises, and it is not difficult to do, using passages from the newspaper or from a class text. In fact, students also enjoy designing these exercises for each other, using a textbook from another course. This is an excellent way for students to learn to apply their knowledge of pronouns, synonyms, and hyponyms.

After students have worked on pronouns, synonyms, and hyponyms as devices of textual cohesion, they should be asked to apply their new knowledge to a longer text, like the one in the following sample exercise.

SAMPLE EXERCISE **D.22.**   APPLYING KNOWLEDGE OF SYNONYMS, HYPONYMS, AND PRONOUNS *(FOR ADVANCED LEVEL STUDENTS)*

Directions: The ideas in a written text are tied together by short, unimportant-looking words. But these little words are very important for understanding. Read the following passage. Then go back and find the words and phrases listed in the table below the text. Write the referents in the table. Work with another student.

THE EFFECTS OF DUMPING HAZARDOUS WASTES

(1) In recent years, concern about the environment has grown as the public has become more aware of many common dangerous dumping practices. (2) These practices, some of which have been going on for years, have increased as the population has grown. (3) Recent publicity has drawn public attention to one form of environmental pollution—the dumping of hazardous chemical wastes. (4) These wastes include heavy metals and other byproducts of technology. (5) Such chemicals often cause cancer, brain damage, and high infant mortality rates.

(6) Dumping of the wastes is difficult to monitor, and quite often even careful dumping has resulted in the destruction of whole areas. (7) When the wastes are first put into a dump, they are usually sealed in large metal drums. (8) As time passes, the metal rusts and the waste materials begin to leak out into the surrounding soil. (9) This has two effects on the environment. (10) First, the local soil is often permanently destroyed, and it must be removed. (11) It thus becomes additional hazardous waste to be stored somewhere else. (12) Second, the chemical waste can sink lower and lower into the soil and reach the water tables deep in the earth's surface. (13) The latter effect produces pollution of the water sources for many miles around. (14) In cases where the wastes leach into a river bed, they can be carried to one of the oceans, thus spreading the pollution globally.

(From E. Mikulecky, 1985, used by permission)

Sentence	Word or Words	Referent
2	these	
2	some of which	
4	these	
5	such chemicals	
7	they	
9	this	
10	it	
11	it	
13	the latter effect	

Summary Words

Summary words are collective nouns and other general words that are used to refer to a number of details or steps. These synonyms are particularly challenging for ESL/EFL and other limited English proficient students. As with other referents, students may not realize that one word is summarizing several others in a passage. For example, the word *process* in the following passage is a word used to summarize a series of steps.

> First, she boiled the water. Then she added a drop of vinegar and six eggs, and she let them boil for ten minutes. She placed the eggs in ice cold water for half an hour to cool them. Then she chopped them and added them to the salad. The whole *process* took about an hour.

Collective nouns and words used to summarize or generalize are easy to teach if you begin by teaching hyponyms as described on page 107. And because these kinds of synonyms require thinking in terms of generalizations and examples, categorization exercises can be effective, too. To teach summary words and phrases, teachers can begin by giving students a rationale such as the following. Then students can perform activities such as Sample Exercises D.23 and D24.

SAMPLE RATIONALE

Writers often use a single word or phrase (a summary word) to name a whole collection of ideas or examples. You can improve your reading if you learn to recognize these summary words and phrases. They name a general idea in a passage that has many examples of that idea.

SAMPLE EXERCISE D.23.   NAMING A GROUP

Directions: The words in each list are members of the same group. Write the name for each group. The first one is done for you. Work with a partner.

1. _Planets in the solar system_

   Mars   Uranus   Jupiter   Saturn   Mercury

2. _____

   tennis   basketball   football   baseball   swimming

3. _____

   Russian   Greek   Polish   Chinese   Italian

4. _____

   cathedral   church   temple   mosque   chapel

5. _____

   malaria   tuberculosis   AIDS   measles   chicken pox

SAMPLE EXERCISE D.24.   IDENTIFYING THE REFERENTS OF A SUMMARY WORD
(*FOR INTERMEDIATE LEVEL STUDENTS*)

Directions: Read each short passage. The underlined word is a summary word that stands for several details in the passage. Write each summary word and then list the parts named in the passage. The first summary word is done for you. Work with a partner.

1. The Flynn family's house was robbed last week. Robbers broke in while the family was out and stole a television set, a Tivo box, some jewelry, and their silver teapot from France. The police are working on this case and they hope to recover the Flynn's belongings.

   Summary word: _belongings_

   Parts: _television set, Tivo box, jewelry, silver teapot_

2. Kilgore Trout's home library is well stocked. There are mystery books, novels, biographies, travel books, how-to manuals, science fiction thrillers, and reference books. This <u>collection</u> is the result of a lifelong habit of reading for pleasure.

Summary word: _____

Parts: _____

3. Susan Diamond got her new SPEND credit card in the mail. She went shopping immediately. She bought groceries at the supermarket, shoes at the department store, and a set of new tires for her car at the auto supply store. She did not spend any cash. The <u>purchases</u> were all made with her new credit card.

Summary word: _____

Parts: _____

4. For quite a long time, it has been known that sulfur dioxide is dangerous for people with sensitive respiratory systems. And some studies have shown a connection between increased levels of sulfur dioxide in the air and large numbers of premature deaths. If the government does not stop the factories from polluting the air, many more <u>health problems</u> could arise.

Summary word: _____

Parts: _____

5. During the summer, the music in Massachusetts moves outdoors. Special concerts are performed in the Hatch Shell on the banks of the Charles River and in a special fenced-in part of Boston Common. The Boston Symphony Orchestra moves out to Tanglewood, an outdoor concert park in the Berkshire Mountains. Jazz, rock, classical, and big-band music can be enjoyed while sailing in Boston Harbor. These <u>musical events</u> help New Englanders forget the long, cold winter.

Summary word: _____

Parts: _____

LEXICAL ITEMS THAT SIGNAL TEXTUAL ORGANIZATION

Often called *transition (or signal) words*, these lexical items serve as signals of text structure and divisions. For example, the terms *first, next, then,* and *finally* are signals to the reader that the contents of a passage are organized chronologically.

Such vocabulary items are best learned within the context of texts that are "ideal types" of various organizational patterns in English. Therefore, these vocabulary items are introduced in Part III: Section G (pages 163–194). In that part of the book, sample exercises are shown for various pattern types including chronology, listing, comparison/contrast, and cause/effect, and signal words for the patterns are introduced there.

ESL/EFL students face an enormous challenge in this area. Research indicates that a five-year-old English speaker begins school with a vocabulary of about 4,000–5,000 word families, and that about another 1,000 word families are added every year. This means that a native English-speaking college graduate will have a vocabulary of about 20,000 word families (Schmitt, 2000, p. 3). A word family consists of a headword (e.g., *context*) plus all of its inflections (e.g., *contextualize*) and closely related derivations (e.g., *decontextualization*); so a student who knows 20,000 word families understands about 100,000 words. If ESL/EFL students learned forty lexical units every single day for four years, which is not very likely, they would learn about 58,400 words.

Vocabulary knowledge is the basis of effective and high-speed bottom-up processing during reading. The larger the vocabulary, the more swiftly the reader can make accurate associations with prior knowledge and comprehend a text. Therefore, vocabulary development is a necessary part of the reading class. Section E addresses the following topics:

- Choosing the most useful words for students to learn from their reading.
- Principles of vocabulary teaching and learning.
- Vocabulary learning strategies.

SOURCES OF WORDS FOR VOCABULARY TEACHING AND LEARNING

Teachers often preteach the words that they think are most useful in the context of a specific article or story that students will read. This is helpful if there are several major concepts in a text that students need to understand. But, in general, the words selected for preteaching (1) may already be known by the students and (2) may be content-specific and not likely to be encountered in future reading. Furthermore, when a teacher begins a reading lesson by preteaching the meanings of specific words, students might get the erroneous impression that the meaning of a text can be found by simply knowing the meaning of every word.

If, on the other hand, students choose the words that they want to learn, they are more likely to be motivated to learn them, but they are likely to select words that they might rarely encounter again in their reading. With a limited amount of time, students need to learn to focus their vocabulary learning on the words that will be most useful in future reading—namely, high frequency words.

High Frequency Words

Recent theory and research in corpus linguistics and vocabulary learning have provided exciting ideas about vocabulary acquisition and its relationship to reading in a second language. Corpus linguistics is the analysis of large samples of texts from a variety of sources. Before the advent of computer technology, such work was time-consuming and difficult. But, today, researchers can download a body (corpus) of texts containing millions of words and analyze the language in many ways. The texts can be corpora of academic texts (as Coxhead worked on in her study of academic words), medical corpora, or any other domain. (To explore this topic, see *The International Journal of Corpus Linguistics*.)

One of the most useful outcomes of corpus linguistics is the development of high frequency word lists. While similar lists have existed for many years, it is the emergence of corpus linguistics and the computer-based analysis of millions of pages of text that have made it possible to develop computer programs that will identify accurately the high frequency words in any text. For example, it is possible to analyze (at no expense) any selected text in a few seconds using the program found at www.lextutor.ca.

According to Nation (2001), about 2,000 high frequency words constitute 80 percent of all texts in English. (The list of the 2,000 high frequency words is included in Appendix III on page 234.) An Academic Word List (AWL), developed by Coxhead (2000), provides an additional 570 high frequency words found in academic texts. (For the AWL, see Appendix III on page 241.) A student who knows all 2,570 words will be familiar with about 85 to 90 percent of the words in any text he or she reads in English!

The following chart shows the percentage of words from each list that is found in English in conversations, fiction, newspapers, and academic texts. This figure shows that even academic texts are composed primarily of the first 1,000 high frequency words.

	Conversations	Fiction	Newspapers	Academic Text
First 1,000 words	84.3%	82.3%	75.6%	73.5%
Second 1,000 words	6%	5.1%	4.7%	4.6%
Academic words	1.9%	1.7%	3.9%	8.5%
Other words	7.8%	10.9%	15.7%	13.3%

(From I.S.P. Nation, Learning Vocabulary in a Second Language, *2001, p. 17. Reprinted with the permission of Cambridge University Press.)*

In Nation's words: "High frequency words are so important that anything that teachers and students can do to make sure they are learned is worth doing" (2001, p. 16). Schmitt (2000, p. 143) maintains that it would be possible for students to learn the 2,000 high frequency words in one school year if they learned fifty of the high frequency words every week for forty weeks.

Reading teachers can use high frequency word lists in several ways.

- First, they can give a copy of the relevant lists to their students so that they are aware of the words and begin to notice them in their reading. Students at the beginning level, for example, may only need to receive the list of the first 1,000 high frequency words.

- Second, teachers can instruct the students to refer to the lists when they are deciding which new words they want to learn from their reading.

- Third, teachers can select words from the lists for the direct teaching of vocabulary, focusing on words that the students will encounter in the context of other course readings.

- In addition, when working on any reading passage, teachers can identify the high frequency words in the text ahead of time and focus students' attention on learning those words. A helpful feature of the Lextutor Web site is a program called "Vocabprofile" (www.lextutor.ca) that makes it possible to analyze any text for word frequency and other information. Users simply paste in a passage or download a longer text and within about three seconds an incredible amount of information appears on the computer screen, including categorization of the words in the text into first and second thousand levels, academic words, and the remainder, or "offlist" words.

Here is a short passage and some of the information that was produced by Vocabprofile.

WHY IS READING IN A SECOND LANGUAGE SOMETIMES DIFFICULT?

Cross-cultural research shows that cultures have varying attitudes about language in general and that these differences are reflected in the printed word. As a result, the way ideas are organized in expository writing (e.g., in essays) varies across cultures. Originally called to our attention by Kaplan (1966), this suggestion has inspired research in several different languages. Ostler, for example, found that the patterns of expository writing in a language "reflect the patterns valued in the native culture." Researchers have found significant differences in text organization between English and the Korean, German, Japanese, Arabic, and Athabaskan languages. It is logical to conclude from this that when people read in a second language they comprehend best the texts that meet their beliefs and expectations about the patterns of written language. To the extent that the patterns in the text of a second language are different from those of the first language, the reader is likely to have difficulty comprehending.

Figure 3.1 Web VP Output

WEB VP OUTPUT:

	Families	Types	Tokens	Percent
K1 Words (1-1000):	53	66	**128**	**77.11%**
Function:	...	...	(77)	(46.39%)
Content:	...	...	(51)	(30.72%)
> Anglo-Sax =Not Greco-Lat/Fr Cog:	...	...	(15)	(9.04%)
K2 Words (1001-2000):	5	6	**9**	**5.42%**
> Anglo-Sax:	...	...	(1)	(0.60%)
1k+2k		...	...	(82.53%)
AWL Words (academic):	8	13	**16**	**9.64%**
> Anglo-Sax:	...	...	( )	(0.00%)
Off-List Words:	?	12	13	7.83%
	66+?	97	166	100%

Words in text (tokens): 166
Different words (types): 97
Type-token ratio: 0.58
Tokens per type: 1.71
Lex density (content words/total): 0.54

Pertaining to onlist only:

Tokens: 153
Types: 85
Families: 66
Tokens per family: 2.32
Types per family: 1.29

(From T. Cobb, VOCAB-PROFILER-BNC, www.lextutor.ca/vp/bc/)

In the Web VP output, we see that the text consists of 166 words. Of these, 77% of the words are found in the K1 list (first 1,000 high frequency words), 5.42% are words found in the K2 list, and 9.64% are found in the AWL.

Here are some definitions that might help interpret the output. A *word family* consists of a headword (an uninflected word), its inflected forms, and its closely related derived forms. A *type* is an individual word. When counting the number of types in a text, repeated words are not counted. When counting tokens in a text, every word is counted, even if it is repeated many times (Nation, 2001 p. 8). The notation *>Anglo-Sax* identifies words that are not Greco-Latin or French cognates.

Extensive Reading as a Source of New Vocabulary

Early work by Krashen (1985) promoted the idea that reading provides "comprehensible input" and hence is an excellent way to acquire English. Research in extensive reading and in vocabulary learning has supported the notion that the more students read, the more exposure they have to the grammar, vocabulary, and structure of a language (Grabe, 1991). Several studies showing vocabulary gains from extensive reading are cited by Day and Bamford (1998, p. 34), although Nation remarks that there have not been many carefully designed experimental studies of second language learner's vocabulary learning from reading.

Extensive reading can be a rich source of general vocabulary knowledge because the reader encounters new words in context, and the words are often repeated in the same book. In order to follow a story or an explanation when reading, the student is motivated to guess and then fine-tune his or her guesses about the meanings of new words. As Nation (2001) points out,

> The most important finding from first language studies is that this vocabulary learning is not an all-or-nothing piece of learning for any particular word, but that it is a gradual process of one meeting with a word adding to or strengthening the small amount of knowledge [about the word] gained from previous meetings. . . . Essentially, vocabulary learning from extensive reading is very fragile. If the small amount of learning of a word is not soon reinforced by another meeting, then that learning will be lost. It is thus critically important in an extensive reading programme that learners have the opportunity to keep meeting the words that they have met before. (p. 155)

Nation suggests that there are two ways to ensure that students have multiple encounters with their new vocabulary items:

- Have students do large amounts of extensive reading at suitable vocabulary levels to ensure repeated encounters with the same words. Research has shown that in order to gain new vocabulary from extensive reading, students should read books in which only about 5 percent of the words are unknown to them. Hence, for a student with a vocabulary of fewer than 2,000 words, a good choice for extensive reading are graded readers with a carefully controlled vocabulary.
- Complement extensive reading with direct study of selected vocabulary items from the high frequency words lists.

DIRECT INSTRUCTION OF SELECTED VOCABULARY

Improving reading depends on vocabulary development. Building on the ideas of Nation and others, it is clear that in order to facilitate vocabulary learning, teachers need to provide direct instruction in high frequency words and lexical chunks, such as collocations.

No matter what students read for extensive reading, they can also benefit from direct teaching of vocabulary. According to Nation (2001), direct teaching of vocabulary should constitute about 25 percent of a vocabulary program. Instruction should be planned so that the students are exposed to new words at least *ten times* in meaningful contexts in order to construct and remember a reliable sense of its meaning. This can include encounters in other parts of the same text, but also in activities such as identifying word parts, using the dictionary, finding word families, looking for collocations that include the word, and productive activities such as doing crossword puzzles, writing, and speaking. To motivate students, it is important to explain why the high frequency words are so important and why learning them will improve their reading comprehension.

Repeated encounters with a target word or phrase in a variety of contexts are necessary to allow the brain to make solid connections in the neural networks. As explained in Part I, numerous parts of the brain are involved in learning, and with each encounter the neural circuits connecting these parts are strengthened to the point where, after sufficient repetitions, there is a solid network for the new word. (See the information on brain-based learning on pages 41–42.)

Coxhead (2006) and Nation (2001) mention three essential aspects of building word knowledge:

1. *Noticing* a new word in a text.
2. *Retrieving* it again and again in meaningful contexts.
3. Using the word *generatively* in many contexts.

Noticing means becoming aware of a specific word. The student might notice an unfamiliar word in a text, either because its meaning is necessary for understanding a passage or because the word is interesting or intriguing to the student. Perhaps the noticed word was underlined or glossed. Alternatively, the teacher might have written it on the board and given a brief definition. The act of noticing is a metalinguistic action: although the word is noticed in a context, it is taken out of that context (decontextualized) and examined for its meaning as a separate language feature (Nation, 2001, p. 64).

Noticing is a powerful step in vocabulary learning. Almost everyone has had the experience of reading a news article about a disease or problem that they had never heard of before and then noticing references to it in their reading. Students who are encouraged to read the list of high frequency words can have a similar experience and begin to notice those essential words in their reading.

Retrieval is required for a word to stay in memory, and it involves repeated timely encounters with the same word. This can be accomplished by rereading the same text or by reading a long story or a book in which the same word appears numerous times. In retrieval, the student encounters the word in a variety of contexts and needs to remember the meaning or, vice versa, is given the meaning and needs to remember the word. Clearly, word cards (flash cards) are one way to increase opportunities for retrieval, and instructions for making and using word cards are given on pages 134–135.

Generation involves meeting, using, and manipulating a word in new contexts and conditions. This includes having students retell in groups the contents of a text, role-play based on a text, or complete writing and speaking assignments that require the use of the target word.

STRATEGIES FOR VOCABULARY BUILDING

For vocabulary building in the context of a reading class, it is important to maintain the general approach of instructing students in using strategies. Vocabulary learning strategies are important for students at all levels, but they become especially important for students who have already mastered the 2,000 high frequency words. As students continue to add to their vocabulary, the words that they learn at the 3,000-word level and up are encountered infrequently in their reading, so direct instruction to the whole class in the same words is not an efficient approach. Hence, for advanced students, vocabulary learning strategies will be the primary means of individual vocabulary growth (Schmitt, 2000, p. 144).

The strategies described here are useful for students at all levels. As with any new activity, the teacher should introduce the strategies with a rationale or a discussion about the benefits of applying them.

Two types of strategies are discussed in the following section:

1. Strategies for dealing with an unknown word while reading.
2. Strategies for choosing and learning new words from reading materials.

Dealing with Unknown Words While Reading

Strategies 1 and 2 address the students' need to deal with unknown words in their reading. Although Nation and others have pointed out that students develop reading fluency most readily when their reading materials contain only a very few unknown words, it is a fact of life that most ESL/EFL students find themselves in situations that require them to read materials with many more unfamiliar words. They are responsible for learning the material, and they need to know how to deal with unknown words that they encounter.

In order to begin a discussion, the teacher can informally poll the class to find out what they do when they encounter an unknown word. It is important for students to realize that they have several options for dealing with these words, and what they decide depends on the word, the material, and their purpose for reading. Then the teacher can discuss this list of strategies with the class:

POSSIBLE WAYS TO DEAL WITH AN UNKNOWN WORD

- Underline the unknown word and keep on reading.
- Stop and ask your teacher or another student for a quick definition.
- Stop and look up the definition in the dictionary.
- Try to figure out the meaning from the context.
- Look at the meaning of parts of the word as a clue to its meaning.

The teacher should discuss the choices briefly and explain that some are more helpful than others. For example, the teacher should point out that stopping to ask someone or looking up the word in the dictionary are both distracting and take time. Often underlining the word and continuing to read (skipping over the word) is a better choice.

Strategy 1. Skip over an unknown word.

Some ESL/EFL students are unwilling to skip over unknown words when reading in English, perhaps because such skipping would not be possible in their first language. However, English discourse is usually redundant (several words convey the same general meaning), so if the student skips over one word, the information is likely to show up elsewhere in the passage. If students in the class resist skipping over words, the teacher can use a cloze exercise such as Sample Exercise E.1 to show students that even with every fifth word removed, they can still get the general meaning of a passage in English.

SAMPLE EXERCISE E.1.   SKIPPING OVER WORDS

*Directions: In this paragraph, every fifth word is replaced by a series of x's. Read the paragraph and do **not** try to figure out the missing words. Then, working with another student, answer the questions that follow. Discuss your answers with another pair of students.*

FUTURE LUNAR MISSIONS

In planning for future xxxxxx missions, scientists are faced xxxxxx one serious limitation to xxxxxx on the moon, and xxxxxx is the lack of xxxxxx. So far no evidence xxxxxx been found of the xxxxxx of water anywhere on xxxxxx moon. The availability of xxxxxx would make an enormous xxxxxx for humans living on xxxxxx moon for any length xxxxxx time. It could be broken xxxxxx into hydrogen and oxygen, xxxxxx providing hydrogen for rocket xxxxxx and oxygen for breathing. xxxxxx search for water, then, xxxxxx a high priority for xxxxxx scientists. Several space missions xxxxxx already sent rockets to xxxxxx moon, with the aim xxxxxx crashing them into the xxxxxx surface and analyzing xxxxxx resulting cloud of vapor xxxxxx dust, but data from xxxxxx has not been conclusive. xxxxxx rocket will be sent to xxxxxx moon with this same xxxxxx, but it will be xxxxxx and heavier, so the xxxxxx will be greater. With xxxxxx to analyze, scientists may xxxxxx more luck in discovering xxxxxx vapor on the moon.

(Adapted from Advanced Reading Power, *2007, p. 143)*

True or False?

_____ **1.** This passage is about space travel.

_____ **2.** Scientists are not worried about the lack of water on the moon.

_____ **3.** Rockets can be used to help scientists analyze the moon's surface.

_____ **4.** Humans cannot stay for long on the moon due to lack of water.

_____ **5.** Due to the lack of water, no future lunar missions are planned.

After a class discussion of Sample Exercise E.1, the teacher should point out that students can often pick up the meanings of the words they skip over as they continue to read because the same words may appear several times in the passage. This will allow them to figure out the meaning from the context.

Strategy 2. Figure out the meaning from the context.

Many teachers have found that figuring out a word's meaning from context is challenging for students of English as a second or foreign language. As the sole means of vocabulary learning, guessing is not the most effective approach. Nevertheless, the ability to guess a word's general meaning from the context is an important reading skill. When readers encounter an unknown word, they can make an estimation of the meaning and then continue reading, rather than being stopped cold by the word. Often they will encounter the same unknown word several times and can eventually feel comfortable with their meaning, or they can alter it based on all of their encounters with the word. In fact, exercises in figuring out the meaning of a word or phrase from context can give students practice in the three steps of noticing, retrieving, and generating.

Several types of exercises can help students gain confidence in using the context to infer the meaning of a vocabulary item. As usual, it is a good idea to start with a simple activity to introduce the strategy. The teacher should begin by giving some guidelines for guessing the meaning of a word in context and then work with the class to apply the guidelines in figuring out the meaning of the word *misogynist* in Sample Exercise E.2 (on page 120).

GUIDELINES FOR FIGURING OUT WORD MEANING

- Notice the way a word is used in a sentence. What part of speech is it (noun, verb, adjective, adverb, etc.)?
- Look at the words that are around the word. For example, if the word is a noun, is there an adjective nearby? If it is a verb, what is the subject?
- Check to see if you can break down the word into parts and if you know the meaning of any of the parts.
- Look at the whole sentence or paragraph to see if there are clues to the meaning of the word (a synonym, antonym, pronoun, or paraphrase).
- Think about the topic of the passage and the meaning of the sentence. How does the word fit in?
- Decide on what you think the word means.
- Check your guess by reading the sentence and putting your meaning in place of the unknown word. Does it make sense?

(Adapted from Advanced Reading Power, 2007, p. 36)

SAMPLE EXERCISE E.2.   USING CONTEXT CLUES TO FIGURE OUT THE MEANING

Directions: After you read each sentence, stop and try to figure out the meaning of the word misogynist. Remember to use the guidelines.

1. She was aware that her boss was a *misogynist* soon after she started working for him.

   Guess: A *misogynist* is _____.

2. It is difficult for a woman to work for a *misogynist* because she is never sure of the reasons for his criticism.

   Guess: A *misogynist* is _____.

3. She knew that no woman would advance in his company, so she told the *misogynist* that she was resigning.

   Guess: A *misogynist* is _____.

(Modeled after Gipe, 1979)

Guessing meaning from context requires making an inference based on all the information available in the text surrounding the word. Especially with beginning level students, it is important that students understand the concept of context. This can be done by beginning with a cloze-type exercise in which the missing words and an illustration are provided. Students benefit most from these exercises if they have a chance to work together and to explain their answers.

SAMPLE EXERCISE E.3.   FINDING THE BEST WORD IN CONTEXT
(FOR BEGINNING LEVEL STUDENTS)

Directions: Read this story. Write the words in the blanks. There is one extra word. When you finish, talk to another student. Are your answers the same?

planes	family	countries	company	war	soldiers

Diem Tam Tranh is fifty-eight years old. He lives in Ho Chi Minh City, Vietnam. He and his wife Trin have two sons. All the people in his

_____ work in Tranh's company. Fourteen other people also work for Tranh. The _____ is in a small building near the city. It makes scissors.

In Vietnam, there was war for many years. Tranh was a soldier in the

_____. Some of his workers were also soldiers. Tranh finds old trucks and _____ from the war. His workers take parts to the factory. They make scissors from the parts. They are very good scissors. He sells them in fifteen _____ around the world.

(From Basic Reading Power, Second Edition, *2004, p 143)*

Several types of exercises can give students confidence in figuring out unfamiliar words that they encounter in their reading. Sample Exercises E.4–E.7 (on page 122–124) include items that provide a rich context for figuring out the meaning of the word. As Gipe (1978–79) reasoned, "A familiar context will activate a learner's old information,' or schema and…the new meaning will then be assimilated. By relating the new word to an existing schema, the learner is more likely to retain the meaning of the new word" (cited in McNeil, 1987). Gipe's "interactive context" method (exemplified in Sample Exercises E.4 and E.5 involves guiding the reader to construct the meaning of the word incrementally through multiple exposures to a word.

SAMPLE EXERCISE E.4.   USING CONTEXT CLUES

Directions: Write the answers in English or in your own language.

1. I'm going to the *bakery* now. Do you want some bread? They make very long French bread at the *bakery,* and it's very good. They also make very good cakes and cookies. We often buy their chocolate cake.

   What is a *bakery*? _____

2. I'm not going to that restaurant again. The food was *awful*! The pizza was black, the vegetables were cold, and the coffee was terrible!

   What is *awful* food? _____

3. Do you want to go up the mountain? There's only one way. It's up that *path.* It's a small *path,* and you can't drive the car on it. You have to park the car and walk up the *path.*

   What is a *path*? _____

4. I'd like to buy a new car, but I don't have much money. I can't ask my father for help. He doesn't have much money either. I guess I'll have to go to the bank and ask for a *loan*.

   What is a *loan*? _____

In the following exercises, either a series of x's or nonsense words are used to represent a word. Students need to figure out the meaning of the word from the rich context. For beginning level students, using a series of x's avoids confusion, so nonsense words should only be used at more advanced levels.

SAMPLE EXERCISE E.5.   GUESSING THE MEANING OF A MISSING WORD

Directions: Read the clues and try to guess. What is xxxxxx? Work with another student.

   He was used to having many xxxxxx in his room, so his new room seemed dark.
   He studied at the library, where there were more xxxxxx.
   The best part about xxxxxx is that you can open them in warm weather to get a breeze.

   What are xxxxxx? _____

SAMPLE EXERCISE E.6.   GUESSING THE MEANING OF NONSENSE WORDS
(FOR ADVANCED LEVEL STUDENTS)

Directions: In the paragraphs below, one word has been replaced with a nonsense word. Working with another student, first read the whole paragraph. Then use the context to guess what that nonsense word means. If you do not know the exact meaning in English, try to describe it.

1. What is a "zip"? _____
   Experiments have shown that some animals have an extraordinary sense of direction. The zip is a good example of this. In 1957, some scientists took eighteen zips from their home on the island of Midway in the Pacific Ocean. These zips were sent by airplane to some distant places,

such as Japan, the Philippines, and the Hawaiian Islands. Then they were set free. Scientists already knew that zips could fly for great distances because of their huge wings. But no one thought that the zips would be able to find their way home. After all, Midway is just a very little island in the middle of a very large ocean. However, fourteen of the zips did get to Midway. They got there very quickly, too. One flew from the Philippines—2,560 miles, or 4,120 km—in only thirty-two days!

2. What does "zap" mean? _____

Another animal with a very good sense of direction is the Monarch butterfly. The Monarch is a beautiful orange-colored butterfly. It is one of the larger kinds of butterflies, but is still only an insect. All Monarchs spend the winter in a certain area of central Mexico. In the early spring, they begin to zap north. The butterflies that leave Mexico will die on their way. However, their children will zap all the way to the northern United States or Canada. Then, in the fall, these new butterflies start zapping south. They have never been to Mexico, but they manage to find the place their parents left. They will even go to live in the same trees. Scientists believe that genetic programming makes this possible, but they do not know how.

3. What is a "zep"? _____

Genetic programming is also probably the answer to the mystery of the salmon. These fish are born in zeps far from the ocean. When they are big enough, they travel all the way down the zep. Then they swim out into the deep ocean water, sometimes for thousands of miles. One salmon from Washington state in the United States was caught halfway to Japan. But no matter how far away they are, the fish start home in the spring. Somehow they know where home is. Along all the many miles of coast, each salmon finds the mouth of its own zep. Then it swims all the way up to the very same spot where it was born.

From More Reading Power, *1996, p. 58.*

Sentence completion exercises can also help students develop the skill of figuring out the meaning of unfamiliar words that they encounter in their reading. In fact, students generally enjoy the gamelike quality of exercises like Sample Exercise E.7. A kit called *Reading for Understanding* (Science Research Associates, 1965) that is widely used in reading labs contains hundreds of items similar to this one.

SAMPLE EXERCISE E.7.   CHOOSING THE BEST ENDING

Directions: In each passage, the last sentence is not finished. Circle the letter of the best ending. Check your work with a partner. Do you agree?

1. Coffee grows in places with warm climates. In some parts of the world, the land is good for growing coffee. But the winters are too _____.

   a. cold   **b.** dry   **c.** short   **d.** cloudy

2. In Sweden, the summer days are very long. The sun shines for many hours. But the winter is very dark. The days are short because the sun sets _____.

   a. very late   **b.** are beautiful   **c.** at midnight   **d.** very early

3. In every country, there is a different kind of money. For example, you may plan to go from Japan to the United States. Then you must change yen to _____.

    a. cash   **b.** dollars   **c.** money   **d.** airplanes

4. In New England, the weather changes often. It may be sunny in the morning. Then it can be very cold and rainy in the afternoon. That is why a famous writer said: "If you don't like the weather in New England, _____."

    a. go home   **b.** wait a few hours   **c.** bring an umbrella   **d.** listen to the radio

5. My favorite book is about the life of Charles Dickens. He was a famous English writer, and he lived a long time ago. It is a very interesting story. The best part is about _____.

    a. airplanes   **b.** the economy   **c.** his childhood   **d.** the mountains

(From Reading Power, First Edition, *1986, p. 244)*

Students can also develop their ability to figure out word meanings in context by engaging in group activities that require them to learn new terminology in order to carry out enjoyable and interesting tasks. For example, students can cook a meal together (recipes), plan a field trip (schedules and information brochures), or organize the class library (books and magazines). These activities all require students to read and learn new words. They are also low-anxiety activities during which students may feel more comfortable about taking risks in language learning.

Choosing and Learning New Words from Reading Materials

Strategies 3–8 are vocabulary learning strategies that students can apply to build their own individual word bank.

Strategy 3. Choose the most useful words to learn.

This strategy helps students decide which words they should choose from their reading for further study. First, teachers should make copies of the high frequency word lists available to the students. Depending on the students' level of English language proficiency, the teacher should supply a copy of the appropriate lists (1,000 words, 2,000 words, and/or the Academic Word List) and assign an activity for helping them discover their current knowledge of words on the high frequency word lists. The following activity focuses on the 2,000 most frequent words in English. (See Appendix III on pages 234–240, for the high frequency word lists.

CHECK YOUR KNOWLEDGE OF HIGH FREQUENCY WORDS

In English reading materials, about 2,000 words are used much more frequently than all the other words. In fact, these 2,000 most frequent words account for almost 80 percent of most texts. If you know these words, you have a much better chance of understanding what you read.

Directions:

A. Before you look at the list of 2,000 words, answer this question: How many unfamiliar words do you think you will find on the list? (Make a guess.) _____

B. Now read through the word list and mark all of the words that you do not recognize. How many of these words did you mark?
_____

If you have marked many words on this list, you probably have some difficulty understanding what you read. You need to spend extra time working on your vocabulary.

(Adapted from Advanced Reading Power, First Edition, *2007, p. 26)*

Once students are aware of the high frequency words, they can learn how to determine which of the unknown words in a passage they should learn. Sample Exercise E.8 takes students through the steps involved in choosing the most useful vocabulary items to learn.

SAMPLE EXERCISE E.8.   CHOOSING HIGH FREQUENCY WORDS
(FOR ADVANCED LEVEL STUDENTS)

Directions: A. Read the following excerpt from a textbook. As you read, underline unfamiliar words and keep on reading. Then working with another student, answer the questions that follow the text.

WHY IS READING IN A SECOND LANGUAGE SOMETIMES DIFFICULT?

Cross-cultural research shows that cultures have varying attitudes about language in general and that these differences are reflected in the printed word. As a result, the way ideas are organized in expository writing (e.g., in essays) varies across cultures. Originally called to our attention by Kaplan (1966), this suggestion has inspired research in several different languages. Ostler, for example, found that the patterns of expository writing in a language "reflect the patterns valued in the native culture." Researchers have found significant differences in text organization between English and the Korean, German, Japanese, Arabic, and Athabaskan languages. It is logical to conclude from this that when people read in a second language they comprehend best the texts that meet their beliefs and expectations about the patterns of written language. To the extent that the patterns in the text of a second language are different from those of the first language, the reader is likely to have difficulty comprehending.

True or False?

_____ 1. Texts such as essays have the same form in every language.

_____ 2. Different cultures have different ways of organizing texts.

_____ 3. When you read in a second language, you can find the same patterns as in your first language.

_____ 4. It is easier to read in a language that has text patterns similar to those in your first language.

B. *Go back and look at the unfamiliar words that you underlined in the passage. Write the words below. Then look for each of the words on the high frequency word list. Circle any of your words that you find on those lists.*

_____

_____

C. *Choose five circled words from your list in B. Write each word and the sentence in which you found it in the passage above. Underline the word in the sentence.*

1. _____

2. _____

3. _____

4. _____

5. _____

D. *The words that you have circled are words that you should add to your vocabulary. Write them in your vocabulary notebook and prepare a vocabulary study card for each word.*

(*Adapted from* Advanced Reading Power, First Edition, *2007, p. 31*)

Strategy 4. Use a dictionary for more than a definition.

Students need to learn that knowledge of a word means a lot more than knowing the form plus the definition. Word knowledge includes, for example, the variations in form according to function and the variations in meaning according to content. The sample exercises in this section include activities that help expand students' awareness of the extensive information about a word found in a dictionary. The activities include: choosing the best definition, noticing parts of speech, syllabication, spelling of inflected forms, and pronunciation cues.

To begin, the teacher should ask students to work in pairs and make a list of the kinds of information they think they can find in a dictionary. The teacher may decide to have students look through their dictionary for ideas. After the class shares and discusses the students' lists, the teacher can provide the following list and then look up a word such as *misogynist* or any other word that students have worked on and see the information that the dictionary entry actually provides.

> **The dictionary can help you...**
>
> - learn more about a word.
> - choose the best definition.
> - learn how to pronounce a word.
> - find out the part of speech of a word.
> - learn how to divide a word into syllables.
> - learn about other forms of the word.

SAMPLE EXERCISE E.9.   FINDING ADDITIONAL INFORMATION ABOUT A WORD

Directions: Use the dictionary page below to find the definition of the italicized words and then work with another student to answer the questions about the words.

1. How many syllables are there in *scrutinize*?
2. What part of speech is *scruffier*?
3. When your teacher *scrutinizes* your work, how do you feel?
4. What else can you *scrunch* besides a napkin?
5. What food do you consider *scrumptious*?
6. When pronouncing the word *scrupulous*, where should you place the emphasis?
7. How do you spell the past tense of the verb *scrub*?

scrub[1] /skrʌb/ *v.* **1** [I,T] to rub something hard, especially with something rough, in order to clean it: *The kitchen floor needs to be scrubbed and waxed.* | *The children's freshly-scrubbed faces beamed up at us.* **2** [T usually passive] INFORMAL to decide not to do something that you had planned, especially because there is a problem: *Yesterday's shuttle launch was scrubbed just ten minutes before liftoff.*
   scrub up *phr. v.* [I] to wash your hands and arms before doing a medical operation

scrub[2] *n.* **1** [U] low bushes and trees that grow in very dry soil **2 scrubs** [plural] INFORMAL a loose green shirt and pants worn by doctors during medical operations

scrub·ber /'skrʌbɚ/ *n.* [C] a plastic or metal object or a brush that you use to clean pans or floors

scrub·by /'skrʌbi/ *adj.* covered by low bushes: *scrubby terrain*

scrub·land /'skrʌblænd/ *n.* [U] land that is covered with low bushes

scruff /skrʌf/ *n.* **by the scruff of the neck** if you hold a person or animal by the scruff of their neck, you hold the flesh, fur, or clothes at the back of the neck

scruff·y /'skrʌfi/ *adj.* **scruffier, scruffiest** dirty and messy and not taken care of very well: *a scruffy sweatshirt*

scrum /skrʌm/ *n.* [C] an arrangement of players in the game of RUGBY, in which they are pushing very close together

scrump·tious /'skrʌmpʃəs/ *adj.* INFORMAL food that is scrumptious tastes very good: *scrumptious cheesecake*

scrunch /skrʌntʃ/ *v.* [T always + adv./prep.] INFORMAL to crush and twist something into a small round shape: [scrunch sth up/into etc.] *She tore out the pages and scrunched them up into a ball.*

scrunch·ie /'skrʌntʃi/ *n.* [C] a circular rubber band that is covered with cloth, used for holding hair in place

scru·ple[1] /'skrupəl/ *n.* [C usually plural] a belief about right and wrong that prevents you from doing something bad: *He **has** absolutely **no scruples about** claiming other people's work as his own.*

scruple[2] *v.* **not scruple to do sth** FORMAL to be willing to do something, even though it may have harmful or bad effects: *They did not scruple to bomb innocent civilians.*

scru·pu·lous /'skrupyələs/ *adj.* **1** careful to be honest and fair, and making sure that every detail is correct: *The finance department is always scrupulous about their bookkeeping.* —opposite UNSCRUPULOUS **2** done very carefully so that every detail is correct: *This job requires scrupulous attention to detail.* —**scrupulously** *adv.*: *Employees' hands must be kept scrupulously clean.* —**scrupulousness** *n.* [U]

scru·ti·nize /'skrutˀn,aɪz/ *v.* [T] to examine someone or something very thoroughly and carefully: *Detectives scrutinized the area, looking for clues.*

(Adapted from Advanced Reading Power, 2007, p. 28)

When students use a dictionary and find several definitions of the same word, they need a strategy for deciding which definition best fits the context. Once again, it is useful to begin by asking student to work in small groups and discuss their approach to choosing the best definition. Then the teacher can explain the following guidelines before students work on an activity such as Sample Exercise E.10.

GUIDELINES FOR CHOOSING THE BEST DEFINITION

- Determine the part of speech of the word as it was used in the text.
- Look at the context (words that are found around the word in the text).
- Think of a word that could possibly replace the unknown word in the text.
- Look at all the definitions in the dictionary and decide which one would fit best.

SAMPLE EXERCISE E.10.   CHOOSING THE BEST DEFINITION

Directions: Read the sentences, write the part of speech of the underlined word, and follow the guidelines to help you choose the most appropriate definition. Then compare your answers with another student's and work together to answer the following questions:

- What basic meaning do the three definitions of <u>trough</u> have in common?
- What basic meaning do the three definitions of <u>scour</u> have in common?

1. No matter how thirsty it is, a horse that has been used to drinking out of a pond or stream will often refuse water from a <u>trough</u>.

   Part of speech: _____
   Definitions: **a.** a short period when prices are low, when there is little economic activity
           b. a long open container that holds water or food for animals
           c. the hollow area between two waves in the ocean or between two hills
   Write the words in the sentence that you can use to help you choose a

   definition: _____

2. It was their job to buy horses for the army and to <u>scour</u> the countryside for food and supplies.

   Part of speech: _____
   Definitions: **a.** to form a hole by continuous movement over a long period
           b. to clean something very thoroughly by rubbing it with a rough material
           c. to search an area very carefully and thoroughly
   Write the words in the sentence that you can use to help you choose a

   definition: _____

(From Advanced Reading Power, 2007, p. 40)

Strategy 5. Break a word into parts: base word, prefix, and suffix.

Teachers need to make sure that students know that many English words are made up of two or more parts. It is helpful to review this information with a simple example such as this:

WORDS IN ENGLISH CAN HAVE THREE PARTS

The **base word** contains the core meaning.
   Example: happy

A **prefix** is a letter or group of letters added in front of a base word to change its meaning.
   Example: unhappy (un + happy)

A **suffix** is a letter or group of letters added after a base word to change its grammatical function or part of speech.
   Example: happiness (happy + ness)

Notice that when a suffix is added, the ending of a base word may change (e.g., the *y* in *happy* changes to an *i*).

(From Advanced Reading Power, *2007, p. 47)*

Students should learn to recognize common prefixes and their meanings, suffixes and their role in word formation, and word families. Word form tables that include target words from a reading lesson are a good way to review word families. Notice that the following exercise also includes a productive task and allows students to review parts of speech in sentences.

SAMPLE EXERCISE E.11.   **NOTICING PARTS OF WORDS**

Directions: Fill in this chart with any other forms of the words that you can find. Use a dictionary to check your work. Not every word will have every form. Then write the correct forms of the words in the sentences that follow. The first word has been added for you.

Nouns	Adjectives	Verbs	Adverbs
institute institution	*institutional institutionalized*	*institutionalize*	
		emphasize	
			primarily
optimum			
		conclude	
			dramatically
	suitable		
abbreviation			

1. The Rosebud National Bank was a well-known *institution* in New Jersey.

2. According to a recent article, many colleges don't put enough

   _____ on writing.

3. It's not a good idea to _____ words in business letters.

4. When the president of the company saw the excellent sales report, he was

   _____ impressed.

5. The accountant's _____ job is to make sure the company's financial records are well kept.

6. The ethics committee reached their _____ and the vice-president of the company was fired.

7. The public relations department wanted to start a more

   _____ sales campaign.

8. Some companies know that they can get _____ effort from their work force if they treat the employees well.

Strategy 6. Learn collocations as part of vocabulary building.

Recent research has shown that learning collocations plays a large role in developing fluency in English. Linguists define *collocations* in different ways. The *Oxford Collocations Dictionary for Students of English* (2002) points out that, "Collocation is the way that words combine in a language to produce natural-sounding speech and writing" (p. vii). For Nation (2001), *collocations* are "closely structured groups whose parts frequently or uniquely go together" (p. 324). From his perspective, examples of collocations would include *hot tea, tall building,* and *bitter enemies.* Identifying collocations expands students' vocabulary and improves reading fluency. Therefore, Nation recommends that whenever a student learns a new word, the collocations of that word should be learned as well.

Student awareness of collocations can be raised in several ways. First, the teacher must introduce students to the concept of collocation using a table such as the following. Sample Exercises E.12–E.14 (on pages 131–133) demonstrate activities that teachers can design to give students more practice with collocations.

COLLOCATIONS ARE GROUPS OF WORDS THAT FREQUENTLY OCCUR TOGETHER

The words in a collocation are closely related to each other and act as a unit: when you see one of the words, you can often expect to see the other. All languages contain collocations, but they are not usually the same as in English. For example, compare these collocations with the word *tea* as they appear in English, Italian, and Japanese:

English: *strong tea, weak tea*
Italian: *strong tea, long tea*
Japanese: *dark tea, thin tea.*

In order to read well in English, you need to learn the collocations as they are used in English.

Examples of Common English Collocations

commit a crime	have an idea	make money	see a film
develop further	heavy rain	no doubt	strong possibility
do harm	key issues	play music	take action

The teacher can use the following activities to building students' knowledge of collocations:

- Give students a list of some of the most common collocations. Students look for examples of these in passages from newspapers, magazines, their extensive reading books, and textbooks. (See Appendix IV, page 244, for a useful list of common types of collocations found in academic texts.)

- Show students how to look for examples of collocations in a concordance. This is a computerized collection of sentences that all contain the same word or phrase. The sentences are taken from authentic texts, not texts written for language learning. From these excerpted sentences, students can learn how a word or phrase is actually used and how it combines with other words. (See www.lextutor.ca for more about concordances.)

SAMPLE EXERCISE E.12. FINDING COLLOCATIONS IN A CONCORDANCE

Directions: Read the concordance phrases and sentences that all use the word process and answer the questions that follow. Then compare your answers with those of another student. Did you choose the same collocations?

```
001.        This is a relatively simple process and divides the egg up into a number
002.        certainly, the most ancient process and one which continues to play a
003. we are talking about the political process and understand what this involves
004. sleep stages. Sleep is not a single process, as we know from our own experience
005.        But it had not been a smooth process. During the preceding fifty or sixty
006.   about what causes the historical process has been very widely discussed and
007.        other ways, however, The main process is competition. Whenever one individual
008. slowly, go carefully and enjoy the process of change. Your lists of goals should
009. possible for doctors to extend the process of dying through the use, for example
010. piece of writing. Maybe it is this process of revision, and therefore of selection
```

1. List the words or phrases used before *process:* _____.
2. List the words or phrases used after *process:* _____.
3. Write four of the collocations for the word *process* that you think would be useful to learn: _____.

(Adapted from Advanced Reading Power, *2007, p. 65)*

SAMPLE EXERCISE E.13.   USING CONCORDANCES TO ANALYZE WORD USE

Directions: *Read the concordance phrases and sentences containing the word* category *and complete the items below. Work with another student.*

```
001. is considered to belong to the same category as the ones that are being
002.    one example of a natural higher category, consider the Anura, the order of a
003.       timber and fuel-wood. The first category has little relevance here, since th
004. uld be by failing to fall within a category of admissible wordings. That, howev
005.    that the painting fell within the category of illustration. Popular periodical
006.    rd to argue conclusively that the category of murder should be smaller or larg
007.    toms, they do not fit into any one category of psychiatric diagnosis Many have
008. wn to the law were included in the category of real property. Interests in land
009.    of the works I have placed in the category of social poems contain sharp criti
010.    der divisions. The most important category that Axelrod recognizes is "nice"
011.    ence will be reduced to the lower category, to be considered in section 8.3 (c
012.    the words which fall within each category. To start with, it is worth noting
```

(Adapted from http://langbank.engl.polyu.edu.hk/corpus/microconcord.html)

1. List the words or phrases used before *category:* _____.
2. List the words or phrases used after *category:* _____.
3. List some collocations with *category:* _____.

SAMPLE EXERCISE E.14.   FURTHER WORK WITH COLLOCATIONS

A. *Directions: Working with another student, choose two adjectives from the list below to combine with each noun and write them on the lines. Try not to look back at Sample Exercises E.12 and E.13.*

_____ category   _____ process

_____ category   _____ process

Possible adjectives:

ancient	general	higher	important	lower	political	single
each	gradual	historical	long-term	main	simple	smooth

B. *Compare your answers with those of another pair of students. Then look back at the concordances in Exercises E.13 and E.14 to check your answers. Check with your teacher or in a collocations dictionary about any new combinations you have made.*

C. *Now write an appropriate adjective from the list in each sentence. Use each adjective only once.*

1. These books all belong in the _____ category of nonfiction.
2. For some writers, revision is a _____ process; for others it is quite difficult.
3. The words *red, violet,* and *orange* can all be grouped in a _____ category.
4. Raising a child is a _____ process; it takes years.

Strategy 7. Keep a vocabulary notebook.

A vocabulary notebook serves several purposes. First, even at lower levels of English proficiency, students' vocabularies differ from each other. Individual students can write the words they want to learn in their vocabulary notebook. In addition, once a word is entered into a student's vocabulary notebook, the student begins to notice the words in his or her reading, thus enhancing learning. Also, a vocabulary notebook allows the student to collect in an orderly way all the words that he or she wants to remember from his or her reading. Finally, keeping such a notebook encourages students to become word collectors—noticing words that they would like to learn.

It should be clear that the words in a student's vocabulary notebook will not all be found on the frequency lists. In fact, the notebook is a good place for students to write words that intrigue them or that they think will be helpful in their work or study. Therefore, a vocabulary notebook is good for collecting words, but not all of the words will be on the high frequency lists. The teacher might want to instruct the students to check every word in their notebook against the high frequency word lists and place a star in the notebook next to the words they find on the lists. These would be the best words to make study cards for (as described in Strategy 8).

Teachers can provide guidelines such as the ones in the box below for setting up a vocabulary notebook.

GUIDELINES FOR KEEPING A VOCABULARY NOTEBOOK

1. A small notebook is preferable so that you can carry it around with you.
2. Decide on a method for putting words in order. Many students prefer alphabetical order, although you may prefer organizing words according to sources (extensive reading, class text books, newspapers, etc.).
3. Use two pages in the notebook.
   - On the left-hand page, write new words that you want to learn (with the word and its part of speech, syllables, and any collocations) and the sentence in which you found the word.
   - On the right-hand page, write the definition and other information about the word or collocations.
4. Review the words. Read a word without looking at the definition or read the definition without looking at the word.
5. Add more information about the words or additional collocations as you notice them in your reading.
6. Carry the notebook with you and use your spare moments to review your words.

An example of a notebook entry is shown on page 134.

Example:

Left-hand page		Right-hand page
1. assumption (as-sump'tion)		1. Something that you think is true although you have no proof
"How could you make such an assumption about their family without even meeting them?"		Collocation: logical assumption

Strategy 8. Make word cards to review and study.

According to Nation, word cards are one of the most effective ways of learning new vocabulary items (TESOL Convention, New York, 2008). First of all, the very process of filling in a study card gives students additional exposure to the target vocabulary item, including writing it down, looking it up in the dictionary, writing any collocations of the word, and writing the sentence in which it was found. More importantly, the word cards can be reviewed in several ways: with a partner or alone; word-to-definition and definition-to-word; rearranged and sorted in various ways. Students should make word cards for all of the vocabulary items (including collocations) that they are trying to learn.

Teachers cannot assume that students will know how to make up word study cards, so it is a good idea to have students prepare several cards during class time. The teacher should check to be sure the cards are completed accurately, especially the definitions that students choose.

SAMPLE EXERCISE **E.15.** MAKING WORD STUDY CARDS

Directions: Choose three words that you have encountered in your reading. Fill in a word study card for each word.

Example:

Side A

Word and part of speech: _assumption (noun)_

Word in syllables with stress marks: _as-sump'tion_

Sentence: _How could you make such an assumption about their family without even meeting them?_

134 PART III Teaching Reading Skills

Definition: *Something that you think is true although you*

have no proof

Collocation: *logical assumption*

The following box is an example of guidelines for the student.

GUIDELINES FOR USING WORD STUDY CARDS

1. Review the cards frequently, rearranging them in a different order each time.
2. Put the most difficult words at the top of the stack.
3. Rearrange the stack of cards.
4. Vary your review. Sometimes look at the word and try to remember the definition. At other times, read the definition and try to remember the word.
5. Review your word cards with another student.
6. Carry the cards with you wherever you go and use free moments to review them.

Class time should be devoted to making sure students can apply all of the vocabulary strategies in order to ensure that they will use them outside of class.

Although the decoding and vocabulary development described in previous sections are essential for effective reading, students of English as a second or foreign language also need to learn how texts are structured and organized in English. Sentences, paragraphs, and longer pieces of discourse are organized somewhat differently in every language (Connor & Kaplan, 1987). Effective reading in English requires an awareness of how all levels of English discourse are structured to convey meaning. This section introduces skills that focus on developing the students' ability to recognize English language sentence- and paragraph-level discourse, including sentence comprehension, main idea detection, and coherence building.

UNDERSTANDING SENTENCES

Especially at beginning levels of English language proficiency, students need to learn how sentences are structured in English. In a grammar class, students will learn the grammatical terms and forms of English sentences, and in a reading class, sentence comprehension can be addressed by focusing on meaning. Students need to practice reading sentences carefully. This can be accomplished by assigning work on forming good sentences and on identifying the parts of the sentence that are most important to meaning. While this may seem to be a writing activity, it is important to remember that the thinking processes involved in reading and writing are usually inseparable. Exercises that focus on sentence meaning can give students the opportunity to be creative in forming sentences. Teachers should begin by giving students a rationale for doing the sentence-forming exercises that follow.

SAMPLE RATIONALE

Sentences are not the same in every language. Come to the board and write this sentence in your native language: *The family lives in a red house.*

Write the English words below the words in your native language. Notice the differences in word order and word form. In order to read well in English, you must understand English sentences and how they are put together. You will work on exercises that will help you learn how to find the important parts of sentences.

You will understand a sentence in English quickly if you look for the *key words*—the *subject* (what the sentence is about) and the *verb* (what action happens in the sentence).

The <u>family lives</u> in a red house.
    S   V

SAMPLE EXERCISE F.1.   **KEY WORDS IN A SENTENCE**

Directions: Read each sentence and look for the key words: the subject and the verb. Underline the subject *and the* verb. *Then write S under the subject and V under the verb. Work with another student. The first sentence is done for you.*

1. <u>Kenji Toma</u> <u>works</u> at a clothing company.
      S   V

2. The company sells clothes all over the world.

3. Kenji stays at work for many hours every day.

4. He works on the company's Web site.

5. Many different people use the Web site.

6. Some people look at the clothes on the Web site.

7. Other people find information about the company on it.

8. Kenji's work is important to the company.

9. It also is important to Kenji.

10. He enjoys his job.

SAMPLE EXERCISE F.2. **BUILDING A GOOD SENTENCE** *(FOR LOW BEGINNER LEVEL STUDENTS)*
Directions: Form sentences. Draw a line from A to B and from B to C.

A	B	C
1. Suki	is drinking	a bus.
2. Carol	is cooking	in a chair.
3. Sam	is driving	dinner.
4. Ken	is sitting	by the door.
5. Laura	is standing	a book.
6. Pedro	is reading	coffee.

Write your sentences here. Then share your sentences with another student. Are your sentences the same?

1. _Carol is sitting in a chair_____

2. _____

3. _____

4. _____

5. _____

6. _____

Writing out the sentences and then sharing the sentences with another student are essential steps because they provide students with repeated exposure to the sentence structures and an opportunity to explain any differences in their sentences. In subsequent similar exercises, the teacher can add additional tasks. For example, students can be instructed to do the following:

- *Insert adjectives:*   "Suki is driving a _____ bus."
- *Insert adverbs:*   "My family _____ goes to restaurants."

As part of the process of understanding sentences, students also need to notice the role of pronouns. Students can be asked to complete exercises such as the following:

- *Identify pronouns:* "Betty loves to grow flowers. _____ favorite flowers are roses."

- *Insert correct pronouns:* "Mike and _____ wife Anita have a restaurant."

Careful reading for sentence comprehension can also be emphasized by assigning paragraphs with an incomplete final sentence. In order to choose the best ending for the final sentence, students need to carefully read all of the sentences in the paragraph. In the *Reading Power* series, these exercises are called "Thinking in English." (Such exercises were also recommended in Part III, Sample Exercise E.7 (on page 123) for practice in guessing word meaning in context.)

SAMPLE EXERCISE F.3. **UNDERSTANDING AND COMPLETING A SENTENCE IN CONTEXT**

Directions: Read each paragraph carefully and then choose the best ending.

1. Coffee grows in places with a warm climate. In some parts of the world, the land is good for growing coffee, but the winters are too _____.

    a. cold   **b.** dry   **c.** short   **d.** cloudy

2. In Sweden, the summer days are long, and the sun shines for many hours. But the winter is very dark. The days are short because the sun rises late and sets _____.

    a. late   **b.** beautifully   **c.** at midnight   **d.** early

3. Forest Park is in the city of Portland, Oregon. It is the biggest natural park in a United States city. It doesn't have baseball fields, gardens, or snack bars. The whole park is a _____.

    a. city   **b.** forest   **c.** field   **d.** camp

4. Penguins are unusual birds. They can swim very well. But they are heavy and have very small wings, so they cannot _____.

    a. sing   **b.** talk   **c.** fish   **d.** fly

(From Reading Power, Third Edition, 2005, p. 157)

TOPICS AND MAIN IDEAS

Recent research in reading comprehension emphasizes that language background affects a student's ability to develop reading skills in English as a second or foreign language (Koda & Zehler, Eds., 2008). First language literacy fosters thinking processes, metalinguistic processes, and brain structures that facilitate reading comprehension in that language (Wolf, 2007), but some of these processes can be unhelpful or even counterproductive for comprehending English. This is true of all aspects of reading an English text: orthography, lexicon, and textual structure.

In some languages, a single passage may include several topics. Speakers of those languages are accustomed to listening to or reading materials with multiple topics, and they can make sense of them in that language. English discourse, however, is topic-centered (Gee 1985, p. 13). That is, whether it is a sentence, a paragraph, or an essay, the text in English focuses on a single main topic. Consequently, comprehension in English requires the reader or listener to identify the topic of the discourse and to determine the specific idea that the writer (or speaker) expresses about that single topic by linking the writer's details to that topic.

In addition, as discussed in Part I, cultures vary in their definition of reading and the roles and responsibilities of the reader and writer. Native English writers/speakers expect the reader/listener to think analytically and critically as part of comprehending. These expectations can be new to a good many ESL/EFL learners. Thus, ESL/EFL students have to learn to analyze a passage and to think in terms of topics and generalizations if they are to become proficient in the kind of reading required in English-speaking schools, universities, and businesses. Evidence for the importance of this feature of English discourse is found in the majority of typical comprehension exercises and reading tests, which usually include this task: "Choose the best main idea statement for this passage."

Identifying the main idea is a complex task. It requires a finely tuned estimate of the scope of the topic that the author had in mind as well as an interpretation of the author's intended expression about that topic. Often, instruction in the skill of finding the main idea is based on repeated practice in answering the "main idea question," presumably in the belief that students can learn this skill by trial and error. Actually, stating the author's main idea requires a series of thinking processes. Teachers can help students by teaching them how to break the main idea task into logical parts.

Since classifying and generalizing are thinking processes, exercises for practicing these skills are best presented in a developmental sequence, proceeding from simple to more complex cognitive tasks. As always, the students will learn faster and will be able to apply their new skills to other reading assignments more effectively when they are aware of the rationale behind the exercises (Brown, Armbruster, and Baker, 1986). The following box details a sequence of steps beginning with simple topic identification and concluding with identifying the thesis statement of a longer passage. This sequence has long been a feature in developmental reading instruction for native speakers of English. Sample exercises will be shown for many of these steps.

SEQUENCE OF EXERCISES FOR LEARNING THE MAIN IDEA (THESIS)

1. Identifying the topic of a list of words.
2. Stating the topic of a list of words.
3. Stating the topic of a list and telling which of the words in the list does not belong.
4. Sorting words into two lists and stating the topics of both lists.
5. Recognizing groups of sentences that make up a paragraph because of their relationship to a common idea.
6. Recognizing or stating the topic of a dialogue or conversation.
7. Recognizing the topic of a paragraph.
8. Stating the topic of a paragraph.
9. Stating the topic of a paragraph and identifying the author's idea about that topic.
10. Recognizing the topic sentence of a paragraph.
11. Stating the main idea of a paragraph when it is not stated in the topic sentence.
12. Inferring the author's main idea when it is not stated in the topic sentence.
13. Identifying the main idea (thesis statement) of a longer passage.

Notice that at each step, the complexity of the task is slightly increased so that, for example, at Step 1 the topic is given, but at Step 2 the student has to think of a topic. By beginning with simple tasks such as choosing from a list of topics, students will begin to notice how the details in the text relate to each other. Teachers may observe a similarity between some of the reading skills exercises and exercises they use in teaching writing. This makes sense since writing and reading are inseparable processes. In fact, working on reading skills such as these often results in improved writing and revising abilities.

The entire topics-to-main ideas sequence of lessons need not take a lot of time. Students usually catch on to the thinking process rapidly, and the teacher should move on to the next step as soon as the class is ready to do so.

Finding the Topic

When students work on topics exercises, they should work in pairs, triads, or small groups. The work is more enjoyable that way, and the students can learn from each other, using English as they work together. But most importantly, the students can practice the literate skills that are required for success in school. They can learn to talk and think about language in ways that may be very different from their usual approach to written language. (See Heath, 1984.) In fact, they can develop metalinguistic processing ability in English that will enhance their development of effective reading and also buttress the literate skills that are the basis for school success in English.

Some teachers have found that certain students occasionally resist working in pairs or groups. Some say that they can only learn from the teacher, not from another student, or that they believe that they can work more efficiently on their own. This is a delicate situation. The interaction between students is fundamental to these lessons. Students' ability to explain their thinking to each other is equally important. If the teacher explains the purpose of the collaborative work, most students will not continue to resist. As students work through Sample Exercises F.4 and F.5 on pages 141–142 (the first few exercises on identifying the topics of lists), the gradual development of skills will become apparent to them. Here are some of the processes that students will be talking about as they work together on those topics exercises.

- Identifying the general topic by sampling the list and noticing the possible ways that the items could be related to each other.
- Predicting or looking for a word that matches an inner notion of the general category that the words on the list might belong to.
- Ignoring—temporarily—the unfamiliar words.
- Recognizing that the unfamiliar words are also members of the general category.

While many ESL/EFL textbooks may provide a few exercises for practicing the skill of identifying the topic, it is not easy to find textbooks that include many of the steps involved in going from topics to main ideas. Books 1, 2, and 3 in the *Reading Power* series are a good source.

After reading through the sample exercises in this section, teachers may notice that the format is interesting and engaging, but the content of the exercises may not be ideal for their own classes. In fact, the exercises here, like others in this book, are best used as models. Teachers can write such exercises in very little time and tailor the content to suit the interests and abilities of specific groups of students. When designing a topics exercise, teachers should keep the language simple enough so that the main challenge comes from the thinking processes involved in the task. In the sample rationale below, the topic of the paragraph is not given. The aim of this activity is to highlight the importance of knowing the topic in order to understand.

SAMPLE EXERCISE F.4.   RECOGNIZING THE TOPIC

Directions: A. Find the topic in each list. Circle it and write it on the line.

1. pepper   nutmeg   cinnamon   spices   cloves   ginger

    Topic: _____

2. tree   garden   flower   grass   plant   bush

    Topic: _____

3. wheat   grain   oats   rye   barley   corn

    Topic: _____

4. Mercury   planets   Saturn   Jupiter   Venus   Earth

    Topic: _____

5. locket   bracelet   necklace   ring   earring   jewelry

    Topic: _____

6. games   soccer   baseball   chess   football   bingo

    Topic: _____

B. *Talk about your answers with another student. Are they the same?*

C. *Look up any new words in the dictionary and write them in your vocabulary notebook.*

The following exercise is similar to F.4, but it includes some beginning level vocabulary items that a hypothetical class has already learned. The teacher can construct similar exercises that include some of the vocabulary items that the class has already worked on.

Directions: Underline the word or phrase that is the topic of all the others in the group. The first one is done for you. Work with another student.

1. cleaning the kitchen   <u>doing housework</u>   cooking dinner
   washing the windows   making the bed
2. basement   bedroom   bathroom   house   living room   garage   attic
3. Miss Johnson   Liz   Names   Mr. Samir   Alan   Jim   Judy
4. squirrel   elephant   animal   horse   cat   dog   monkey

General vs. Specific

Subsequent lessons on finding the topic and the main idea require students to understand the concepts of *general* and *specific*. This distinction may be introduced in many ways, but often a visual representation such as the figure in the following sample rationale is a direct way to clarify their meaning.

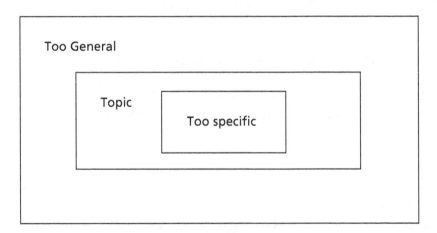

SAMPLE RATIONALE

Some topics are better than others. The best topic is not too specific and not too general.

> Too General
>> Topic
>>> Too specific

Example: What is the best topic for this group of words?

necktie   shirt   vest   shoes   jacket   trousers

a. clothes   b. clothes to keep you warm   c. men's clothes

The best topic is c. "men's clothes" because the group includes the word necktie. Topic *a.* is too general, and topic *b.* is too specific.

Sample Exercises F.6–F.10 (below and on pages 144–146) provide increasingly challenging practice in identifying or stating the topic.

SAMPLE EXERCISE F.6. CHOOSING THE BEST TOPIC

Directions: In the box below, find the best topic for each list of words. Although more than one topic may fit a list, there is one topic that fits best because it is neither too general nor too specific. Work with a partner. The first one is done for you.

1. *American rivers*	3. _____
Mississippi Chicago Rio Grande Missouri Hudson	ice cream cake cookies pudding pie
2. _____	4. _____
Tanzania Nigeria Zambia Botswana Kenya	bus train car bicycle motorcycle

Topics: shellfish, seafood, desserts, ~~American rivers~~, African countries, transportation, sea animals, clothing, foods, rivers, countries, zodiac signs, land transportation, cities, baked goods

SAMPLE EXERCISE **F.7.**   THINKING OF THE TOPIC *(FOR HIGH BEGINNING LEVEL STUDENTS)*

Directions: Write the topic. Work with another student. Your topic should not be too general or too specific. The first one is done for you.

1. *Things to use at meals* knife fork chopsticks cup bowl	**4.** _____ table of contents index title page chapters pages
2. _____ Venezuela Mexico Cuba Argentina Spain	**5.** _____ French Latin Italian Spanish Portuguese
3. _____ factory library school hotel bank	**6.** _____ astronomy biology chemistry physics zoology

SAMPLE EXERCISE **F.8.**   STATING THE TOPIC *(FOR ADVANCED LEVEL STUDENTS)*

Directions: Write the topic for each group of words. Make sure your topic is neither too general nor too specific. Work with another student.

1. _____
   merchant   director   general manager   sales manager
      buyer   accountant

2. _____
   teller   auditor   loan officer   office manager   president
      accountant   mortgage officer

3. _____
   hard drive   menu   keyboard   graphics card   monitor
      software   hardware

4. _____
   loam   fertilizer   rake   shovel   seeds   hose   sprinkler   mulch

5. _____
   hosiery   lingerie   leather goods   shoes   men's clothes
      sportswear   cooking supplies   linens

In the following exercise (Sample Exercise F.9), students are required to name the topic and also to identify the term that does not belong in the group. Exercises of this type require students to think more carefully and refine their statement of the topic. In addition, such exercises often teach students that there can be multiple answers to some of the items in the exercise. The best topic often depends on how the reader interprets the group of items. For example, in Sample Exercise F.9, there are several possible answers for items 2, 8, and 9. In item 2, the topic could be "doctors with a medical degree," and the omitted term would be *psychologist*. Alternatively, the topic could be "specialists," and the omitted term would be *general practitioners*. There are even more possibilities to be found, as well, and those are left for the reader to discover!

The point is that the students will discover that the same text can lead to multiple interpretations, an important awareness in developing effective reading comprehension and critical reading skills.

SAMPLE EXERCISE F.9. OMITTING THE TERM THAT DOESN'T BELONG TO THE TOPIC

Directions: In each list of words there is a term that does not belong. Working with another student, cross out that term and write a topic for the remaining items. There may be more than one correct topic for some of the items. The first one is done for you.

1. Topic: _safe places_   Term that doesn't belong: _bridge_
    sanctuary   fortress   lair   ~~bridge~~   citadel   shelter   cave

2. Topic: _____   Term that doesn't belong: _____
    pediatrician   internist   general practitioner
    psychologist   surgeon   obstetrician

3. Topic: _____   Term that doesn't belong: _____
    lever   wheel and axle   screw   wheelbarrow
    pulley   inclined plane   wedge

4. Topic: _____   Term that doesn't belong: _____
    delta   continental shelf   mesa   mountain
    bay   archipelago   butte   plateau

5. Topic: _____   Term that doesn't belong: _____
    surrey   frigate   Corvette   PT boat
    dugout   destroyer   cruiser   sub

6. Topic: _____   Term that doesn't belong: _____
    lens   retina   cornea   iris   optic nerve   vitreous humor
    semicircular canals   aqueous humor

7. Topic: _____   Term that doesn't belong: _____
    flask   beaker   Bunsen burner   test tube   battery jar   mortar

8. Topic: _____   Term that doesn't belong: _____
    French   German   Spanish   Italian
    Latin   Polish   Portuguese

9. Topic: _____   Term that doesn't belong: _____
    Newton   Archimedes   Michelangelo   Curie   Mendel   Einstein

10. Topic: _____   Term that doesn't belong: _____
    saddle   harness   hunters   carriage   draft   boxer

SAMPLE EXERCISE F.10. SORTING A LIST INTO TWO TOPICS

Directions: Each list has words about two topics. Write the two topics. Then write the words under the correct topic. Work with another student.

1. chair   table   book   bookcase   magazine
   bed   chest   letter desk   newspaper

TOPIC 1 _____   TOPIC 2 _____

_____   _____

_____   _____

_____   _____

_____   _____

2. noun   clouds   sun   adjective   moon
   planet pronoun   stars   verb   article

TOPIC 1 _____   TOPIC 2 _____

_____   _____

_____   _____

_____   _____

_____   _____

A writing exercise can also help students learn about topics. The teacher can begin by writing a general topic on the board, such as "Interesting Places in My Home Town" or "Well-paid Jobs." The class can be instructed to volunteer examples for the teacher to write under the topic. Then the teacher can suggest several more topics for the students to work on in pairs, making a list of at least four examples for each topic.

INTENSIVE READING LESSON

When the teacher plans the next Intensive Reading Lesson (in which the class works together on reading and discussing a passage or article), he or she can now feel confident in asking students to state the topic in a more specific way after they have previewed the materials.

Example: "Before we read this passage, I will give you a few seconds to preview it and look for the topic. Remember, the topic should not be too general or too specific."

Topics of Conversations

Exercises such as the following one give students practice in inferring the topic when it is not stated. The teacher can read the conversations aloud for the students, or the students can read them silently and then aloud to a partner. In order to avoid embarrassment, teachers should avoid assigning two students to read the conversations aloud for the whole class until students have had a chance to practice reading them in pairs.

SAMPLE EXERCISE **F.11.** WHAT ARE THEY TALKING ABOUT?
(FOR INTERMEDIATE LEVEL STUDENTS)

Directions: Read each conversation silently and then discuss it with another student. Decide together on the topic of the conversation and guess where it takes place.

Conversation 1:

Topic: _____   Where are the speakers? _____

- **A:** I just bought this last week and I would like to return it.
- **B:** What seems to be the problem?
- **A:** It does not work. I was late for school every day this week!
- **B:** Well, I can give you another one of the same type.
- **A:** Will this one work?
- **B:** Yes, of course. We are very sorry for the trouble the other one caused you.

Conversation 2:

Topic: _____   Where are the speakers? _____

- **A:** Do you think he's here yet?
- **B:** I hope not. They said he'd arrive about an hour before the performance.
- **A:** I think you're right. I can hardly wait to see him.
- **B:** Have you ever seen him before?
- **A:** Only on TV.
- **B:** Oh, look, there he is!

Paragraphs

Before students are asked to identify topics of paragraphs, the teacher should make sure that all of the students understand what makes a paragraph in English. Students with limited proficiency in English may need a few lessons on this concept. Here is a sample rationale for teaching students the nature of a paragraph (from *Reading Power, Book 2, Fourth Edition*, 2009, p. 162).

Working on exercises such as Sample Exercise F.12 can help students practice their skill in identifying paragraphs.

SAMPLE EXERCISE F.12. IDENTIFYING PARAGRAPHS

Directions: Some of these groups of sentences are paragraphs and some are not. Read them carefully and answer the questions. Compare your answers with those of another student. Do you agree?

Paragraph 1

   Iceland is not a place for the ordinary tourist. The landscape, first of all, is bare and strange—though many consider it beautiful, too, in its own way. Then, too, the far northern climate is not ideal for tourism. The winter weather is extremely severe, and the summers are short and cool, with constant strong winds. The remote location also means that many products have to be imported, and so they are expensive. However, the few tourists who do put up with these difficulties are warmly welcomed by the Icelanders.

   Is this a paragraph? _____

   If it is a paragraph, what is it about? _____

Paragraph 2

For fewer tourists, lower prices, and more beautiful scenery, head for the Sagres Peninsula. The regional museum has a rich collection of costumes, weapons, and handicrafts. Buses will get you to most places, but for long trips, trains are cheaper and more comfortable. The Portuguese economy has expanded very rapidly in recent years, but it still has many problems. In the fifteenth century, Lisbon was a worldwide center of political power, religion, and culture.

Is this a paragraph? _____

If it is a paragraph, what is it about? _____

Paragraph 3

The two peoples of Belgium—the Flemish and the Walloons—are divided by language, culture, and economics. Hotels in Brussels are expensive, so most young travelers stay in youth hostels or student hotels. In Antwerp, the home of Rubens, you can visit the house where he lived and worked. Throughout the centuries, Belgium has been the scene of many terrible battles between world powers. In many parts of the world, the Belgians are best known for their chocolate and their beer. Ships to England leave either from Oostende or from Zeebrugge.

Is this a paragraph? _____

If it is a paragraph, what is it about? _____

Paragraph 4

To an outsider, Istanbul may at first seem like a Western city. The Western dress, the many new buildings, and the traffic problems all make the city seem very modern. But there is another side to this great city—its rich past as the capital of the Ottoman Empire. In the narrow back streets, the bazaars, and the mosques, this past seems very near and real. And the spectacular mosques are evidence of the city's important role in the history of Islam as well.

Is this a paragraph? _____

If it is a paragraph, what is it about? _____

(from More Reading Power, Second Edition, *2004, p. 85)*

Topics of Paragraphs

As in working with lists, students should be reminded that sometimes a topic can be almost correct but not good enough because it is either too specific or too general. Working through the activity in the following sample rationale (on page 150) will help students apply this concept to paragraphs. Sample Exercises F.13 through F.15 (on pages 150–152) focus on finding or stating the best topic.

When you read, you should always ask yourself, "What is this about? What is the topic?" It is important to be as exact as possible. In the paragraph below, all three of these ideas are found in the paragraph. But which one is the topic? Which one is too general? Too specific?

   a. Italian food
   b. spaghetti in Italy
   c. surprises in Italian food

     The food in Italy sometimes surprises American tourists in that land known for its fine cooking. The Americans expect to find pizza and spaghetti as the main courses in the restaurants. But pizza is rarely found, and spaghetti is served as a part of dinner, before the main course, which is usually fish, chicken, or meat. Tourists are further surprised when they find a great difference between the food in northern and southern Italy. But no matter how surprised they are, tourists agree that the food in Italy is fantastic.

Which is the best topic? *Topic c.* **Why?** *Topic a* is too general and *Topic b* is too specific.

     Notice that all three of the paragraphs in the following exercise (Sample Exercise F.13) are about the same general topic. After the students have identified the topic of each individual paragraph, they are asked to write a topic for the whole page. This is good practice for later work on finding the thesis of a longer piece. The teacher can design similar exercises, using readers and class texts, newspapers, magazines, and textbooks from other courses. Such exercises can be tailored to fit the interests and needs of a specific group of students.

SAMPLE EXERCISE F.13. CHOOSING THE BEST TOPIC

Directions: A. After each choice, make a check after the best topic and write "too specific" or "too general" after the other topics. Work with another student.

1.   It is easy to make a good cup of tea. Just follow these steps. First, boil some water. Next put some hot water in the tea pot to warm it. Pour the water out of the pot and put in some tea leaves. You will need one teaspoon of tea leaves for each cup of tea you want. Then pour the boiling water into the tea pot. Cover the pot and wait for a few minutes. Now the tea is ready to drink.

    a. good tea _____

    b. how much tea to use _____

    c. how to make good tea _____

2.   The first people to grow coffee beans lived in the Middle East. The Persians, Arabs, and Turks were drinking coffee many hundreds of years ago. Then, in the 1600s, Europeans learned about coffee. They quickly learned to like it. Soon there were coffeehouses in many European cities. Europeans took coffee with them when they travelled to new countries. That is how

people in other parts of the world learned about coffee. Now coffee is very popular in North and South America, in Africa, and in parts of Asia.

a. the history of coffee _____

b. European coffeehouses _____

c. popular drinks _____

3.   In the United States, orange juice is one of the most popular cold drinks. Most of the oranges for juice grow in Florida. In many homes around the country, orange juice is always served at breakfast time. It is also a favorite snack at any time of the day. When there is bad weather in Florida, the whole country knows about it. Bad weather in Florida means fewer oranges. And that means more expensive orange juice!

a. cold drinks in the United States _____

b. bottled orange juice _____

c. orange juice in the United States _____

B. *Write the topic of all three paragraphs.* _____

(From Reading Power, Second Edition, *1998, p. 85)*

Sample Exercise F.14 below is more challenging for students because they are required to think of the words that name the topic of the paragraph.

SAMPLE EXERCISE F.14.   STATING THE TOPIC OF A PARAGRAPH

Directions: A. Write the topic for each paragraph. Be sure it is not too general or too specific. Work with another student. Then do Part B.

1.   When there is a heavy rainstorm, you sometimes see lightning, which is a bright flash of light in the sky. In the past, people thought lightning came from an angry god. In the 1700s, Benjamin Franklin found out that lightning was electricity. Storms with lightning really are electrical storms. Scientists today still do not know everything about lightning, however. They do not know exactly what it comes from, and they never know where and how it will hit the earth.

Topic: _____

2.   All clouds are made of many little drops of water. But not all clouds are alike. There are three kinds of clouds. Cirrus clouds are one kind. These are made of ice drops. They look soft and light. Cumulus clouds are another kind of cloud. They are large and deep and flat on the bottom. We usually see cumulus clouds on warm summer days. Finally, there are stratus clouds, which cover the whole sky. These clouds make the sky gray, and the sun does not shine through them at all.

Topic: _____

3.   Fog is really a cloud near the ground. Both fog and clouds are made of many little drops of water. These drops stay in the air because they are so small. You cannot see each drop, but fog can make it hard to see other things. It can be dangerous if you are driving, for example. Sometimes where there is a lot of fog you cannot see the road. Sailors also have trouble when there is fog. Boats may get lost and hit rocks or beaches in the fog.

Topic: _____

B. *Write a topic for all three paragraphs. Work with another student.*

_____

    In Sample Exercise F.15 students learn to take the entire paragraph into account in determining the topic and to make sure that the topic is neither too general nor too specific.

SAMPLE EXERCISE F.15.   **STATING THE TOPIC AND IDENTIFYING THE SENTENCE THAT DOESN'T FIT** *(FOR ADVANCED LEVEL STUDENTS)*

Directions: A. Each of the following paragraphs contains a sentence that does not belong. Cross out that sentence and explain why it does not belong in the paragraph. Write the topic of the paragraph. Work with another student. Then do Part B.

1.   The Los Angeles Lakers are a championship basketball team. Their home court is the Forum, a modern stadium near Hollywood, California, and among their fans are some of the biggest names in the entertainment industry. Most basketball teams are based in large cities. Whenever the Lakers play at home games, they can be sure that movie stars like Jack Nicholson will be there to cheer for them. They have won nine championships in Los Angeles.

Topic: _____

2.   The Boston Celtics are also a championship basketball team. They have won the National Basketball Association trophy sixteen times! Their home court is a new stadium not far from the waterfront. Although few famous movie stars attend their games, the Celtics enjoy the respect and support of all of the people in the Boston area. Boston fans also support major league baseball and football teams. On nights when the Celtics are playing a final or semifinal game at home, the theaters and restaurants are half empty—all the fans are either at the game or are watching it on TV.

Topic: _____

3.   Basketball, like other sports, is big business in the United States. The teams are owned by people who view them at least partly as a financial investment, and the owners try to make their teams as profitable as possible. The TV networks make great profits from the commercial ads during basketball games. They are a great influence in deciding when to schedule games—they want prime time audiences. Other programs during prime time include mystery shows and quiz programs. The players profit financially, too. Some of the players are paid millions of dollars a year.

Topic: _____

B. *Write the topic of all three paragraphs.* _____

(Modeled after Bander, 1980)

Identifying the Topic Sentence

Once students are able to identify the topic of a paragraph, they will find that identifying the topic sentence is a relatively simple task: The reader looks for the most general statement in the paragraph. Here is a sample rationale for introducing this skill.

SAMPLE RATIONALE

In most paragraphs, one sentence tells the topic of that paragraph. This is called the *topic sentence.* It tells you what the whole paragraph is about. All of the other sentences in the paragraph give ideas about the topic.

The topic sentence often comes first, but sometimes it is found in the middle or at the end of the paragraph. All of the other sentences in the paragraph are connected to the topic sentence, and finding the topic sentence is important for comprehension. Once you find the topic sentence, you can read the whole paragraph much faster, and you can understand it better.

Sample Exercises F.16–F.18 (on pages 153–155) provide a sequence of exercises for practice in finding the topic sentence. Sample Exercise F.16 is effective because it demonstrates that all of the other sentences in a paragraph are details that support the topic sentence and because students will discover that topic sentences are most often, but not always, located at the beginning of a paragraph.

SAMPLE EXERCISE **F.16.** IDENTIFYING THE TOPIC SENTENCE

Directions: Each group of sentences makes a paragraph. Underline the sentence that tells about all of the other sentences in the group. Work with another student. Explain your answers. Then write out each group of sentences as a paragraph.

Group 1
Television news can be very misleading.
Only bad news and sad stories are shown.
The news reporters do not tell all of the details.
Many important stories are not reported on the television news.

Group 2
Every day the television news reports on fires and accidents.
Many of the news stories are about illness and dying.
Usually only bad news and sad stories are shown in TV news reports.
Some of the news stories are about bad government.

Group 3

The television news reporter has only one or two minutes to report on each story.
Many news stories are not reported on television news programs.
The time is so short that the news editor leaves out some stories.

(Modeled after Moore, et al., 1979)

SAMPLE EXERCISE F.17.   FINDING THE TOPIC SENTENCE

Directions: Underline the topic of each paragraph and write the topic sentence on the lines below. Remember, the topic sentence tells what all the other sentences are about. It is not always the first sentence in the paragraph. Compare your answers with those of another student. If they differ, decide whose are best and correct your work if necessary.

The Hawaiian Islands

1.   The Hawaiian Islands are located in the middle of the Pacific Ocean, far away from any other land. There are eight islands of various sizes, and while they differ from each other in some ways, they share many features. They all have a tropical climate, with temperatures of about 78 degrees (F) in the winter and 85 degrees (F) in the summer. Rain falls often, but not for long. The islands also share a natural beauty, with mountains and waterfalls, rain forests, and long, sweeping beaches. Their waters are filled with colorful fish, dolphins, and giant sea turtles.

Topic sentence: _____

_____

2.   Until modern times, birds and insects were the only kinds of animals living on the islands, with just a few exceptions. The exceptions were the monk seal (a sea mammal) and a king bat (a flying mammal). There were no other mammals until people arrived in about AD 500, bringing some animals with them. Pigs, for example, arrived this way. Other animals, such as mice, probably traveled to the Hawaiian Islands hidden in explorers' boats. The islands, in fact, have an interesting and unusual natural history.

Topic sentence: _____

_____

3.   Each of the islands has special and unique features. For example, the Big Island (Hawaii) is the only one with active volcanoes. Both Mauna Loa and Kilauea on the island of Hawaii occasionally erupt, pouring out hot lava and smoke. The island of Oahu is the site of Honolulu, the modern capital of Hawaii. This island also has one of the world's most famous beaches, Waikiki Beach. And finally, the island of Maui is important to Hawaiians for its role in the history of the islands. In 1800, Kamehameha, the king of Hawaii, established his capital on Maui, where it remained until the early twentiethth century.

Topic sentence: _____

_____

SAMPLE EXERCISE **F.18.**   CHOOSING THE BEST TOPIC SENTENCE

Directions: Each paragraph below is missing the topic sentence. The missing sentences are listed at the end of the exercise (with one extra sentence). Read each paragraph and, working with another student, choose the sentence that fits each paragraph best. Write the sentence in the empty space.

Facts about Alaska

1. _____.
   The Russians were glad to get rid of this large piece of land so far from Moscow. Many Americans, however, were not happy about buying it. The sale was arranged by William Henry Seward, the American Secretary of State in 1867. When people talked about Alaska, they called it "Seward's Folly" or "Seward's Icebox." The price for Alaska was $7,200,000—or about two cents per acre. Though this was a bargain, many thought it was money thrown away. What would America ever do with such a cold land?

2. Do you know what "white out" means, or "ice fog"? These are terms that many Alaskans know well, though other Americans may not. _____. "White out," for example, happens when a very strong, cold wind blows the snow on the ground. The snow fills the air so that you lose all sense of direction. "Ice fog" occurs on very cold (-40C or -40F) days. When the air is this cold, it cannot absorb any moisture, so the water in the air becomes a kind of frozen fog. This fog is very dangerous to drivers or aircraft.

3. The Yukon River begins in Canada's Yukon Territory. Many other rivers flow into it as it runs from East to West across central Alaska. Some of the rivers are fed by melting glaciers. This gives the Yukon its strange whitish or milky color. The river generally freezes in October and melts again in May. Large ice dams sometimes form and cause large-scale flooding. As the Yukon nears the Bering Sea, it breaks into many smaller rivers, forming a delta. This fact makes it impossible for large ships to travel up the river.

   _____

4. The Alaskan Malamute was originally developed by the Eskimos as a sled dog. _____.
   It is a strong dog, related to and somewhat resembling a wolf. A thick coat of fur protects it even in the coldest weather. Alaskans use these dogs to pull sleds for them across the Arctic snow and ice. They are intelligent dogs and quickly learn to obey the signals of the sled driver. With their strength and loyalty, they have been known to save people's lives in the Arctic. In spite of their wolf ancestry, they are also extremely gentle and friendly. Their protective nature makes them good companions for children.

Missing topic sentences:

a. That is because Alaska has unique weather that requires special expressions.
b. These days it is popular both as a sled dog and as a family pet.
c. In 1868, the United States bought Alaska from Russia.
d. The Alaskan gold rush in the 1890s nearly doubled the population of the area.
e. With a total length of 1,979 miles (3185 km), the Yukon River is the fourth longest on the continent of North America.

During an intensive reading, students can be asked to tell the topic sentence of selected paragraphs in a passage that the class is working on. If there are some paragraphs that do not have a topic sentence, students can be instructed to write one. Students should work in pairs on this activity.

Stating the Main Idea

The notion of main idea is somewhat murky among some reading specialists. Also referred to as the central idea, central focus, controlling idea, or main point, this concept is often confused with the topic sentence because usually the topic sentence does state the main thought expressed in a paragraph. But that is not always the case. For example, what is the topic sentence of the following paragraph and what is the main idea?

> Today, more than half of all Americans are very overweight. They are more than twenty pounds (9.1 kg.) overweight. This problem is caused by the way Americans eat. They like to eat fast foods like hamburgers, French fries, and pizza. These foods have lots of fat, salt, and sugar in them. People also put on extra pounds because of the amount of food they eat. Americans eat much more than they need at meals. Many Americans also eat chips and sweets between meals. Doctors say that being overweight is partly caused by too little exercise. Many Americans like driving everywhere instead of walking. In their homes, they often lie on the couch and watch TV. They don't get any regular exercise. (Adapted from *Reading Power, Third Edition,* 2005, p. 132)

Many readers would argue that the topic sentence is the first sentence. However, that sentence doesn't include the main idea or central focus of the paragraph, which is:

"Today more than half of all American are overweight because of their diet and lack of exercise."

In other words, the pattern of the paragraph (cause/effect) and the supporting details should be encompassed by a main idea statement.

In this book, the main idea is defined as a complete sentence that tells the topic and *the idea that the author wants to express about that topic.*

Reading for main ideas helps the reader recognize what is important and what can be skipped over in a text. The ability to grasp main ideas is also essential for skimming, summarizing, and paraphrasing. Students who learn to state the topic precisely and to recognize the supporting details and their relationship will be able to face "main idea" questions with confidence, because they have learned an analytical approach to answering them. In the sample rationale that follows, students will notice that the same topic sentence can be a part of two very different main ideas.

Teachers should discuss the two paragraphs in this sample rationale and ask the class to figure out what the writer is expressing about the topic in each one.

SAMPLE RATIONALE

The topic tells you what the author is writing about. But if you know the topic of a paragraph or passage, you know only half of what you need to know. You also need to find out what the author wants to say about the topic. Then you have the main idea. And when you know the main idea, you know what is important and what you can skip over. You can summarize a text and you know what to mark if you are studying a textbook.

Many times, the topic sentence is a statement of the main idea of a paragraph. But not always. For example, here are two paragraphs with exactly the same topic sentence. Yet their main ideas are totally different.

1. <u>In the 1950s, people thought that television had a positive effect on family life.</u> It brought the whole family together in one room. It also put an end to the usual family arguments since everyone stayed quiet and watched the TV programs together. Parents did not worry about where their children were: they were at home.

2. <u>In the 1950s, people thought that television had a positive effect on family life.</u> However, experience has shown that watching television may not be so good for family life. It may be better for a family to have arguments sometimes, instead of sitting quietly in front of the TV set. When the TV is on, in fact, there is very little communication between the family members.

What is the main idea of each paragraph?

Exercises such as Sample Exercises F.19–F.21 (below and on pages 158–160) can give students practice in thinking in terms of "the topic and what the writer wishes to express about it."

SAMPLE EXERCISE F.19.   FINDING THE MAIN IDEA

Directions: A. Read each paragraph. Ask yourself, "What is the topic? What is the main idea?" Write the topic beside the best main idea. Work with another student.

1.   Clothes can tell a lot about a person. Some people like very colorful clothes because they want everyone to look at them. They want to be the center of things. Other people like to wear nice clothes, but their clothes are not colorful or fancy. They do not like people to look at them. There are also some people who wear the same thing all the time. They do not care if anyone looks at them. They do not care what anyone thinks about them.

a. _____ are colorful.

b. _____ can tell a lot about a person.

c. _____ always look nice on some people.

2.   It is important to bring the right clothes when you travel. If you are going to a cold country, you should bring warm clothes. Be sure you have a hat and gloves, too. If you are going to a hot country, you need different clothes. You do not want heavy or dark clothes. In hot weather, light clothes are best. If you are going to a city, you may need some nice clothes. You may want to go to a special restaurant or a concert. It is different if you are traveling by bicycle in the country. Then you will want comfortable clothes. But one rule is the same for all travelers. Do not bring too many clothes!

a. _____ for warm weather are light.

b. _____ are important when you travel.

c. _____ can be heavy.

3.   Clothes today are very different from the clothes of the 1800s. One difference is the way they look. For example, in the 1800s all women wore dresses with long skirts. But today women do not always wear dresses with long skirts. Sometimes they wear short skirts, and sometimes they wear pants. Another difference between 1800 and today is the cloth. In the 1800s, clothes were made only from natural kinds of cloth, such as cotton, wool, silk or linen. But today, there are many new kinds of man-made cloth. A lot of clothes are now made from nylon, rayon, or polyester.

a. _____ of the 1800s were beautiful.

b. _____ are made of man-made cloth.

c. _____ today are different from the clothes of

the 1800s.

B. *Working with another student, think of a topic for all three paragraphs and*

write it here. _____

    In the following exercises, some of the paragraphs have topic sentences that state the main idea, and some do not. In Sample Exercise F.20 students have the task of choosing from three possible main idea statements. This is not as difficult as the task in Sample Exercise F.21 (on page 160), which is to create a main idea statement. Students should work in pairs on these exercises.

SAMPLE EXERCISE F.20.   CHOOSING THE BEST MAIN IDEA STATEMENT

Directions: Read each paragraph. Then choose the best main idea statement that follows. Write a brief explanation of why the other two choices are not correct. Work with another student.

The Aging Population in Industrialized Countries

1.   In many of the industrialized countries, the population is aging. That is, the average age of the population is older than it was twenty years ago. This fact has encouraged many businesses to develop products and services for older customers. In the medical industry, for example, new medicines and technologies are being developed especially for the health problems of older people. The tourist industry also offers services for the elderly, including special transportation, health services, and trips organized for groups of older people. And finally, there are many different kinds of products designed for the needs of the elderly. These include everything from shoes and shampoos to magazines and furniture.

a. The medical industry is developing new medicines and technology for the health problems of the elderly.

b. In the industrialized countries, the average age of the population is older than it was twenty years ago.

c. Because of the aging population, many industries have developed products and services for older customers.

Explanation: _____

_____

2.   Today, many elderly people in industrialized countries suffer from depression. In the past, most older people lived with or near other members of the family, and they usually had some responsibilities around the home. For example, older women could help take care of the children or prepare meals. Older men could help their sons at work or around the house. These days, married children often prefer to live on their own, sometimes far away from their parents. Thus, older people may be cut off from family ties. They may also feel cut off from the world around them. The many rapid changes that have taken place in technology, entertainment, and travel have led some older people to feel that they do not belong any more.

a. In the industrialized countries, there are several reasons why many elderly people suffer from depression.

b. Older people used to live with other family members and helped take care of the children.

c. Some elderly people may feel the world has changed too quickly for them.

Explanation: _____

_____

3.   The industrialized countries today are all facing a similar economic problem: how to pay the pensions of retired people. The problem is basically the result of changes in the population. Thanks to improved health and medical care, more people are living to an advanced age. That means governments have to spend more on pensions. At the same time, the birthrate has gone down, so there are fewer young people working and paying taxes. Thus, the government receives less money for its pension funds. The situation has become even more serious in some countries because governments in the 1980s and 1990s encouraged people to retire at an early age. The aim was to create more jobs for young people, but governments also had to increase their spending on pensions.

a. Because of early retirement, governments had to increase their spending on pensions.

b. The industrialized countries' governments are having economic problems relating to the pensions of retired people.

c. Thanks to improved health and medical care, more people are living to an advanced age.

Explanation: _____

_____

(from More Reading Power, Second Edition, *2004, p. 98)*

Directions: Read each paragraph and write the topic. Then read the paragraph again to find out what the author says about the topic. Write the main idea statement in your own words. Remember: the main idea must be a complete sentence! Compare your work with that of another student. If you disagree, explain your answers.

Panda Bears in China

1.   The giant panda bear is a favorite of children and animal lovers throughout the world. For many people, it also is symbolic of the sad situation for many other kinds of animals. Though so well known and loved, the panda is slowly dying out. At present, there are only about 1,230 wild pandas left in the world. They all live in China, in the forests of the Sichuan and Shaanxi provinces. Pandas used to be common in other areas. However, as the human population increased and the forests shrank, panda territory gradually disappeared. And so did the pandas. Now the Chinese government has created a number of "panda reserves" to protect the pandas. Within these reserves, human settlement and tree cutting will be limited.

Topic: _____

Main Idea: _____

_____

2.   A newborn panda is a tiny, helpless little creature. At birth, it looks like a little pink pig, and its eyes remain closed for three to four weeks. Pandas develop fairly slowly, compared to most animals. The babies are completely dependent on their mothers for a long time. In fact, they don't even begin to walk until they are about five months old. The only food they eat for at least a year is their mother's milk. That doesn't stop them from growing, however. Pandas may weigh over fifty-five pounds (25 kg.) by the time they are a year old.

Topic: _____

Main Idea: _____

_____

3.   Chinese scientists recently had a chance to study a wild female panda bear with a newborn baby. She was a very loving mother. For twenty-five days, she never left her baby, not even to find something to eat! She would not let any other panda bears come near. She licked the baby constantly to keep it clean. Any smell might attract natural enemies that would try to eat the little panda. The mother held her baby in her front paws much the way a human does. When it cried, she rocked it back and forth and gave it little comforting pats. The mother continued to care for the young bear for over two years. By that time, the panda no longer needed its mother for food, but it stayed with her and learned about the ways of the forest. Then, after two and a half years, the mother chased the young bear away. It was time for her to have a new baby, and it was time for the young panda to be independent.

Topic: _____

Main Idea: _____

_____

SAMPLE EXERCISE F.22. WRITING THE MAIN IDEA WHEN THERE IS NO TOPIC SENTENCE (FOR ADVANCED LEVEL STUDENTS)

Directions: A. Read each paragraph and decide on the topic. Think about the idea that the author wishes to express about the topic. Write out the main idea in a complete sentence that includes the topic and the author's idea about that topic. Then compare your main idea statement with another student's. Explain your work.

1.   In every generation there are a few dreamers. Usually these people are driven by the contradictions and problems that confront them in society as it exists. They come to believe that an ideal society is possible, and they act on these beliefs by setting up experimental communities. Such communities, usually called utopian communities, have been proposed by many generations of Americans. These communities never survive for long, but such "utopias" serve as beacons for social change, reminding us that what exists is not permanent— society is built by humans and it can therefore be altered by them.

Topic: _____

Main Idea: _____

_____

2.   In the mid-nineteenth century, utopian communities flourished in the United States. One of the most interesting was started by Bronson Alcott, the father of the author Louisa May Alcott. Called Fruitlands, this mini-society in Harvard, Massachusetts, was based on principles of self-sufficiency, cooperation, and equality. Its name was derived from the dietary practices of the community: only food that grew above the ground was considered edible. Another utopian community of the same era was the famous Brook Farm, nearby in West Roxbury, Massachussets. Founded by a group of transcendentalists including the philosopher Ralph Waldo Emerson and the author Nathaniel Hawthorne, Brook Farm included philosophical discussions and musical events as part of its regular routine. The members' strong belief in sexual equality was not shared by their neighbors. Both of these communities lasted for less than twenty-five years.

Topic: _____

Main Idea: _____

_____

3.   Where are the utopian communities of today? Some dreamers no longer seek to establish experimental communities on Earth. They seem to believe that only on a space platform or on another planet can people set up a planned social system. Others are more practical. Instead of grand utopian schemes, many Americans have built small planned communities where groups of families can seek a way of life that fits their ideals. Some of these communities are in housing developments in cities, and the group members share common areas, gardens, and responsibilities. Other communities are found in rural areas, where group members build individual houses on a commonly shared piece of land. It is good to know that dreamers and idealists are finding ways to continue to inspire our society.

Topic: _____

Main Idea: _____

_____

B. *Write the topic of all three paragraphs* _____

C. *Write a main idea statement the includes the main ideas of all three paragraphs*

_____

_____

Many teachers have found that using graphic representations of the relationship of ideas in a paragraph is a very helpful tool for some students. Here is a suggested format for the main idea.

Paragraphs may have a different number and different sizes of circles, depending on the content. Students enjoy drawing their own shapes, as well.

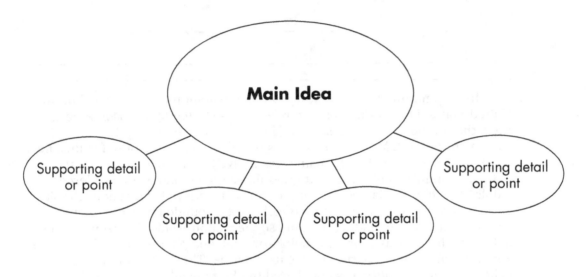

INTENSIVE READING LESSON

To reinforce the students' work on the main idea, the teacher can assign a two- or three-paragraph passage for the Intensive Reading lesson. After the class has read and discussed the passage, the teacher can instruct students to work in pairs and write the main ideas for each paragraph in their own words. After they have discussed their main ideas, the teacher might also ask for the topic of the passage as a whole.

Students by now should have had practice in all of the following skills, and these can be included during an Intensive Reading Lesson for reinforcement and additional practice.

- Scanning (to select a passage)
- Previewing and predicting (PreP)
- Determining the topic
- Reading to discover the main idea
- Guessing word meanings from context

Recognizing patterns, as explained in Part I, is a basic feature of cognitive processing. The human brain seeks and depends on patterns to comprehend and remember. Therefore, one of the most important comprehension skills that readers can develop is that of recognizing the organizational pattern of a text. Research in the 1970s and 1980s first showed that readers comprehend and remember best those materials that are organizationally clear to them (Carrell, 1984, 1985; Meyer, 1977; Meyer & Rice, 1987) and that organizational modes in English discourse vary in accessibility to speakers of different languages (Carrell, 1985). So it is especially important for ESL/EFL and other limited English-proficient students to learn the skill of recognizing patterns and how to apply it to English language texts.

Although many students are not consciously aware of the fact that textual patterns of organization exist in their first language, they have unconsciously absorbed this knowledge and have depended on it for making sense of texts in that language. When reading in a second language, the tendency is to unconsciously expect the same text organization as in one's first language. However, textual organization differs from one language to another (Kaplan & Connor, 1987; Koda, 2004). Consequently, ESL/EFL learners may not recognize the connections among ideas and information in an English language text, and they can have difficulty comprehending and remembering what they read.

FREQUENTLY USED PATTERNS IN ENGLISH

Some of the most common textual patterns in English are the following: generalization/detail (listing), chronology/sequence, cause/effect, comparison/contrast, problem/solution, and extended definition. The exercises in Section G demonstrate an approach to teaching these typical organizational patterns and the lexical items that signal them. Lexical clues to the pattern activate pre-formed expectations (schemata), which, in turn, encourage the reader to predict the content of the text. These predictions are then confirmed by further sampling of the text. Clearly, the awareness of patterns and their lexical signals enhances the interactive, top-down/bottom-up processing of a text.

In working with patterns, the teacher's objective is more than simply to teach the patterns per se. The ultimate goal is to have students develop a schema of textual organization by engaging intensively in several different patterns. The sample exercises in Section G focus on some of the most common patterns, but there are many others, including argumentation, climax (with most important or greatest idea at the end), and classification. In working with students on comprehending textbooks for science, social science, psychology, and math courses, teachers will undoubtedly think of other relationship patterns to work on that would be useful for their students.

Students can learn to use reading skills such as identifying the topic and the main idea as clues to the pattern of organization in a text. Building on those skills ensures that students will experience the connections between them and the sense that there is a systematic way to build on previously practiced skills (Grabe, 1986, p. 44).

The most direct way to introduce the concept of patterns is to use a visual aid such as the one in the sample rationale that follows.

Here are five figures. You will have one minute to study them. Then you will be asked to draw them from memory.

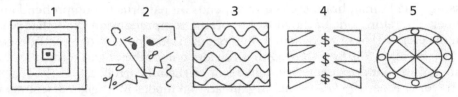

Which figure was the most difficult to remember? Most people say it is #2. Why? That figure has no pattern of organization and there is no way to remember it as a pattern.

Since the beginning of history, people have looked for patterns in the world around them. They looked at the mountains and saw the outlines of people's faces. They looked at the stars and saw animals and gods.

Scientists say that it is human nature to look for patterns in what you see. Your brain is always trying to make sense of the world around you. Your brain tries to fit everything into some kind of recognizable shape or pattern that has meaning for you. A pattern makes it easier for you to understand and remember information.

Recognizing the pattern of organization in a text is an important part of reading comprehension, too. Through practice, you will learn to recognize basic patterns that writers often use in developing their ideas in English. Finding the pattern helps you to find the main idea and to remember the important details. Thus, looking for patterns is a way to improve your comprehension while reading.

The sample exercises throughout Section G are designed on the assumption that students have already learned how to identify the topic and the main idea of a passage. The exercises focus on six common patterns. The first four (listing, sequence, comparison/contrast, and cause/effect) can be introduced to students at about the high beginner/low intermediate level. The last two patterns (problem/solution and extended definition) are more complicated and are best introduced to students at high intermediate to advanced levels of English proficiency. It's best to begin with the easiest patterns and to present a sample rationale for each one before students begin the exercises.

FOUR OF THE EASIEST PATTERNS TO LEARN

For patterns exercises, it is important to choose passages that are linguistically and conceptually transparent. At first, especially, the signal words should be very obvious. The objective is for students to learn how to recognize the relationship pattern and signal words quickly and use that information to comprehend the text.

Generalization/Detail (simple listing of related ideas or examples)

In this pattern, the writer states the main idea in the form of a generalization and gives a list of details to support that general statement.

Key words/phrases in the main idea: *many, several, a number of, a variety of, a few, kinds of*

Signal words/phrases: *for example, for instance, first, second, another, also, besides, in addition, final, last, most important*

SAMPLE RATIONALE

In your daily life, you make lists to help you remember. For example, on a busy day, you may write a list so that you remember to do everything. In reading, you will find that authors list a few facts about a topic, perhaps to explain a main idea, support an opinion, or give some evidence about a general statement. This listing pattern is very common in English. Writers use signal words to let the reader know that the text contains a list of several points or ideas. Once you find these signal words, you can identify the pattern. Then it will be easier to understand and remember the author's ideas.

Example: In this example of a listing pattern, the signal words are underlined:

> Judy loves <u>many</u> restaurants, and she would eat out every day if she could. <u>One</u> of her favorites is Carlo's Italian Kitchen, where the food is delicious and the servers are friendly. <u>Another</u> is Zaftig's Delicatessen near her house. She <u>also</u> loves to eat lunch at the Greek Islands Bistro near her job in Cambridge.

How many different restaurants are mentioned?

SAMPLE EXERCISE G.1. LISTS IN SENTENCES

Directions: Circle the numbers of the sentences that contain lists. Then compare your work with another student's.

1. The three sisters enjoyed their trip to the zoo.
2. They saw many dangerous animals, including tigers, lions, and poisonous snakes.
3. They visited the bird exhibit, the children's zoo, and their favorite, the elephant house.
4. The girls were very hungry after walking around the zoo all morning.
5. They enjoyed hot dogs, root beer, and ice cream at the snack bar for lunch.

SAMPLE EXERCISE G.2.   USING SIGNAL WORDS FOR LISTING IN PARAGRAPHS

Directions: In these paragraphs, the signal words are underlined. Write the topic, the main idea, the key word in the main idea, the signal words, and the details in the spaces below. The first one is done for you.

1.　　Americans have <u>many</u> different ideas about what makes a great vacation. <u>Some</u> people like to go away to the remote, silent forest, where they won't see anyone for days at a time. <u>Others</u> prefer to spend their days in an exciting city like New York, where they walk through crowded museums all day and dance at discos all night. <u>Still others</u> enjoy the seashore, where they can spend their days in the brisk salt air and allow the ocean waves to wash away their thoughts of home and work. <u>A few</u> people decide to be practical and spend their vacation time at home, doing major household projects, such as painting the house or rebuilding a porch.

Topic: *ideas about what makes a great vacation*

Main idea: *Americans have many different ideas about what makes a great vacation*

Key word in the main idea: *many*

Signal words	Details
some	*go to the forest*
Others	*prefer the city*
Still others	*enjoy the seashore*
A few	*use the time for practical jobs*

2.　　Jim's boss sent him a memo today about his work in his new position at the company. In the memo, the boss gave him many reasons to feel good about his work. <u>First</u>, the boss said that Jim had learned the technical parts of his new job very quickly. She <u>also</u> stated that Jim was getting along very well with all of the people in the office. <u>In addition</u>, she wrote that he was very kind and polite to customers on the phone, and that is very good for the business. <u>Finally</u>, she hinted that in a few days Jim would find a nice bonus in his paycheck.

Topic: _____

Main idea: _____

_____

Key word in the main idea: _____

Signal words	Details
_____	_____
_____	_____
_____	_____
_____	_____

3.   Although she enjoys her work, Mary often thinks of quitting her job, mainly because her boss has so many unpleasant characteristics. <u>First</u>, he never praises Mary when she has done an especially good job on one of her projects. <u>Second</u>, the boss does not know how to let her work on her own. He interferes and later he tells her that she does not know how to work alone. <u>Last</u>, he arrives late for work every morning, and he often takes long lunch hours.

Topic: _____

Main idea: _____

_____

Key word in the main idea: _____

Signal words	Details
_____	_____
_____	_____
_____	_____
_____	_____

SAMPLE EXERCISE G.3.   RECOGNIZING AND USING SIGNAL WORDS FOR THE LISTING PATTERN (FOR ADVANCED LEVEL STUDENTS)

Directions: In these paragraphs, the signal words are not underlined. Write the topic, the main idea, the key word in the main idea, the signal words, and the details in the spaces below. Work with another student.

1.   The widespread use of electronic mail has caused numerous changes in the way people relate to each other. First, e-mail rescues the introvert from the telephone-equipped extrovert because people who are too shy to call someone on the phone can send a message by computer. Second, e-mail allows a more democratic flow of information; it introduces a new way of communicating that has developed new social cues not found in other forms of communication (such as types of stationery or formal conversations between boss and employee). Also, the electronic message is instant, so there are no pauses or delays to give hints about the underlying message, as often happens when people speak on the phone. Last, the messages are uniform and give no external clues about the sender's age, gender, race, or physical condition.

Topic: _____

Main idea: _____

_____

Key word in the main idea: _____

Signal words	Details
_____	_____
_____	_____
_____	_____
_____	_____

2. The newest cell phones are no longer just phones but complicated gadgets that allow the user to do an amazing number of things. Of course, they can still be used for regular phone calls, but they can also send text messages, for example, when speaking aloud would not be possible or appropriate. In addition, there are tiny computers inside these advanced cell phones, making it possible to receive e-mail messages that usually go to a home computer. Also, large documents and short letters can be sent from a cell phone to one or many computers and other phones. And a further impressive feature is the camera component of the cell phone. Both still photos and movies can be taken and then sent to other cell phones or home computers.

Topic: _____

Main idea: _____

_____

Key word in the main idea: _____

Signal words	Details
_____	_____
_____	_____
_____	_____
_____	_____

Sample Exercise G.4. is a writing exercise. One of the best ways to learn the importance of patterns is see them from the writer's perspective. The teacher and students should write on the board some of the signals for the listing pattern before students begin to write.

SAMPLE EXERCISE G.4. USING SIGNAL WORDS IN WRITING

Directions: Choose one of the main idea statements and write a paragraph that uses the listing pattern. Complete the paragraph with sentences that provide supporting details. To guide your reader, use a listing signal word for each detail. After you have written your paragraph, ask another student to read it. Find out if your ideas are clear and interesting. Then rewrite the paragraph to include any suggestions from your partner.

Main idea statements:

1. Working as a pilot of a jet plane is dangerous for several reasons.
2. In the late twentieth century, there were several important new developments in science and technology.
3. The environment is in danger in many ways.
4. My hometown has many wonderful features.
5. Grandmothers are important to the family for many reasons.

(*Adapted from* More Reading Power, Second Edition, *2004, p. 112*)

Some students learn best through visual imagery. Here is a suggested format for a graphic organizer for the listing pattern.

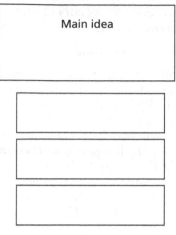

(Continue with as many boxes as needed. Students will also enjoy using other shapes.)

Chronology/Sequence (time order, steps in a process)

In this pattern, the writer explains the main idea with a series of events or steps that follow one after the other in time order.

Key words/phrases in the main idea: *began, account, story, process, history, sequence*

Signal words/phrases: *first, second, then, next, after, while, since, then, soon, finally, at last, in [year], last month, later, over time, the next step, the following week*

SAMPLE RATIONALE

When you read a history book or a recipe book, you usually find a sequence of events or steps. Once you notice this pattern, you can follow the author's ideas and remember them. Texts can be organized in two general types of sequence patterns:

- Stories, history books, biographies, and news articles are usually presented in *chronological (time) order.*
- Scientific experiments, directions for making something, directions to find someplace, and recipes are usually presented as a *series of steps* in a process.

The important point to remember is that things happen in a certain order, and the writer uses signal words to help you follow along the way.

Example: In this example, the signal words are underlined. Is this an example of time order or steps in a series?

Alan was planning to ride his bicycle to work, so he decided to check his bike to make sure he could ride it safely. <u>First,</u> he checked the amount of air in the tires. <u>Then</u> he cleaned the frame and the rims of the tires. <u>Next,</u> he oiled the axle. <u>After that,</u> he tightened the cable for the gears. And <u>finally,</u> he examined the brakes to make sure they were adjusted for quick stops in city traffic.

SAMPLE EXERCISE G.5. **USING SEQUENCE SIGNALS**

Directions: In each paragraph, the signal words are underlined. Fill in the information on the lines below and write the events or steps next to the signal words on the lines below. Then compare your work with another student's.

Example a: Chronological Order (time)

Franklin D. Roosevelt, the thirty-second president of the United States, served his country for <u>most of his life</u>. He was the only president to be elected four times. He was born in Hyde Park, New York, on <u>January 30, 1882</u>, and he began his studies at Harvard in <u>1903</u>. In <u>1905</u>, he married Eleanor Roosevelt, a distant cousin. <u>During</u> their marriage, they had six children. <u>After</u> serving in the New York State Senate, Mr. Roosevelt worked in Washington as Secretary of the Navy until <u>1921</u>. <u>At that time</u>, he became very ill with polio and lost the use of his legs. <u>In 1928</u>, Mr. Roosevelt ran for governor of New York. <u>After</u> serving two terms as governor, he was elected to the presidency <u>in 1933</u>. President Roosevelt died in office on <u>April 12, 1945</u>.

Main idea:

_____

_____

Key word in the main idea: _____

Signal words	Events
January 30, 1882	*He was born in Hyde Park, New York.*
1903	_____
1905	_____
During	_____
After	_____
1921	_____
At that time,	_____
In 1928,	_____
After	_____
in 1933	_____
April 12, 1945	_____

Example b: Steps in a Process

Using a digital camera and a computer is an easy and enjoyable <u>way to make</u> good photographs. <u>First</u>, you must install the computer program that is sold with the camera. <u>Then</u> take some pictures and connect your camera to the computer, using the cables provided with the camera. <u>Next</u>, open the program on the computer and save the pictures on the hard disk or a CD. <u>After that</u>, you can edit the pictures as desired, using the photo editing tools on the program. You can make your photos lighter or darker, for example, or you can change the size. <u>At this point</u>, be sure to save the edited photos and then, <u>finally</u>, you are ready to print them.

Main idea:

_____

_____

Key word in the main idea: _____

Signal words	Steps
First,	*install the computer program.* _____
Then	_____
Next,	_____
After that,	_____
At this point,	_____
then, finally,	_____

SAMPLE EXERCISE G.6. FINDING AND USING TIME ORDER SIGNAL WORDS

Directions: Read each paragraph and underline the signal words. Then fill in the lines below, write the signal words and the events or steps in the spaces below. Compare your work with another student's.

1.   The Vietnam War began soon after World War II. At first, in 1946, the war was between the Vietnamese and the French. The government was French, but many Vietnamese people did not want a French government. They wanted the French to leave so they could have their own government. The Vietnamese fought hard, and slowly they won more and more land. By 1953, the French army was in trouble. They were not winning the war. French soldiers were dying, and the war was costing a lot of money. So, in 1954, the French army stopped fighting and left Vietnam. That was the end of the first part of the Vietnam War.

Main idea:

_____

_____

Key word in the main idea: _____

Signal words	Events
_____	_____
_____	_____
_____	_____

2.   The second part of the Vietnam War began in 1954. After the French army left, there were two Vietnams: North Vietnam and South Vietnam. There were also two governments, but both governments wanted to be the only government for all of Vietnam. So from 1954 until 1960, the North and the South were fighting all the time. The North Vietnamese grew slowly stronger. By the beginning of 1965, the North Vietnamese were winning the war. However, the United States government did not want the North Viet-

namese to win. So in March 1965, the United States began to help South Vietnam. They sent guns and airplanes to help the South. At first, the United States sent only a few soldiers. But by July 1965, there were about 75,000 American soldiers in Vietnam.

Main idea:

_____

_____

Key word in the main idea: _____

Signal words   Events

_____   _____

_____   _____

_____   _____

_____   _____

_____   _____

(From Reading Power, Third Edition, *2005, p. 117)*

SAMPLE EXERCISE **G.7.**   FINDING AND USING SIGNAL WORDS FOR STEPS IN A PROCESS

Directions: Read this paragraph and underline the signal words. Write the main idea and the signal words below. Then write a step in the sequence of steps for each signal word. Work with a partner.

When you decide to take a trip, the planning can be fun. First, you have to decide where to go. Next, you need to look at maps and books about the place and figure out how to use your time while you are there. Soon after that, you should talk to a travel agent to find out how you will travel and how much it will cost. Then, if you are going to a country with a language different from yours, you may decide to learn a few phrases in that language. Finally, you need to make a packing list and check to be sure that you have everything you need. After all of this, you can relax and have a great trip.

Main idea: _____

_____

Key word in the main idea: _____

Signal words   Events or steps

_____   _____

_____   _____

_____   _____

_____   _____

_____   _____

Before beginning to work on Exercise G.8 (on page 173), the teacher should ask students to supply some time order and sequence signal words and write them on the board. Then students can use them as they proceed to do the activity. As they work together in sorting out the list of steps, they will use time order signal words orally in a natural way. The teacher should listen in and point out how often the students use the signal words as they discuss the steps.

SAMPLE EXERCISE G.8. **STEPS IN A LONG PROCESS**

Directions: A. Read the passage and try to remember the order of steps in making a submarine sandwich.

HOT SUBS FOR LUNCH

The name may be different in other parts of the world, but in Boston they are known as "subs," or submarine sandwiches. One of the most popular lunch items in town, a sub for lunch is typical for people from all walks of life, from the governor on down.

The best way to find out about subs is to go to a sub shop, where these wonderful sandwiches are the specialty. You will find huge ovens right behind the counter, because a real sub is served hot.

The sub sandwich maker usually says, "What kind of sub do you want?" The customer might answer, "Large Italian."

The man begins by taking a large, long bread roll from a plastic bag under the counter. He slices it lengthwise and puts in layers of Genoa salami, mortadella, and other cold meats, and tops that with provolone cheese.

Leaving the sandwich open, the sandwich chef places it on a metal tray and slides it into the oven. He bakes it until the meat is warm, the roll is toasty, and the cheese has begun to melt. Then he takes it out and calls out, "What do you want on the large Italian?"

"Everything," is often the reply. "Everything" means that he adds mayonnaise, salt, pepper, oil, and a sprinkling of oregano. But that is not all. He also puts in lots of chopped pickles, sliced onions, pickled hot peppers, sliced tomatoes, and crunchy chopped iceberg lettuce.

Finally, taking the sandwich in his hand, the sandwich maker folds the two sides together, carefully slices it in half, and wraps it in waxed paper. "For here or to go?" he asks. No matter which way you take it, you can be sure that you will enjoy lunch that day!

B. *How did he make the submarine sandwich?*

Below are the steps involved in making a submarine sandwich, but they are out of order. Do not look back at the passage. Working with a group of three or four students, write the numbers of the steps in the correct order on the line below.

1. He carefully slices it in half.
2. He adds liberal portions of chopped pickles.
3. He places it on a metal tray.
4. He wraps it in waxed paper.
5. He takes a large bread roll out of a plastic bag.
6. He folds the two sides together.
7. He slices the roll in half lengthwise.
8. He asks, "For here or to go?"
9. He calls out "What do you want on the large Italian?"
10. He allows it to bake until the meat is warm.

The correct order of steps: _____

Sample Exercise G.9 is a writing exercise that will help students reinforce the use of the sequence pattern. The teacher should review the sequence signal words before students begin working.

SAMPLE EXERCISE G.9.   WRITING A PARAGRAPH IN THE SEQUENCE PATTERN

Directions: On a separate sheet of paper, write a paragraph in the time order/ sequence pattern. Begin with one of the main idea statements below and complete the paragraph with sentences describing events or steps. To guide your reader, use a sequence signal word for each event or step. After you have written your paragraph, ask another student to read it and underline the signal words. Ask if he or she thinks the paragraph is in time order or in a series of steps. Find out if your ideas were clear and interesting. Then rewrite the paragraph to include any suggestions from your partner.

Main idea statements:

1. It is easy to make a cup of tea.

2. A trip to another country requires a lot of planning.

3. Learning how to play _____ is a long process. (Add the name of a sport.)

4. My daily schedule is busy and complicated.

5. _____'s musical career began at a very young age. (Add the name of a famous musician.)

As with all of the patterns, the chronology/sequence pattern can be shown in the form of a graphic organizer such as the following:

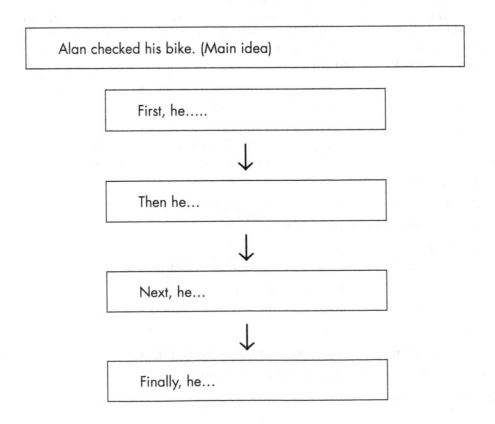

Now that students have worked on the sequence pattern, help them to apply their knowledge in the next Intensive Reading Lesson. Offer the class a choice of several different time-order and process passages. Students should be able to apply these skills:

- Preview and predict
- Scan for specific information
- State the topic
- State the main idea
- Recognize the sequence pattern and tell the steps or events in order

Comparison and Contrast

In this pattern, the writer's main idea is a general statement about two things that are similar and/or different. Specific details about similarities and/or differences are given.

Key words/phrases in the main idea: *similarities, differences, both, in common, same, different, compare, comparison, contrast.*

Signal words/phrases for similarities: *similarly, also, in the same way, as, like, both, in common.*

Signal words/phrases for differences: *however, but, on the other hand, although, while, in contrast, than, conversely, yet, unlike.*

SAMPLE RATIONALE

You can recognize the comparison/contrast pattern by noticing that the paragraph or passage is about two things and by noticing the signal words. Once you have learned how to recognize this pattern, you will be able to understand and remember more when you read.

A. To show how two things are alike in some ways and different in others, writers use a comparison pattern.

    Example: Comparison of a jet plane and a helicopter (signal words are underlined)

      1. How are they <u>alike</u>?
        a. <u>Both</u> have engines that need fuel.
        b. <u>Both</u> have wheels.
        c. <u>Both</u> are used for air transportation.
        d. <u>Both</u> require pilots with special training.
      2. How are they different?
        a. A jet plane is <u>larger than</u> a helicopter.
        b. <u>While</u> a plane takes off horizontally, a helicopter goes straight up vertically.
        c. A jet plane can carry <u>more passengers</u> than a helicopter.
        d. A helicopter can land in <u>more kinds of places</u> than a jet plane.

B. To show only how two things are different, writers use a contrast pattern.

    Example: Contrast your country and the United States. How are they different?

      a.

      b.

      c.

Directions: In these paragraphs, the comparison/contrast signal words are under-
lined. Working with another student, write the main idea and signal words on
the lines below. Then write the appropriate detail next to each signal word. Some
parts are done for you.

1. Comparison (similarities and differences)

<u>Both</u> New York City and Paris depend on vast subway lines to transport their millions of commuters. In <u>both</u> cities, the subways are often crowded, especially at rush hours. <u>Another likeness</u> is the terrible noise level in the trains. <u>A further similarity</u> is that the two subway systems both cover a wide area at little expense for commuters. <u>However</u>, the differences between the two are quite striking. <u>While</u> subway stations in New York tend to be plain except for some decorative tiles, Paris stations are generally attractive. Many of the French stations are filled with works of art. In Paris, the subway trains are clean and they run every few minutes. <u>On the other hand</u>, New York's trains can sometimes be less clean and reliable.

Does this paragraph include similarities, differences, or both? _____

Topic: _____

Main idea: _____

_____

Key word in the main idea: _____

Signal words	Details
both	*subways are often crowded*
Another likeness	_____
A further similarity	_____
However,	_____
While	*New York stations tend to be plain/Paris stations* *are generally attractive*
On the other hand,	_____

2. Comparison (similarities only)

The Ukraine and Japan are very far away from each other, and the cultural traditions in each place are generally very different. But the people who live in both places do have one thing in common. They both like to eat pastries filled with meat. Ukrainian pastries are called pilmeni and Japanese pastries are called gyoza, and they are remarkably similar. Both are made of pieces of flat dough folded around a spicy meat filling. In both countries, people usually eat their pastries with sauce. The Ukrainians use sour cream and the Japanese use soy sauce.

Topic: _____

Main idea: _____

_____

Key word in the main idea: _____

Does this paragraph include similarities, differences, or both? _____

Signal words	Details
both	_____
similar	_____
Both	_____
both	_____

3. Contrast (differences only)

When the first baby arrives in a family, everything changes. In the past, the parents needed an alarm clock in the morning, <u>but</u> now the baby decides when they should wake up. Formerly, the parents spent their evenings watching TV or reading, <u>but</u> now all their free time is spent admiring their infant. <u>In contrast</u> to pre-baby days, their life is more carefully planned. <u>While</u> they used to go out to see friends whenever they wanted to, that is no longer possible. If they want to go out without the baby, they must arrange for a babysitter. <u>Unlike</u> the neat and tidy rooms of the past, these days their apartment is full of baby things. Their friends have even noticed a <u>difference</u> in the topic of conversation: it's always about the baby!

Topic: _____

Main idea: _____

_____

Key word in the main idea: _____

Does this paragraph include similarities, differences, or both? _____

Signal words	Details
but	<u>*in the past, needed alarm clock/now baby wakes them*</u>
but	_____
In contrast	_____
While	_____
Unlike	_____
difference	_____

SAMPLE EXERCISE G.11. USING COMPARISON/CONTRAST SIGNAL WORDS

Directions: Read these paragraphs and underline the comparison/contrast signal words. Then, working with another student, write the answers and fill in the information on the lines below.

1. In some ways, English breakfasts are similar to American breakfasts. In both England and the United States, people usually eat large breakfasts. English and American breakfasts both include several dishes. They may include some fruit juice, cereal, and then eggs and toast. In both places, there may also be some meat with the breakfast. However, there are also some differences between American and English breakfasts. In England, people usually drink tea in the morning. However, most Americans prefer coffee. The English usually do not eat sweet things for breakfast, but many Americans like sweet bread or coffee cake.

What is this paragraph comparing? _____

Main idea: _____

_____

Key word in the main idea: _____

Signal words	Details	Likenesses
_____	_____	_____
_____	_____	_____
_____	_____	_____
_____	_____	_____

2.   American breakfasts are very different from breakfasts in Italy. In general, American breakfasts are much larger than Italian breakfasts. Americans may eat several different foods for breakfast. They may eat cereal and eggs and toast. But Italians usually just have bread and coffee. Many Americans also like to eat some kind of meat. Italians almost never eat meat early in the morning. Finally, American coffee is different from Italian coffee. Many Americans do not drink strong coffee in the morning. Italians always like their coffee strong and dark.

What is this paragraph contrasting? _____

Main idea: _____

_____

Key word in the main idea: _____

Signal words	Details	Differences
_____	_____	_____
_____	_____	_____
_____	_____	_____
_____	_____	_____

(From More Reading Power, Second Edition, *2004, p. 118*)

SAMPLE EXERCISE G.12.   USING SIGNAL WORDS

Directions: Read each paragraph and underline the comparison/contrast signal words. On the lines below, write the main idea, the signal words, and the details. Compare your work with another student's.

Ideas about Education

1.   High school graduates are sometimes nervous about attending college because they fear that everything will be different. In fact, there are some important similarities between college and high school. In both places, academic success depends on being a responsible student. This means attending classes regularly, doing your homework, and studying new materials carefully. The social situation in college is also like high school. If you had friends in high school, chances are you will have friends in college, too. The activities in college also closely resemble the activities in high school. Musical groups, sports teams, special interest clubs, and other activities are found in both institutions.

Main idea: _____

_____

Does this paragraph include similarities, differences, or both? _____

Signal words   Details

_____   _____

_____   _____

_____   _____

_____   _____

2.   The University of Bologna in northern Italy is different from most North American universities. One major difference is its age. Founded in the tenth century, it is the oldest university in Europe and its ancient halls give students an appreciation of history. North American universities, on the other hand, are all relatively new, and generally students are surrounded by more modern buildings. Another difference is the campus. The buildings that make up the University of Bologna are scattered around the center of the city. There is no campus or special university area, as there usually is at North American universities. Unlike the North American university campus, there are no trees or open spaces for students to meet in near this old Italian institution. Instead, students meet on the streets, in cafes, and in the courtyards of the historic buildings.

Main idea: _____

_____

Does this paragraph include similarities, differences, or both? _____

Signal words   Details

_____   _____

_____   _____

_____   _____

_____   _____

3.   In Russia, there has always been a strong tradition of learning foreign languages. This led to the development of specialized foreign language schools. These schools teach the same subjects as all other Russian public schools. However, unlike most public schools, many of the subjects are taught in French, German, or English at the foreign language schools. The students are different, too. Unlike the regular Russian language schools, students must be selected to attend specialized schools. Quite often these students come from families with higher levels of education. The greatest difference lies in the language abilities of the students. Students in specialized language schools learn to express themselves fluently in a foreign language.

Main idea: _____

_____

Does this paragraph include similarities, differences, or both? _____

Signal words   Details

_____   _____
_____   _____
_____   _____
_____   _____

(From More Reading Power, Second Edition, *2004, p. 119)*

Sample Exercise G.13 (on page 181) is a writing exercise that will help students consolidate their work on the comparison/contrast pattern. Before working on it, the teacher and students should review the signal words for the comparison/contrast pattern.

SAMPLE EXERCISE **G.13.**   WRITING A COMPARISON/CONTRAST PARAGRAPH

Directions: On a separate sheet of paper, write a paragraph about one of the following topics, using the comparison/contrast pattern. Your main idea statement should let your reader know whether you are writing about similarities, differences, or both. Complete the paragraph with sentences that give details to support the main idea. Remember to use signal words to guide your reader. After you have written your paragraph, ask another student to read it and underline the main idea and the signal words. Find out if your ideas were clear and interesting. Then rewrite the paragraph to include any suggestions from your partner.

Topics:

a. The city you live in and another city
b. Movies and real life
c. Being a student and being a full-time worker
d. Male friends and female friends
e. Business management in your country and another country

The comparison/contrast pattern can be represented in a graphic organizer such as the one below, which shows both similarities and differences.

A jet plane and a helicopter are similar in some ways, but different in others. (Main idea)

Jet Plane	Helicopter
Similarities	Similarities
needs fuel has wheels is used for transportation requires special training for pilot	needs fuel has wheels is used for transportation requires special training for pilot
Differences	Differences
larger than helicopter takes off horizontally can carry more passengers	can land in more places takes off vertically

(Design adapted from X. Jiang & W. Grabe, 2010)

INTENSIVE READING LESSON

Once students have learned to use the first three patterns (listing, sequence, and comparison/contrast), it is time to assign one passage of each type. The students should preview the three passages and identify the overall pattern of each one. Then the class should decide as a group which of the passages to read and discuss. And once again, the students should be directed to apply all of the skills they have learned so far:

- predicting
- identifying the topic
- finding the main idea
- recognizing the organizational pattern and signal words

Cause/Effect

In this pattern, the writer's main idea is that one event or action caused another event, situation, or action.

Key words in the main idea and signal words for details are the same and often include: *causes, leads to, is the cause of, creates, brings about, makes, provokes, produces, gives rise to, contributes to, results in, is due to, is the result of, comes from, results from, is produced by, is a consequence of, follows, is caused by.*

Cause/effect may be a difficult pattern for ESL/EFL students for several reasons. First, unlike other patterns, the cause/effect signal words are often verbs. (The strong coffee <u>caused</u> me to stay awake all night.) And as integral parts of sentences, these signal words don't stand out in the same way that signal words for other patterns usually do. Furthermore, verbs forms can express the cause/effect relationship actively (The rain <u>caused</u> the flood.) or passively (The flood <u>was caused by</u> the rain.).

Second, cause/effect relationships are as likely to be single (What caused the flat tire?) as multiple (What were the causes of World War I? What were the effects of the flood?).

There is also the problem of word order. If students mistakenly assume that the thing named first is always the cause and the thing named second is the effect, they are in trouble! It is important to keep these factors in mind when selecting or writing exercises for teaching cause/effect relationship patterns, and it is best to begin with single cause/effect relationships that clearly show the connection between the passing of time and cause and effect (Zupnik, 1988). The following sample rationale is set up to help clarify the time relationship in cause/effect.

SAMPLE RATIONALE

Causes and effects are part of our daily lives. It is important to learn how to recognize the cause/effect pattern when you read. It is not as easy to identify as the other patterns.

   Example: I missed the bus this morning.

   I was late for work.

What happened first?   What happened next?

I missed the bus ———→ I was late for work.

   cause   effect

When you read a passage with a cause/effect pattern, THINK: "What happened first?" Then you will know the cause.

A cause/effect sentence does not always put the cause first.

   Example: Because I missed the bus, I was late for work.

   cause   effect

   I was late for work because I missed the bus.

   effect   cause

In both sentences, *because* is the signal word. It is found in the part of the sentence that tells the cause.

(Adapted from Zupnik, 1988)

SAMPLE EXERCISE G.14.   **IDENTIFYING CAUSES AND EFFECTS**
(FOR INTERMEDIATE LEVEL STUDENTS)

Directions: A. Study the following pairs of words and phrases. Which causes which? THINK: Which one comes first? Then draw an arrow from the cause to the effect. The first one is done. Work with another student.

Column A	Column B
1. viruses ——————→	infectious diseases
2. epidemics	bacteria
3. headaches	colds and flu
4. improperly stored food	food poisoning
5. slow development	improper nutrition
6. swimming in pools	ear infection
7. heart trouble	diet high in fat
8. skin cancer	too much exposure to the sun
9. black lung disease	working in a coal mine
10. skiing	broken leg

B. *For each pair, write a sentence. Begin each sentence with the word or words in Column A (on the left).*

* If the arrow goes from left to right, use these signal words:

causes   lead to   can lead to   is the cause of produces
can cause   gives rise to   brings about results in

* If the arrow goes from right to left, use these signal words:

is due to   results from   can result from   is the result of
is produced by   is caused by   is a consequence of

Examples:

1. _Viruses can cause infectious diseases._

2. _Epidenics are produced by bacteria._

3. _____

4. _____

5. _____

6. _____

7. _____

8. _____

9. _____

10. _____

C. *Compare your sentences with another student's. If you disagree, explain your work.*

(From *More Reading Power*, Second Edition, 2004, p. 123)

SAMPLE EXERCISE G.15. **IDENTIFYING CAUSES AND EFFECTS**
(FOR INTERMEDIATE LEVEL STUDENTS)

Directions: Read each sentence. Underline and label the cause and the effect. Draw an arrow from the cause to the effect. Then compare your work with another student's.

> *Example:* <u>Hepatitis</u> can result in <u>chronic ill health</u>.
>   C   ⟶   E

1. Coal-burning factories cause acid rain.

2. Stricter anti-pollution laws can lead to higher prices for consumers:

3. Acid rain can bring about the death of lakes and streams.

4. Forests have become diseased due to acid rain.

5. Coal burning also results in higher levels of sulfur dioxide in the air.

6. Sulfur dioxide pollution can result in higher infant death rates.

7. Coal burning causes the exterior walls of buildings to decay.
8. Strict anti-pollution controls may cause coal miners to lose their jobs.

Many times, a text describes a situation that has multiple causes or multiple effects. This is complicated for many students, so it is best to introduce this concept separately, after students are already comfortable with the basic notion of cause/effect. The following sample rationale can be used to begin work on multiple causes and effects.

SAMPLE RATIONALE

In many real-life situations, there is not just a single cause and a single effect.

Example a: Sometimes a single cause can produce many effects.

> In 1992, Hurricane Iniki hit the Hawaiian Island of Kauai. As a result, all telephone lines were out of order, the airport was closed, and thousands of homes were damaged. Hotels were washed away, and tourists' holidays were ruined. Many Kauaians lost their jobs.

What is the cause? *Hurricane Iniki*

What are the effects? *telephone out of order, airport closed, homes damaged, hotels washed away, holidays ruined, jobs lost*

Example b: Sometimes a single effect is the result of several causes.

> The Frozen Yogurt Company closed its shop in the center of town. There really was no other choice. The poor economy meant fewer customers and higher prices for supplies. Bills for electricity and water seemed to go up every month. And then the landlord decided to double the rent.

What is the effect? *The Frozen Yogurt Company closed.*

What were the causes? *poor economy; fewer customers; higher price for supplies; higher electric, water, and rent bills*

Example c: Sometimes a single cause leads to an effect that becomes the cause of another effect and so forth. This could be called a "chain of events," with all the causes and effects linked together. Notice how one thing leads to another in this paragraph.

> During the war in Vietnam in the 1970s, many villages were destroyed. People were left homeless, so they moved to the city. The cities were often overcrowded, with little hope for a good life. This led many Vietnamese to leave their homeland and move to the United States. As a result, many schools and colleges in the United States expanded their English language programs.

Chain of events:

War in Vietnam → Villages were destroyed → People were homeless → People moved to cities → Cities became crowded, no hope → Vietnamese moved to the United States → United States needed more English language programs

---

(From More Reading Power, Second Edition, *2004, p. 125)*

Directions: A. On the left, there are two possible causes for the list of effects on the right. Write the letter of the effect that could go with each cause. Work with another student. Explain your choices to the class. Some of the effects can be used twice.

CAUSES	POSSIBLE EFFECTS
1. Learning a new language 2. Living in a new city	a. Many headaches b. Meeting interesting people c. Feeling in danger d. Spending a lot of money e. Going to the language lab f. Feeling confused g. Understanding other's ideas h. Doing homework i. Finding a new job j. Getting married

B. *In this part, two effects are listed in the right-hand column. From the left-hand column, select the causes that could go with each effect. Write the numbers of the probable causes next to one of the effects. Be ready to explain your choices.*

CAUSES	POSSIBLE EFFECTS
1. Smaller rain forests 2. Use of chemical fertilizers 3. Carbon dioxide emissions 4. Lack of good jobs on farms 5. Polluted rivers 6. Wars 7. High birth rates 8. Too many hunters 9. Overcrowded living conditions	a. Many animals have become extinct. b. Many cities are overcrowded.

(From More Reading Power, Second Edition, 2004, p. 125)

Directions: Read each paragraph. Write the topic and main idea. Underline the signal words and then write the causes and effects. Compare your work with another student's and discuss any differences in your answers.

Staying Healthy

1.   In the United States, why do so many people spend millions of dollars on vitamin pills every month? Many Americans buy vitamins and special health products because they want to keep their bodies healthy. Often, they don't eat healthful food, so they take vitamins instead. The big spending on vitamins is also the effect of advertising. Big companies advertise vitamins as the quick and easy cure to many health problems. People often believe these ads, even though they are not always true. As a result, Americans buy more and more vitamins.

Topic: _____

Main Idea: _____

_____

Causes	Effects
_____	_____
_____	_____
_____	_____

2.   Aspirin is a simple drug that has many useful effects. It can stop a headache or an earache. It helps take away pain in the fingers or knees. Aspirin can stop a fever if you have the flu, and it can make you feel better if you have a cold. Some doctors believe that aspirin also can result in a healthy heart. They say that some people should take an aspirin every day. For those people, aspirin could prevent heart disease. Many doctors say that people should take an aspirin immediately after a heart attack. It could save lives.

Topic: _____

Main Idea: _____

_____

Causes	Effects
_____	_____
_____	_____
_____	_____

(From Reading Power, Third Edition, *2005, p. 131)*

Before students work on the writing assignment below, the teacher should help students review the signal words for cause/effect.

SAMPLE EXERCISE **G.18.** WRITING A CAUSE/EFFECT PARAGRAPH

Directions: On a separate sheet of paper, write a paragraph about one of the following topics in a cause/effect pattern. Complete the paragraph with sentences that include causes and effects. To guide your reader, use a signal word for each cause or effect. After you have written your paragraph, ask another student to read it and underline the cause/effect signal words. Find out if your ideas were clear and interesting. Then rewrite the paragraph to include any suggestions from your reader.

Topics:

1. An earthquake in Mexico
2. The AIDS epidemic around the world
3. An election in your country
4. The Internet
5. Doing your homework assignment at the last minute

The following are examples of graphic organizers that students can use for the cause/effect pattern.

• For simple situations with one cause and one effect:

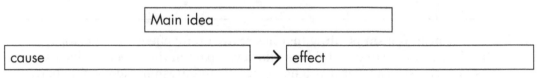

• In situations with one cause and many effects:

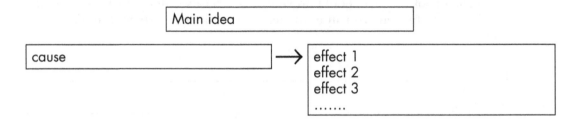

And, of course, with multiple causes and one effect, the same setup (shown above) can be used, with the cause box becoming a list of causes and a smaller box for the effect.

• For more complicated cases of causes and effects in a chain:

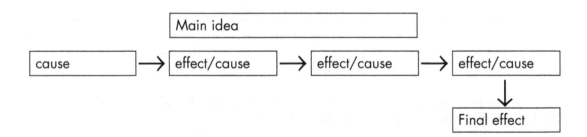

PRACTICE IN IDENTIFYING THE FOUR PATTERNS

Once the students have worked with the first four patterns, the teacher should assign several exercises for practice in identifying and discriminating between them. This helps students to develop the metacognitive skill of thinking in terms of patterns. Sample Exercise G.19 (on page 189) involves identifying the four patterns in sentences, and Sample Exercise G.20 (on pages 189–190) requires students to identify patterns in paragraphs in a longer passage.

SAMPLE EXERCISE G.19. IDENTIFYING PATTERNS IN SENTENCES
(FOR INTERMEDIATE LEVEL STUDENTS)

Directions: Identify the relationship patterns in the following sentences. Underline signal words, and always consider the sense of the sentence as a whole. After each sentence, write TO (Time Order), CC (Comparison/Contrast), CE (Cause/Effect), or S (Sequence). The first one is done for you. After you complete this exercise, compare your answers with another student's and discuss any differences.

1. The tornado <u>came from</u> the collision of the warm low front with the cold high-pressure air mass.   *CE*
2. After the tornado had passed, the city was deluged with torrential rains.
3. The downpour presented disaster victims with the problem of trying to keep dry.
4. Officials said that the storm was worse than any other disaster that had struck the area during the past fifty years.
5. There were not so many injuries as in the 1950 tornado, but the property damage was ten times as great.
6. Two hundred and fifty families were left homeless by the storm.
7. In recent months, the city has had many troubles: record-breaking snows, high unemployment, a water shortage, a flu epidemic, and now a tornado.
8. The people have shown many good traits: patience, courage, ingenuity, and a remarkable sense of humor.
9. The trouble seemed to inspire many people to behave unselfishly.
10. Although most citizens were too stunned to consider what had to be done, a few of the men began to organize volunteer clean-up crews.

SAMPLE EXERCISE G.20. IDENTIFYING PATTERNS IN PARAGRAPHS

Directions: Here are four paragraphs about Sir Isaac Newton; each one has a sentence missing. Read each paragraph and use the signal words to help you decide on a pattern. Then choose one sentence from the extra sentences below. Write the number for that sentence next to the paragraph in which it would fit best. There is one extra sentence. Compare your answers with another student's. If you disagree, explain your answers.

(L = Listing   TO = Time order   CC = Comparison/contrast   CE = Cause/effect)

Paragraph 1

Sir Isaac Newton worked on many important scientific problems. First, there was his development of the laws of motion. He also made important discoveries about optics and the nature of color. His other work included ideas about astronomy, chemistry, and logic. And finally, he produced his *Principia,* a book that explained his law of universal gravitation.

Pattern: _____   Missing sentence: _____

Paragraph 2

Isaac Newton was born in England in 1642. He went to Trinity College, Cambridge University, in 1661, at the age of eighteen. In 1665, the plague swept through England, and Newton left school and returned to his family home in Woolsthorpe. It was there that he began most of his best work. He published his famous book, *Principia,* in 1682. And in 1699, he was made the director of the English Mint. Sir Isaac Newton died in 1727, and he is buried in Westminster Abbey.

Pattern: _____   Missing sentence: _____

Paragraph 3

Although the two men were both geniuses, Isaac Newton and Albert Einstein have very little else in common. True, they both did their most important and famous work before the age of twenty-six. But there are great differences between them. "Proper behavior" was most important to Newton, while Einstein liked to be different. Newton spent his later years working for the government, while Einstein spent his entire life doing science.

Pattern: _____   Missing sentence: _____

Paragraph 4

Newton did most of his best work during his stay in Woolsthrope from 1665 to 1668. Many writers have tried to find out what caused him to produce all of those great ideas in such a short time. Was it the peace and quiet of the small town that caused his creative powers to increase? The causes may never be known, but the effects of Newton's genius are still felt today.

Pattern: _____   Missing sentence: _____

Extra Sentences:

1. Some people think that a falling apple caused Newton to think of the law of universal gravitation.
2. Present-day physicists have discovered limits to the mechanical universe which Newton described.
3. In addition, he invented differential and integral calculus.
4. People say that Isaac Newton never smiled but Albert Einstein had a great sense of humor.
5. In fact, by age twenty-six, he had already completed most of his best scientific work.

TWO MORE DIFFICULT PATTERNS TO LEARN

Sometimes patterns of textual organization are not signaled lexically; instead, they are very subtly shown by the content and the overall organization of a text. This is especially the case with the problem/solution and extended definition text patterns; that is one reason why they are challenging for beginning and intermediate students. In fact, teachers may not find many examples of these patterns in texts that are accessible to such students. On the other hand, these two patterns are often found in academic materials, so it is important to include instruction on them for higher level students.

Problem/Solution

In this pattern, the topic is a problem and the main idea is a statement of both the problem and how it was solved. Problems and solutions are abundant in many textbooks (e.g., science, history, psychology), so knowing how to recognize this pattern is especially relevant for college-level ESL/EFL students.

Key words in the main idea: *situation, trouble, problem, crisis, dilemma, issue.*
Signal words: *solve, solution, resolved.*

This sample rationale introduces the problem/solution pattern. Notice that in working on Sample Exercises G.21 and G.22 (below and on pages 192–194), students are also asked to write the main idea statement. This serves as a review for stating the main idea and also prepares students for learning how to summarize a paragraph.

Teachers can use textbooks that their students are currently reading in other classes as a source of additional examples of the problem/solution pattern. In fact, once students are familiar with this pattern, they should be given a homework assignment to bring in several examples from their reading in textbooks and also in newspapers and magazines.

SAMPLE RATIONALE

Every day, people face a variety of problems, small and large:

- *Who will take care of our two dogs while we are out of town?*

- *How can we stop our neighbors from being noisy late at night?*

- *How can we pay the rent and also pay our doctor bills?*

- *Can governments find a place to store harmful radioactive waste from nuclear power plants?*

The problem/solution pattern is important because it is found in almost every kind of text: in science, history, and social science textbooks, and in novels, newspapers, and magazines. In the problem/solution pattern, the topic sentence usually states a problem to be solved. Often, this is followed by a description of the problem. Then there is either a suggestion for how to solve the problem or a description of how someone solved it.

Unlike the listing, time order, comparison, and cause/effect patterns of organization, the writer of a problem/solution passage may use many different kinds of signal words. For this reason, the problem/solution pattern can be more difficult to recognize than other patterns.

One way to recognize a problem/solution pattern is to look for the word *problem* or one of its synonyms in the topic sentence. These synonyms include *situation, difficulty, trouble, crisis, dilemma, predicament, issue,* or *quandary.* Another way to recognize the pattern is by noticing that the passage begins with a question that states a problem.

SAMPLE EXERCISE G.21. IDENTIFYING THE PROBLEM AND THE SOLUTION

Directions: Read each paragraph and underline the problem. Then, on the lines that follow, write the problem, the solution, and the main idea. Remember to write complete sentences. Compare your work with another student's. The first paragraph is partly done as an example.

1.   <u>How can you keep fruits and vegetables fresh in a hot climate when you do not have a refrigerator?</u> A teacher in Nigeria has invented a new, non-electric cooler that does not need ice. It is a simple device made of a small clay pot that fits inside a larger pot, with wet sand between them and a damp cloth on top. This cooler can keep eggplants, tomatoes, and peppers fresh for three weeks or more. Since the device does not require electricity and it costs little to make, it could be extremely useful in developing countries, where transporting and storing fresh produce is difficult. The Nigerian teacher has won a $75,000 prize for his work. He plans to make and distribute the coolers in Nigeria and other African countries.

Problem: <u>How can you keep fruits and vegetables fresh in a hot climate</u>

<u>when you do not have a refrigerator?</u>

Solution: _____

Main idea: <u>You can keep fruits and vegetables fresh in a hot</u>

<u>climate by</u> _____

2.   As people get older, they usually begin to experience physical problems. They often begin to lose their eyesight, their hearing, and they become less able to get around. Some begin to lose their memory as well. Getting older is a fact of life, of course, and there is nothing you can do to stop the years from passing. However, some scientists at Tufts University in Massachusetts have discovered that there may be a way to prevent some of the physical problems associated with aging. In experiments with rats whose age was the same as humans at sixty-five to seventy-five, the scientists fed the animals half a cup of blueberries every day. After eight weeks, the rats showed improved physical skills. They also showed improved short-term memory, as demonstrated by the fact that they could find their way through mazes more quickly. In fact, blueberries contain antioxidants, which slow the aging process. One leading scientist says he now eats blueberries every day.

Problem: _____

_____

Solution: _____

Main idea: _____

_____

(From Advanced Reading Power, *2007, p. 129)*

Here is an example of a graphic organizer for the problem/solution pattern that teachers can share with students.

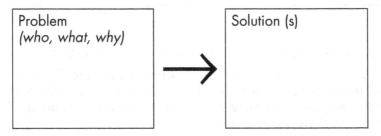

(From Y. Jiang & W. Grabe, 2010)

Extended Definition

In this pattern, the writer names a concept or complicated process that will be defined and explained in the paragraph or passage. Usually, the main idea or first sentence of the paragraph states a dictionary definition, followed by a description and/or other explanation. There are usually no signal words for the details.

Key words in the main idea: *consists of, is, seems to be, are.*

As with the problem/solution pattern, the extended definition is found in many textbooks, and teachers can use examples from these texts with college-level students. And, again, students can be assigned to find examples of this pattern in their reading outside of class. In the following sample rationale, an example is provided for class discussion before the students work on Sample Exercise G.22 below.

SAMPLE RATIONALE

In the extended definition pattern, the writer names a concept or complicated process that will be defined and explained in the paragraph. You will find this pattern in textbooks when the author wishes to define key concepts. Usually, the main idea or first sentence of an extended definition paragraph states a dictionary definition of the concept or process, followed by a description and/ or an explanation. There are usually no signal words for the details. In the main idea, key words/phrases often include the following: *consists of, is, seems to be, are.*

> **Example:** A total solar eclipse is an astronomical event during which the moon seems to cover the sun. When the moon passes between the earth and the sun, all or part of the sun's light is blocked. The moon, of course, is much smaller than the sun, but it is much closer to the earth. For this reason, the sun and the moon appear to be about the same size to us. During a total solar eclipse, the sun, the moon, and the earth are all in a straight line, and the moon completely hides the sun from view.

What is the concept that is being defined? _____

SAMPLE EXERCISE G.22. ANALYZING EXTENDED DEFINITIONS

Directions: These paragraphs have an extended definition pattern. Underline the concept being defined. Then fill in the information in the lines below. The first paragraph is done as an example.

1. A <u>solar eclipse</u> is an astronomical event during which the moon seems to cover the sun. When the moon passes between the earth and the sun, all or part of the sun's light is blotted out. The moon, in fact, is much smaller than the sun, but it is also a great deal closer to the earth. As a result, both the sun and the moon seem to be about the same size to us. During a total eclipse, the sun, the moon and the earth are all in a straight line, and the moon completely hides the sun from view. A partial eclipse occurs when the three bodies are not exactly in a straight line. In an annular solar eclipse, the sun is visible as a bright ring around the moon because the moon is farthest from the earth.

    Concept being defined: *Solar eclipse* _____

    Main idea (basic definition): *A solar eclipse is an astronomical event during*

    which the moon seems to cover the sun. _____

    Explanation and description: *How and why a solar eclipse occurs and*

    three different types of solar eclipses _____

2. Lunar craters make travel on the moon's surface a challenge for astronauts or robotic rovers. The surface of the moon is marked by millions of the deep depressions or holes that are visible from the earth with just

the naked eye. The craters are generally circular, range in size from a few feet (one meter) to many hundreds of feet (500 meters) across, and can be surrounded by sharp mountainous peaks. They have been created by the impact of various objects— asteroids, comets, or meteorites. Since the moon has no atmosphere to protect it from potentially dangerous objects in space, it is exposed to anything that may be in its path. The fact that there is no atmosphere on the moon, and thus no wind or rain, also means that the craters remain unchanged unless another object lands in the same spot.

Concept being defined: _____

Main idea (basic definition): _____

_____

Explanation and description: _____

_____

(From Advanced Reading Power, *2007, p. 144)*

As a graphic organizer, a simple set of boxes can help students visualize the extended definition pattern.

(Name of concept)	is a		that	

(From Y. Jiang & W. Grabe, 2010)

INTENSIVE READING LESSON

For students at the advanced level, the teacher should hand out three different passages at least one page in length from textbooks or magazine articles that might interest the class. Ask the students to carry out the following tasks before the class chooses one of the passages for an in-depth discussion:

- Preview each passage. What is the topic? What do you already know about this topic?
- The class should choose one of the passages to work on.
- Read through the passage. Is it difficult to read? Why?
- Underline any words or phrases that were new to you.
- Find and label one paragraph that has each of the following patterns: Listing, Sequence, Comparison/Contrast, Cause/Effect, Problem/Solution, and Extended Definition.
- Form groups of about five students and compare your work.

The teacher should follow up the group work with an all-class discussion of the passage that was selected by the students.

In Section H—the next and final section of this book—students will learn to apply their text structure skills to longer passages and to several essential study skills.

Study skills lessons should be a part of every teacher's syllabus because students learn study skills most efficiently in the context of a specific subject (e.g., grammar, biology, history, or math). However, in many programs, the reading teacher is designated as, or becomes by default, the study skills instructor. In Section H, a brief overview of a strategic approach to selected study skills is presented. These study skills are further applications of all of the reading skills presented in Sections B through G:

- Applying reading skills to longer passages.
- Summarizing.
- Study reading.
- Critical reading.

READING LONGER PASSAGES

Once students have worked on developing the skills of recognizing the main idea and the pattern of organization in paragraphs, they can learn how to apply the same skills strategically in reading longer passages such as essays. Teachers should begin by pointing out to students the many similarities between paragraphs and longer passages (as shown in the sample rationale that follows).

SAMPLE RATIONALE

A longer reading passage has many of the same features as a paragraph. Therefore, when you are reading a longer passage, you can use many of the same reading skills that you use for understanding paragraphs.

	Paragraph	Longer Passage
Focuses on a single topic	✓	✓
Pattern of organization	✓	✓
Signal words	✓	✓
Main idea	Main idea is a complete sentence.	Thesis statement is a complete sentence.
Supporting ideas	✓	✓

The teacher should explain to the students that:
- The main idea of a longer passage is called the thesis statement.
- Paragraphs in a longer passage may have a variety of patterns that are not the same as the overall pattern of the passage.
- The main idea of each paragraph in a longer passage is a *supporting point* for the thesis statement of the passage.

In Sample Exercise H.1 (on page 196), a paragraph and an essay based on that paragraph will demonstrate to students their parallel structural relationships.

Directions: A. Read the paragraph. Then, working with another student, fill in the missing information on the lines below.

CHICAGO, A GREAT DESTINATION FOR TOURISTS

The city of Chicago, Illinois, is an attractive place to visit because it offers three great features: wonderful architecture, many museums, and beautiful parks. The city's architecture plays an important part in the history of buildings in the United States. The first skyscrapers were built there. The museums include a natural history museum, a museum of science and industry, and a world-famous art museum. Throughout the city, parks play a big role in the lives of Chicagoans, especially Grant Park, which is located along the shore of Lake Michigan. There you can find large public spaces, a huge fountain, and several miles of walking trails. Tourists can find plenty to do in Chicago.

Topic: _____

Topic sentence/Main idea: _____

_____

Key words in the main idea: *three great features* _____

Pattern: _____

Signal words	Details/Examples
Architecture	*skyscrapers were important in history of U.S. buildings*
Museums	*history, science, and art*
Parks	*Grant Park*

Concluding sentence: _____

_____

B. *Read this five-paragraph essay that is based on the paragraph in Part A. Then, working with another student, fill in the information on the lines that follow. (Hint: The thesis statement is the last sentence in the introductory paragraph.)*

CHICAGO, A GREAT DESTINATION FOR TOURISTS

Located in the middle of the United States on the shore of Lake Michigan, Chicago, Illinois, is one of the largest cities in the United States. Because of its location, it became a center of transportation and commerce early in its history, and immigrants were attracted there by the many jobs available. Today, Chicago is the third largest city in America (after New York and Los Angeles). It has become a vibrant and exciting place to live, work, and visit. Three of the top attractions for tourists in Chicago are the wonderful architecture, many museums, and beautiful parks.

One of Chicago's greatest attractions is its architecture, which has played an important role in the history of American buildings. In the 1890s, Louis Sullivan began to design buildings in a new and modern style. While earlier architects designed buildings that were wide, Sullivan began to create beautiful tall structures that led to the development of the skyscraper. Nowadays, you can see some of his early work, as well as the work of other architects who designed some of Chicago's tallest buildings. Tourists can take walking tours of downtown Chicago to visit some of their buildings and learn more about the history of the fabulous skyscrapers.

In addition to its architecture, Chicago is noted for its many museums. Visitors can spend a whole day, for example, at the Field Museum of Natural History. There they can see an exhibit of the earliest residents of North America and another exhibit of Egyptian history including an X-ray of a mummy! Just a few blocks away is the Art Institute of Chicago, which is both a museum with 300,000 works of art and an art school with 3,000 students. The museum is especially famous for its collection of modern art from all around the world. Finally, a short drive along Lake Shore Drive will take tourists to the Museum of Science and Industry. This is a "hands-on" museum where visitors are encouraged to interact with many of the exhibits. One of its unique features is a complete, fully equipped German submarine captured by the United States in 1944. The submarine is located just outside the museum, and groups of visitors can walk through it with a well-informed tour guide.

All of these museums are located in the city's biggest park, Grant Park, which extends for miles along the shore of Lake Michigan. Chicagoans use this park as their "playground." It is large enough to include space for the annual jazz festival as well as miles of walking trails. In the center of the park is the Buckingham Fountain, a beautiful water work that, on summer evenings, is illuminated with multicolored lights that make it a magical place. Further north in the park is the newest addition, a section called Millennium Park, in which visitors can experience a huge modern reflecting sculpture shaped like an arch and known to Chicagoans as "The Bean."

In conclusion, it is clear that Chicago has a lot to offer the tourist. It would take at least a week to study the architecture, visit the museums, and spend time in Grant Park. Once visitors have stayed for a week, they will find that there is even more to see and do in Chicago, and they will want to extend their stay to explore the city.

Topic of this passage: _____

Paragraph 1

Thesis statement: _____

_____

Key words in the thesis statement: _____

Pattern of organization: _____

Paragraph 2

Topic: _____

Main idea: _____

_____

Pattern of organization: _____

Paragraph 3

Topic: _____

Main idea: _____

_____

Pattern of organization: _____

Paragraph 4

Topic: _____

Main idea: _____

_____

Pattern of organization: _____

Paragraph 5

Topic: _____

Main idea: _____

_____

Pattern of organization: _____

Directions: In every essay, book chapter, or magazine article, it is possible to find a single overall pattern for the whole text. However, the individual paragraphs in the text may have different patterns. Read this essay and look for the overall pattern. Then answer the questions that follow. When you have finished, compare your work with that of another student.

WATER SPORTS IN HAWAII

If you enjoy water sports, Hawaii is the place for you! With its tropical climate and warm water, it is possible to be on the water or in the water all year round. Anyone of any age can go swimming at one of the many beautiful Hawaiian beaches. Or you can choose sport fishing from the shore or from a boat. Many people enjoy sailing, but if you prefer, you can go canoeing or wind surfing. Three sports that are especially popular on the islands are surfing, snorkeling, and scuba diving.

Surfing, the islands' most famous sport, started in Hawaii many years ago. The Hawaiians called it "he'enalu," which means "to slide on a wave." Long before the arrival of the Europeans, the Hawaiians would ride on the waves on long, narrow wooden boards. When the first Europeans came to the islands, they were amazed by these surfing Hawaiians. Since that time, surfing has become a very popular sport not only in Hawaii but also on the California coast and in Australia, among other places.

Surfing is a sport that requires you to be a good swimmer. You must also have an excellent sense of balance. To go surfing, you must swim out from the beach with your surfboard under your arm. When you get to the place where the waves begin to break, you have to wait for the right moment—the moment of calm just before a wave arrives. Then you need to try to stand up on the board as the wave begins to rise under you. At the same time, you must try to steer the board with your feet so that you stay on top of the wave. The important thing is to keep your balance and not fall. If you can manage this, you will have an exciting ride all the way in to the shore.

Two additional popular sports in Hawaii are scuba diving and snorkeling. These sports allow you to look at what is under the surface of the ocean. Of the two, scuba diving allows you to see the most interesting undersea sights because you can go further underwater. "SCUBA" means "Self-Contained Underwater Breathing Apparatus," which refers to the equipment used for breathing and swimming around far underwater. In Hawaii, you must take special courses to learn how to scuba dive because it can be dangerous. If you are less adventuresome, you might try snorkeling instead of scuba diving. Less equipment is needed to snorkel—just a face mask, a breathing tube (snorkel), and flippers for your feet. Unlike scuba diving, snorkeling is easy to learn and does not require any special instruction. You breathe through the snorkel, float on the surface of the water, and look down through the mask. Often, fish will come close to you and eat out of your hand.

The ocean around the Hawaiian Islands is clean, clear, and full of hundreds of different kinds of colorful fish. The undersea world is made even more fascinating by the coral reefs, large structures produced by small marine organisms over many, many years. Among the red, gold, white, and light purple reefs, you may also see larger fish and sea turtles. Whether you choose surfing, scuba diving or snorkeling, you will understand why Hawaii is known as a perfect place to enjoy water sports.

Topic of this essay: _____

Paragraph 1

Thesis statement: _____

_____

Pattern of organization: _____

Signal words that helped you decide on the overall pattern: _____

_____

Paragraph 2

Topic: _____

Main idea: _____

_____

Pattern of organization: _____

Paragraph 3

Topic: _____

Main idea: _____

_____

Pattern of organization: _____

Paragraph 4

Topic: _____

Main idea: _____

_____

Pattern of organization: _____

Paragraph 5

Topic: _____

Main idea: _____

_____

Pattern of organization: _____

(Adapted from More Reading Power, Second Edition, *2004, p. 139)*

SUMMARIZING

Once students have learned how to apply reading skills to longer passages, they have the necessary tools for writing a good summary. While summarizing is often considered to be a writing skill or a study skill, it is also an important reading skill. Summary writing requires the reader to apply many of the skills that have been described in this book (e.g., stating the main idea, identifying the pattern of organization, using signal words). In addition, writing a summary reinforces interactive top-down and bottom-up modes of processing and makes readers aware of their own understanding of a text. And, importantly, summarizing leads readers to a conscious awareness of the strategies they apply for comprehending.

Summarizing is a skill that can be taught in a systematic way. Brown and Day (1980) spelled out many of the principles involved in writing a good summary.

RULES FOR SUMMARIZING

1. Delete unnecessary material—information that is trivial.
2. Delete material that is important but redundant (repeated).
3. Substitute a superordinate term for a list of items. For example, if a text contains a list such as *chair, table, and desk,* substitute the word *furniture.*
4. Substitute an encompassing action for a list of subcomponents of that action. For example, *John left the house. He went to the train station. He bought a ticket to London.* The three actions can be combined into a summary: *John went to London.*
5. Identify the topic sentence/main idea statement, if there is one. That sentence is usually the author's summary of the paragraph.
6. If there is no topic sentence/main idea statement, invent your own.
7. Determine the overall pattern of organization of the text.

(Adapted from Brown & Day, 1983)

Day's research on teaching summarizing (1980) demonstrated that junior college students can be trained to produce good summaries by following the rules above, with explicit instruction and modeling at each step. Donant (McNeil & Donant, 1982), working with fifth-grade children, also demonstrated that explicit teaching of such rules was effective in training the children to write good summaries and to better comprehend what they read.

Developing the Concept of Summarizing

Before beginning work on summarizing paragraphs and longer passages, the students need an opportunity to develop the concept of summarizing. First, they should work on exercises that introduce the notion of summary words (e.g., Sample Exercise H.3 on page 202). This requires them to build on their ability to think in terms of general and specific, a skill they already practiced in the exercises in Section F (on pages 142–144). Then they can further develop their skill by working on summarizing a sentence into a single summary word or phrase to replace a group of details (e.g., in Sample Exercise H.4 on pages 203–204).

Directions: Read each group of words and think of a word or phrase that summarizes all of the words in the group. Work with another student. The first one is done for you.

1. <u>sports</u>
   baseball
   basketball
   football
   swimming
   tennis

2. _____
   Mars
   Uranus
   Jupiter
   Saturn
   Mercury

3. _____
   get a shovel
   dig a hole in the ground
   put lots of water in the hole
   unwrap the roots of the tree
   place the roots in the hole
   be sure the tree is straight
   cover the roots with lots of soil
   stamp down the soil
   add more water

4. _____
   clean the house
   buy some chips and salsa
   order some pizza
   bake a cake and decorate it
   wrap the presents
   set the table
   cool the drinks

Summarizing Sentences

Next, students can begin working on summarizing sentences. The sample rationale that follows explains how to summarize a sentence, and exercises such as Sample Exercise H.4 (on pages 203–204) can help students become confident in this skill.

SAMPLE RATIONALE

When you summarize a sentence, you make it much shorter.

   ✓ Use summary words and phrases to take the place of groups of words about the same topic.

   ✓ Leave out descriptive words such as adjectives or adverbs, and keep only the words that tell the main point of the sentence.

   ✓ Use as few words as possible.

   ✓ The summary of a sentence should still be a complete sentence.

    Example: The tall, handsome cowboy put the leather saddle on his black horse, untied him from the wooden fence, waved a hearty good-bye, and rode off into the blazing sunset.

You can leave out all the adjectives. All of the cowboy's actions (put saddle on horse, untied him, waved good-bye, and rode off) can be summarized in one summary word: *left.*

    Summary: The cowboy left. (A complete sentence)

(Adapted from More Reading Power, *Second Edition, 2004, p. 143)*

SAMPLE EXERCISE H.4. SUMMARIZING A SENTENCE *(FOR LOWER LEVEL STUDENTS)*

Directions: Summarize these sentences using summary words and phrases. Remember that a sentence summary must be a complete sentence. Work with another student. The first one is done for you.

1. After she turned on the oven, Yuki mixed the sugar, flour, eggs, milk, oil, and vanilla in the new blender, poured the batter into the buttered pans, and put the cake in the oven.

   Summary: *Yuki baked a cake.*_____

2. As the bus rolled into her hometown, Liz looked around at the familiar streets and shops that she had not seen for two years.

   Summary: _____

3. Geraldo put on his coat, picked up his briefcase from the table near the door, put out the cat, and got ready for his ten-minute walk to the bus stop.

   Summary: _____

4. With her new credit card, Anna bought groceries at the Beacon Supermarket, shoes at Martin's Department Store, and a new set of tires for her red sports car at Ace Auto Supplies.

   Summary: _____

5. After clearing away the old leaves and branches, Jeff dug up the hard ground, mixed in fertilizer and new soil, raked it all smooth, and planted the seeds.

   Summary: _____

6. When they heard the weather forecast, the islanders closed the windows, put tape across the glass, moved all of their plants and chair indoors, and bought lots of freshwater and food supplies.

   Summary: _____

7. Piper put her pens and pencils neatly in a row, turned on the radio, stacked her English books on the desk, got herself a soda, and sat down at her desk.

Summary: _____

(Adapted from More Reading Power, Second Edition, *2004, p. 143)*

Summarizing Paragraphs

Students are now ready to work on the more complex skill of summarizing a paragraph. They will notice that their work in the previous summarizing exercises and their work on finding the topic, main idea, and details of a paragraph will be very useful here. The following sample rationale can be used to introduce students to summarizing paragraphs. Sample Exercise H.5 (on pages 205–206) will give students practice in this skill.

SAMPLE RATIONALE

A paragraph summary should be as short as possible and it must be a complete sentence. The summary should express the main idea in as few words as possible and it should have the same pattern as the paragraph. Follow these steps:

Step 1. Read the paragraph all the way through to be sure you understand it.

Step 2. Check to see if the paragraph contains a topic sentence.

- If you find a topic sentence, does it state the main idea of the paragraph? Does it tell the topic and the idea that the writer wants to express about that topic? If so, you can use it for your summary. Just make the topic sentence shorter by using summary words and phrases and taking out descriptive words.
- If the topic sentence is not a good statement of the main idea, write a main idea statement and then make it shorter using summary words and phrases and leaving out descriptive words.

The teacher should guide the whole class to work together on practicing with the following example.

Example:

Shopping malls have produced a revolution in shopping and living habits in many parts of the world. Before 1950, there were no malls, but now almost every city or region in industrialized countries has at least one. In fact, shopping malls have become a part of daily life. Many people even think of them as social centers. In a way, malls have taken the place of the main streets of a town or city. Shops and services that were once spread over several city blocks are now in one place at the mall. Everyone can save time by shopping at the mall. And people young and old, with time on their hands, often say, "Let's go to the mall!"

Topic sentence: *Shopping malls have produced a revolution in shopping and living habits in many parts of the world.*

Pattern of organization: *Cause/effect*

Summary: *Shopping malls have changed the cultures of many countries.*

Directions: Read these paragraphs carefully and follow the steps for summarizing. Look for the topic sentence and/or main idea. Write a one-sentence summary for each paragraph on the lines below. Make sure that your summary has the same pattern of organization as the paragraph. Then compare your summaries to another student's. Discuss any differences and look back at the paragraph to explain your work.

The Invasion of Alien Species

1.   In many parts of the world, alien species are harming the environment and causing other problems. An alien species is a species of plant or animal that has moved from its original home to a new area. Sometimes people have purposely introduced the new species; sometimes it arrives accidentally, as a side effect of international trade. In its new location, the alien species has no natural enemies, so it can grow and multiply without limit. Over time— sometimes decades, sometimes a few years—the new species takes living space and food away from the native plants and animals. The result can mean drastic changes in the natural landscape and problems for people.

Pattern of organization: _____

Summary sentence: _____

_____

2.   The tiger mosquito is an example of an alien species. This kind of mosquito is common in Asia, but in recent years it has moved to parts of southern Europe. Scientists believe that the eggs of this insect probably arrived inside some car tires that were filled with water. In a few years, the mosquitoes multiplied and spread over large areas of Italy and other countries. Tiger mosquitoes can reproduce faster than the common European mosquito, so they quickly replaced a large percentage of the native mosquitoes. Though they do not cause serious disease in humans, tiger mosquitoes are a serious nuisance. They are far more aggressive than common European mosquitoes, and the effects of their bites are worse.

Pattern of organization: _____

Summary sentence: _____

_____

3.   Another example of a different kind of animal that has recently moved to another continent is the zebra mussel. This small shellfish was first discovered in the Great Lakes of North America in 1986. It may have come over from Russia on a cargo ship. In a very few years, zebra mussels had spread over all the Great Lakes and into many important rivers. They have grown into thick masses, covering many areas of lakes or river bottoms. They have also covered and closed up pipes for power stations and water treatment centers. Government officials say that the mussels have caused many millions of dollars worth of damage.

Pattern of organization: _____

Summary sentence: _____

_____

4. Among the many examples of alien species of mammals that have caused damage is the Indian mongoose. This animal was brought to Hawaii in the 1800s to kill rats in sugarcane fields. Since then, they have grown in numbers so that today they are a major threat to bird life on the islands. One of the mongoose's favorite foods, in fact, is bird's eggs. Thus, the mongoose has caused millions of dollars worth of damage to poultry farmers in Hawaii, and it has greatly reduced the numbers of many native bird species. Many of these species, which are unique to the islands, now risk extinction.

Pattern of organization: _____

Summary sentence: _____

_____

(Adapted from More Reading Power, Second Edition, *2004, p. 150)*

Using the paragraphs in Sample Exercise H.5, the next exercise shows students how to summarize a passage that is a few paragraphs long.

SAMPLE EXERCISE H.6. SUMMARIZING A SHORT PASSAGE

Directions: A. Reread the four paragraphs and your summaries in Sample Exercise H.5. Then put your summary sentences together in one short paragraph. Use only the words that are necessary and connect your ideas using signal words. What is the overall pattern of organization?

Write your summary below:

_____

_____

_____

_____

B. *Ask another student to read your paragraph to find out if your ideas are clear. Then go back and make any changes that will improve your summary.*

Summarizing Longer Passages

The ability to summarize longer passages is essential for students who have been assigned to read and learn the material in articles or textbook chapters. Many good students use summarizing as their primary way of studying textbooks because by summarizing they can determine the key ideas and remember them for later class work. In fact, the physical act of writing out a summary reinforces the information in the brain. In addition, summaries of textbook passages are great resources for reviewing for exams. Once again, it is helpful to provide students with clear steps for this process. Sample Exercise H.7 (on pages 207–209) gives students an opportunity to apply the steps.

SAMPLE EXERCISE H.7.   SUMMARIZING A LONGER PASSAGE

Directions: Write a summary of this article by following the steps.

Step 1. Read the passage all the way through. Determine the overall pattern of organization and write it here _____. Then go back and number the paragraphs.

THE ICEMAN

On a September day in 1991, two Germans were climbing the mountains between Austria and Italy. High up on a mountain pass, they found the body of a man lying on the ice. At that height (10,499 feet, or 3,200 meters), the ice is usually permanent, but 1991 had been an especially warm year. The mountain ice had melted more than usual, so the body had come to the surface.

It was lying face downward. The skeleton was in perfect condition, except for a wound in the` head. There was still skin on the bones and the remains of some clothes. The hands were still holding the wooden handle of an ax and on the feet there were very simple leather and cloth boots. Nearby was a pair of gloves made of tree bark and a holder for arrows.

Named Ötzi the Iceman after the Ötztal area where he was found, he became a worldwide sensation. Who was this man? How and when had he died? Everybody had a different answer to these questions. Some people thought that Ötzi was from this century, perhaps the body of a soldier who died in World War I, since several soldiers had already been found in the area. A Swiss woman believed it might be her father, who had died in those mountains twenty years before and whose body had never been found. The scientists who rushed to look at the body thought it was probably much older, maybe even a thousand years old.

Before they could be sure about this, however, they needed to bring the body down the mountain and study it in their laboratories. The question was, whom did it belong to? It was lying almost exactly on the border between Italy and Austria and of course both countries wanted the Iceman, as he was called. For some time the Austrians kept the body, while the Italians and Austrians argued, but later it was moved to Italy. It now lies in a special refrigerated room in the South Tyrol Museum in Bolzano, Italy.

With modern dating techniques, the scientists soon learned that Ötzi, the Iceman was about 5,300 years old. Born in about 3,300 B.C.E., he lived during the Bronze Age in Europe. At first, scientists thought he was probably a hunter who had died from an accident in the high mountains. More recent evidence, however, tells a different story. A new kind of X-ray shows an arrowhead still stuck in his shoulder. It left only a tiny hole in his skin, but it caused internal damage and bleeding. He almost certainly died from this wound, and not from the wound on the back of his head.

Now scientists can tell a new story of the Iceman's death. Ötzi was attacked and managed to flee. As he ran, he was shot in the back with an arrow. He pulled out the arrow shaft but the head remained stuck in his shoulder. He reached the top of the mountains but was now exhausted and weakened from bleeding. When he could go no further, he lay down and died.

With his clothes and tools, the Iceman has already taught us a great deal about the times in which he lived. We may never know the full story of how he died, but scientists continue to study Ötzi's to learn more about those distant times.

(Adapted from More Reading Power, Second Edition, 2004, p. 151)

Step 2. Working with another student, divide the passage into logical parts. Write a topic for each part. (There may be fewer than five parts.)

Part 1: Paragraphs _1_ –_____   Topic: _____

Part 2: Paragraphs _____ –_____   Topic: _____

Part 3: Paragraphs _____ –_____   Topic: _____

Part 4: Paragraphs _____ –_____   Topic: _____

Part 5: Paragraphs _____ –_____   Topic: _____

Step 3. Write a one-sentence summary of each part:

Part 1: _____

_____

Part 2: _____

_____

Part 3: _____

_____

Part 4: _____

_____

Part 5: _____

_____

Step 4. Write a paragraph that combines all of the summary sentences together. Be sure that your summary paragraph has the same pattern of organization as the passage and use signal words to show the relationship between ideas. Use as few words as possible. Compare your work with another student's.

_____

_____

_____

_____

_____

(Adapted from More Reading Power, Second Edition, *2004, p. 151)*

INTENSIVE READING LESSON

The teacher should plan an Intensive Reading Lesson at this point to review the skills that students have learned so far. In this activity, students realize how much they have learned, and this builds their confidence.

1. As a whole-class activity, ask students to write the names of all of the various reading skills on the board (e.g., finding the topic and stating the main idea). Ask students to volunteer to explain the purpose and value of each skill.
2. Assign a long article and have students work in groups to apply the skills they have listed on the board. In small groups, students should work through the article, checking off each skill as they apply it.
3. When the groups are finished, they should each have a good summary of the article.
4. Ask groups to exchange and compare their summaries.

STUDY READING

Three strategies for study reading are discussed here: marking a text, writing study questions, and using graphics for text comprehension. They all build upon the skills that have been presented in previous parts of this book.

Text Marking

In some cultures, students are taught *not* to write in a textbook. However, strategic text marking can help students pay attention, understand, and remember what they read. Further, by learning to mark only certain text features, students reinforce their skill in discriminating between major and minor details. Accurate text marking also allows a student to rapidly and effectively review a text by simply noticing the marked portions.

After explaining the importance of accurate text marking with the following sample rationale, teachers should train students in the strategy of text marking by working through a text with them. As teachers show students how a specific text can be marked, they should advise students to use a pencil, *not* a pen or a highlighter, for marking the text. There are several sound reasons for this:

- Text markings are often tentative and need to be changed. A pencil (with a good eraser) makes this possible.
- Students often highlight large quantities of a text, and that makes it difficult to review the text for the most important ideas and points.
- With a pencil, the students can use a wider variety of text markings (arrows, circles, etc.) and also write short notes in the margins of the text.

SAMPLE RATIONALE

Marking a text is an essential part of effective study, but you must know *what* to mark and *how* to mark.

What to mark:
The topic of the passage.
The thesis statement.
Signal words for the pattern of the passage.
The main ideas of the paragraphs.
The details that support the thesis statement and the main ideas.
Ideas that seem to differ from what you already know or expect.
Words or ideas that are difficult to understand.

How to mark:
Use a pencil (in case you need to erase).
Do not use a highlighter.
Use circles, arrows, and lines to connect ideas.
Make a star in the margin next to important points.
Write a question mark or an exclamation point to express your reaction.
Write numbers next to points in a series.

The example on page 211 shows some of the features that a student should mark in a text. The students should be instructed to read the passage all the way through before going over the various markings.

The Cultivation of the Pineapple

definition

The pineapple has been cultivated and enjoyed by humans for thousands of years. According to archaeologists, evidence from drawings on ancient Peruvian pottery shows that Native Americans were cultivating the pineapple in about 1,000 C.E. Furthermore, some botanists believe that people in South and Central America began cultivating it much earlier. Cultivated pineapples do not produce seeds. This fact indicates that the plant has been dependent on humans for its reproduction for such a long time that it no longer can reproduce by itself.

When Europeans discovered the pineapple at the end of the fifteenth century, it was a case of love at first sight. Many of the early explorers reported favorably about this new fruit, saying that it had a delightful smell and a sweet, refreshing taste. In fact, of all the new American fruits that were brought back to Europe, the pineapple was the most successful. While other fruits, such as the tomato, were regarded with great suspicion and believed to be poisonous, the pineapple was accepted relatively quickly.

Throughout the sixteenth century, the ships of the European explorers carried pineapples from Central and South America to other parts of the world. During these voyages, the fruit provided an excellent source of fresh food and vitamins for the ship's crew. Furthermore, when they arrived, the travelers found that, if the climate was suitable, it was easy to grow more fruit from the cut-off tops of pineapples. By the end of the sixteenth century, pineapples were being cultivated in parts of India, Africa, and China. In Europe, the climate was generally too cold, so the fruit could be grown only by wealthy people with heated greenhouses.

Pineapples remained a luxury food until the early twentieth century, when they became more easily available. Faster shipping and improved rail and road connections made it possible to bring the pineapples to new markets. Then with the advent of safe industrial canning methods, factories could produce canned pineapple for mass markets. As the fruit became more available and better known, demand rose rapidly for both fresh and canned pineapple. Production quickly expanded to meet that demand, most notably in Hawaii, which dominates the world market. Today, Puerto Rico, the Philippines, Kenya, and Thailand are also important pineapple producers.

---

[1] *advent:* beginning

(From Advanced Reading Power, *2007, p 184)*

Writing Study Questions

Students should learn to write two types of study questions: pre-reading questions and quiz questions. Specialists have long advocated study skills systems that include the activity of asking questions before reading (e.g., "SQ3R"—Scan, Question, Read, Recite, Review). Forming pre-reading questions helps students to set a purpose for reading, activate prior knowledge before they read, and remain engaged in reading the text in order to find the answers to their own pre-reading questions.

Writing quiz questions after reading is another way to promote learning. When students know that they will have to write one or more quiz questions about what they have read, they will have an additional reason to concentrate and read with good comprehension. Forming quiz questions is also a type of review because students often have to look back at the passage to identify the important points in the passage about which they would like to write their questions.

In Sample Exercise H.8 below, the pre-reading and one study question have already been written to get the student started. Then, in Sample Exercise H.9 (on page 214), students practice all of the parts involved in question forming.

SAMPLE EXERCISE H.8. USING STUDY QUESTIONS

Directions: A. Read the pre-reading question. It is based on the title of the article below.

Pre-reading question: <u>*What is the connection between frogs and life on earth?*</u>

B: *Preview the article and then read it carefully. Look for the answer to the pre-reading question. As you read, mark the text.*

- The thesis statement (underline with a double line.)
- Signal words for the pattern of the passage (circle)
- The main ideas of the paragraphs (underline)
- The details that support the thesis statement and the main ideas (arrows, stars, or other marks)
- Ideas that seem to differ from what you already know or expect (question mark or note in margin).
- Words or ideas that are difficult to understand. (underline and question mark)

C. *Write the answer to the pre-reading question here.*

_____

_____

D. *Write three quiz questions about the passage. The first one has been done for you.*

1. <u>*What is one factor in the disappearance of amphibians?*</u>

2. _____

3. _____

E. *Exchange quiz questions with another student and write answers to each other's questions without looking back at the article. Then compare your work and check your answers by rereading the article.*

F. *If you underlined any new words in the article, look them up in a dictionary and write them in your vocabulary notebook.*

FROGS AND LIFE ON EARTH

In the 1980s, scientists around the world began to notice something strange: Frogs were disappearing. More recent research has shown that many kinds of amphibians are declining or have become extinct. Amphibians, such as frogs, are animals that live partly in water and partly on land, and they have been around for a long time—over 350 million years. They have survived three mass extinctions, including the extinction of the dinosaurs. Why are they dying out now?

Scientists are seriously concerned about this question. First of all, amphibians are an important source of scientific and medical knowledge. By studying amphibians, scientists have learned about new substances that could be very useful for treating human diseases. Further research could lead to many more discoveries, but that will be impossible if the amphibians disappear.

The most serious aspect of amphibian loss, however, goes beyond the amphibians themselves. Scientists are beginning to think about what amphibian decline means for the planet as a whole. If the earth is becoming unlivable for amphibians, is it becoming unlivable for other kinds of animals and human beings as well?

Scientists now believe that amphibian decline is due to several environmental factors. One of these factors is the destruction of habitat, the natural area where an animal lives. Amphibians are very sensitive to changes in their habitat. If they cannot find the right conditions, they will not lay their eggs. These days, as wild areas are covered with houses, roads, farms, or factories, many kinds of amphibians are no longer laying eggs. For example, the arroyo toad of southern California will only lay its eggs on the sandy bottom of a slow-moving stream. There are very few streams left in southern California, and those streams are often muddy because of building projects. Not surprisingly, the arroyo toad is now in danger of extinction.

There are a number of other factors in amphibian decline. Pollution is one of them. In many industrial areas, air pollution has poisoned the rain, which then falls on ponds and kills the frogs and toads that live there. In farming areas, the heavy use of chemicals on crops has also killed off amphibians. Another factor is that air pollution has led to increased levels of ultraviolet (UV) light. This endangers amphibians, which seem to be especially sensitive to UV light. And finally, scientists have discovered a new disease that seems to be killing many species of amphibians in different parts of the world.

All these reasons for the disappearance of amphibians are also good reasons for more general concern. The destruction of land, the pollution of the air and the water, the changes in our atmosphere, the spread of diseases—these factors affect human beings, too. Amphibians are especially sensitive to environmental change. Perhaps they are like the canary bird that coal miners once used to take down into the mines to detect poisonous gases. When the canary became ill or died, the miners knew that dangerous gases were near and their own lives were in danger.

(From More Reading Power, Second Edition, *2004, p. 235)*

Connecting Graphs and Illustrations to a Text

Students sometimes ignore graphs and/or illustrations that accompany a passage. They need to learn that they can gain a clearer understanding of a text if they take a moment to notice the connections between the graphics and the text.

Directions A. Read this short excerpt from a report by the United States Bureau of Labor Statistics, "Highlights of Women's Earnings in 2008" (Report #1017, pp. 1, 4. Downloaded 6/7/10 from http://www.bls.gov/cps/cpswom2008.pdf).

PAY LEVELS IN THE UNITED STATES, 2008

This report presents earnings data from the Current Population Survey (CPS), a national monthly survey of approximately 60,000 households conducted by the U.S. Census Bureau for the U.S. Bureau of Labor Statistics. Information on earnings is collected from one-fourth of the CPS sample each month. Readers should note that the comparisons of earnings in this report are on a broad level and do not control for many factors that can be significant in explaining earnings differences.

In 2008, women who were full-time wage and salary workers had median[1] weekly earnings of $638, or about 80 percent of the $798 median for their male counterparts. In 1979, the first year for which comparable earnings data are available, women earned about 62 percent as much as men. After a gradual rise in the 1980s and 1990s, the women's-to-men's earnings ratio peaked at 81 percent in 2005 and 2006.

Asian women and men earned more than their white, black, and Hispanic counterparts in 2008. Among women, whites ($654) earned 87 percent as much as Asians ($753), while blacks ($554) and Hispanics ($501) earned 74 percent and 67 percent as much, respectively. In comparison, white men ($825) earned 85 percent as much as Asian men ($966), black men ($620) earned 64 percent as much, and Hispanic men ($559), 58 percent.

-----

[1]**median** just as many people earn more as earn less

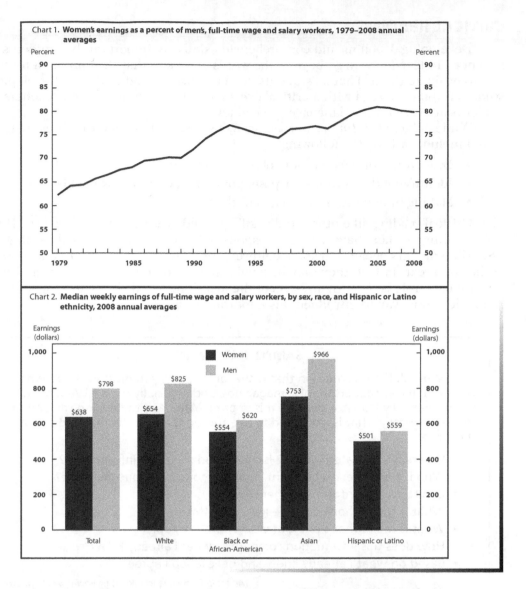

Chart 1. **Women's earnings as a percent of men's, full-time wage and salary workers, 1979–2008 annual averages**

Chart 2. **Median weekly earnings of full-time wage and salary workers, by sex, race, and Hispanic or Latino ethnicity, 2008 annual averages**

B. *Working with another student, read the charts that show differences in earnings for U.S. workers according to gender and ethnicity. Then look back at the passage and underline the parts of the text that relate to the charts.*

C. *Answer the questions.*

1. Which group has the lowest median earnings?
2. Which group has the highest median earnings?
3. Which group has higher median earnings—African American women or African American men?
4. In which group do men and women earn almost the same?
5. In what year were women's earnings the lowest compared to men's earnings?
6. In what year did women's earnings come closest to equaling men's earnings?
7. Which group earned the least in 2008?
8. In 2008, which group earned the most?

D. *Compare your work with that of another pair of students. If you disagree, look back at the reading and charts and explain your work.*

CRITICAL READING

Developing decoding and comprehension skills are important, but students also need to learn how to go beyond the words and ideas that they find in a text and to evaluate them. That is, students need to learn to read critically. Developing students' ability to read with a critical eye should be a high priority for teachers of students at every level of language proficiency.

While *critical reading* is a broad term, a strategic approach to critical reading would include at least the following:

- Evaluating sources (authors of books, Web sites, texts).
- Identifying the author's purpose, point of view, and possible bias.
- Making inferences from what is in the text.

Critical reading, like other study skills, should be a part of every course. However, reading teachers have a special responsibility to introduce critical reading to ESL/EFL students because in some cultures, students are taught *not* to question an author or a text. In fact, they may be taught that the text is the authority, and that the students' role is to learn and accept the ideas presented. The following sample rationale is one way to introduce this important topic.

SAMPLE RATIONALE

With all the information that is available today, you must evaluate what you read in newspapers, books, magazines, and especially on the Web. Nothing is automatically true just because it is in print. You need to develop the ability to *read critically.* That is, you need to ask questions about the text and about the writer.

- Where is this material from? Is this a valid source of information?
- Who is the writer? Is he or she qualified to write about this topic?
- Can I trust the information here?
- What is the author's purpose in writing this?
- What is the author's point of view about the topic?
- How does this information compare to what I already know?
- Based on what I already know and believe, do I agree?

(Adapted from Advanced Reading Power, *2007, p. 216)*

Evaluating Sources

Fiction

Students can learn to evaluate the authors of fiction by learning more about the writer of a book and examining how the author's background influenced the text. Here is a sample rationale that introduces this skill.

SAMPLE RATIONALE

Every writer is influenced by the ideas and events of his or her time, as well as by his or her individual knowledge and experiences. Knowing something about the author of a work of fiction will help you better appreciate the author's work. You can find some information about an author by looking at the back cover or inside of a book. Then you can look for more information by searching the Web.

Directions: A. Read the following descriptions of three authors of mystery novels. Then answer the questions. Work with another student.

- Alexander McCall Smith is the author of the international phenomenon *The No. 1 Ladies Detective Agency* series set in Botswana and featuring an African woman named Mme Ramotswe. Born in what is now known as Zimbabwe (Africa), McCall Smith was a law professor at the University of Botswana. He lives in Scotland, where he is a professor of medical law at Edinburgh University.

- Tess Gerritsen left a successful practice as a doctor of internal medicine to raise her children and concentrate on her writing. She gained nationwide praise for her first novel of medical suspense, *Harvest,* which became a New York Times bestseller, and her second national bestseller, *Life Support*. She lives in Maine in the United States.

- Andrea Camilleri was born in Sicily, Italy. After a long and successful career as a writer and director of film for television, he began to write mysteries at the age of seventy. He has written both historical mysteries and modern detective stories, all set in Sicily. His most famous books include *The Shape of Water* and *The Voice of the Violin,* both from the Inspector Montalbano series.

1. How are the authors alike?
2. How are they different?
3. What are some connections between their personal lives and their books?
4. How might their books be similar?
5. How might they be different?

B. *Compare your answers with those of another pair of students. If you disagree about any of them, explain how you got your answers.*

C. *Choose one of the three authors and find out more about him or her on the Internet. Report to your class about what you found.*

Nonfiction

When students read nonfiction books, it is even more important for them to read with a critical eye, examining the qualifications of the author, the facts presented, and the timeliness of the information in the book. Here is a sample rationale teachers can use to begin a discussion of critical reading of nonfiction.

SAMPLE RATIONALE

Nonfiction books make up the majority of the reading that you do as a student. While all books may claim to be based on facts, these facts may or may not be valid. Before you read a nonfiction book, you should ask the following questions:

- Who is the author? What is his or her professional background?
- Is the author qualified to write about this topic? Why?
- When was this book written? Is the information up-to-date?

SAMPLE EXERCISE H.11. CRITICAL EXAMINATION OF A NONFICTION BOOK

Directions: A. Read the adapted version of a book jacket for Bury Me Standing: The Gypsies and Their Journey *by Isabel Fonseca (1995). Then search the Web for the author's name using Google or another search engine and follow the links to information about the author's life and other works. Working with another student, share the information you find on the Web and then answer the questions below the passage.*

Reviewer's comments about the book Bury Me Standing: The Gypsies and Their Journey:

"...the Gypsies—or Roma—are among the least understood people on earth... their culture remains largely obscure. But in Isabel Fonseca, they have found an eloquent witness." (*The N.Y. Times*)

"A revelation: a hidden world—at once ignored and secretive, persecuted and unknown—is uncovered in these absorbing pages." (S. Rushdie)

"Despite her affection for most Gypsies she encounters, Fonseca resists romanticizing her subject...Sadly, Fonseca discovers that while *gadje* (non-Gypsies) are ignorant of Gypsy life, Gypsies themselves also do not know the full story of their own tragic history." (N. Hunt)

Isabel Fonseca was educated at Columbia University and Oxford University and presently makes her home in London. She has worked as an editor of the *Times Literary Supplement* and she has written for a large number of publications, including *The Wall Street Journal*. Fonseca traveled among the Gypsies (Roma) in Poland, the Czech Republic, Hungary, and several other countries between 1991 and 1995. She lived with a Gypsy family for a summer and found herself walking into a world of conflict in the world's largest oppressed minority who has no homeland.

---

1. What is the professional background of this author?
2. Is the author qualified to write about this topic? Why?
3. Will the information in this book be up-to-date?
4. Would you expect this book to be a reliable source of information about Iran? Why or why not?

B. *Compare your answers with those of another pair of students. If you disagree, explain your answers. Would any of you be interested in reading this book? Why? Why not?*

Websites

Anyone can create a website or put information on the Web! There are no editors to check the reliability of a writer (as in a newspaper or magazine). Therefore, students need to be especially critical. Teachers should give the students guidelines for evaluating websites and then practice the skill with actual sites. The Web and its domains are constantly evolving, so the sample exercise on page 219 demonstrates a format, but the activity is most effective when the teacher writes exercises that are based on up-to-date web addresses that their students are likely to encounter.

GUIDELINES FOR EVALUATING WEBSITES

- Does the writer identify himself or herself and give his or her credentials? Many websites are created by individuals with no special knowledge or experience.
- Does the website belong to an organization that you have heard of? If you have not heard of it, use a search engine (Google or others) to look through the web for more information about the organization.
- What is the stated purpose of the website? Does the material on the site seem suitable for that purpose or could there be a second, hidden purpose (e.g., it appears to simply offer information about an organization, but actually it aims to convince you to join the organization).
- Does the website refer to any reliable, outside sources of information (such as well-known organizations) or just to the writer's opinions?
- Is this an open-source website (i.e., one that anyone can add information to)? Open-source websites can provide lots of information, but they are not always completely reliable. *Wikipedia,* the online encyclopedia, is a good example of this. It is best to double-check any information and consider *Wikipedia* as only one of several sources.

(Adapted from Advanced Reading Power, *2007, p. 216)*

The websites in Sample Exercises H.12 and H.13 below, are known to the author. Teachers should always visit a website first before they decide to use it with their students.

SAMPLE EXERCISE **H.12.** EVALUATING WEBSITES

Directions: A. Working with another student, go to these sites on the web and for each site, answer these questions:

1. What is the purpose of the website?
2. Would you trust the website to have reliable information?
   a. www.ESLmonkeys.com
   b. www.fidelity.com
   c. www.longman.com
   d. www.mass.gov
   e. www.lextutor.ca
   f. www.target.com
   g. www.winikermusic.com

B. *Compare your answers with those of another pair of students. Are they the same?*

SAMPLE EXERCISE H.13. EVALUATING WEB SITES ABOUT A SPECIFIC TOPIC

Directions: A. Imagine that you are doing research on the Hubble Space Telescope. Look at these web addresses for sites with information about Hubble. Do not go to the actual websites. Make predictions about the sites by answering the questions that follow.

1. www.boston.com/bigpicture/2008/12/hubble_space_telescope_advent.html
2. hubble.nasa.gov/
3. imagine-hawaii.com/hubble.html
4. www.howstuffworks.com/hubble.htm
5. scitech.blogs.cnn.com/category/hubble-space-telescope/
6. acrosstheuniverse.blogs.nytimes.com/tag/hubble-space-telescope/

   a. Which of these websites appears to belong to an individual? How can you tell?
   b. Which of these websites appears to belong to an organization? Circle the name or abbreviation of the organization.
   c. Which of these websites do you think provides reliable information? Why?
   d. Which of these websites would you consult to find out the history of the Hubble Space Telescope?

B. *Now visit the actual websites. Check your predictions. Were they accurate?*

C. *Compare your results with those of another student.*

Evaluating Author's Purpose, Point of View, and Possible Bias

In addition to evaluating the sources of reading materials, students need to learn to identify and evaluate the author's purpose, point of view, and possible bias. A sample rationale and exercise are included here for each of these critical thinking skills. In designing exercises, the teacher should first provide several articles or textual passages for practice. Then students can be asked to bring in additional passages from print or online newspapers, magazines, and textbooks for evaluating each of the three features.

SAMPLE RATIONALE

Identifying the Writer's Purpose

To evaluate a piece of writing, you need to ask not only who wrote it, but also why it was written—the writer's *purpose*. The three main purposes for writing are the following:

1. To inform. The author presents facts and explains ideas to the reader.
2. To persuade. The author uses facts and opinions to argue for or against some idea.
3. To entertain. The author tries to amuse or interest the reader with humor, suspense, and stories.

A piece of writing can often fulfill more than one purpose. It can, in fact, be informative, persuasive, and entertaining all at once. However, the writer usually has one main purpose in writing it.

SAMPLE EXERCISE H.14. DISCOVERING THE WRITER'S MAIN PURPOSE

Directions: Preview and then read this newspaper article. Mark the main ideas and key details. What is the writer's main purpose? To inform, to persuade, or to entertain? Write the answer below the text and explain your answer.

Burning Trees to Save a Forest

by Liz Westfield

Burning trees to save a forest! Strange as it sounds, that is the United States Forest Service's new idea for saving America's forests.

For more than a hundred years, Americans were taught that fires in a forest were always bad. When trees burned in the forest, it was a disaster that would ruin the forest. The Forest Service promoted this idea in many ways. They even invented a character named Smokey the Bear, who always said, "Remember, only *you* can prevent forest fires."

In the past, whenever there was a fire in the forest, the rangers immediately put it out. No fires were allowed to burn, even in places where many of the trees were dead or diseased. This did not help the forests, however. In fact, with so many dead and diseased trees, the forest fires in the western United States have been far worse in recent years.

The new chief of the U.S. Forest Service recently explained that there is a new and better way to save our forests. He said, "Small, limited fires are part of nature. That is the way that old, dead, and diseased trees are cleared away to make room for new trees."

Now the Forest Service has new plans. They will start small fires in forests, but they will control the fires. The fires will be started in parts of the forest which are old and full of diseased trees. The rangers plan to burn about 30,000 acres a year for the next 20 years.

As the chief said, "It took many years for the forests to become old and diseased, and so it will take more than twenty years to correct the problem by using controlled fires."

1. What is the author's main purpose? _____
2. How can you tell? _____
3. Compare your answers with another student's. Are they the same?

SAMPLE RATIONALE

Identifying the Writer's Point of View

All writers have a *point of view*—or way of thinking—about their topic that has developed because of their particular experiences and background. When you read critically, you need to identify a writer's point of view and consider how it affects the facts or arguments that are presented. You can identify the point of view by first looking at the main idea or thesis of a passage and then examining the kind of support that the writer gives for it.

SAMPLE EXERCISE H.15. **IDENTIFYING THE WRITER'S POINT OF VIEW**

Directions: A. Read each paragraph carefully and underline the main idea of the passage. Identify the writer's point of view about the topic. Underline the words or phrases that help you decide and then answer the questions. (The helpful words are underlined in paragraph one.)

1. Children and Television

According to recent statistics, the average American, including children, watches four hours of television a day. This cannot be beneficial for the children. Among the many consequences of this situation are the rising levels of obesity among children and the increasing risk of heart disease and diabetes. Spending long hours in front of the television also means that children read less than they did in the past and this has negatively affected their level of achievement in school. Furthermore, the violence in many programs viewed by children has led to an increase in violent behavior on the part of children.

Topic: _____

Point of view about the topic: _____

How can you tell? _____

2. Fast Food and Obesity

Can we blame McDonald's and fast food in general for the fact that many Americans are overweight? Many people would say yes, and lawyers are now trying to force changes in the way fast food is made. But let's fact it—we can't blame the restaurants. They're just serving what people buy. We should blame ourselves. No one forces us to buy those cheeseburgers and fries! We would all be much healthier and thinner if we went to the supermarket instead and cooked a healthy meal at home

Topic: _____

Point of view about the topic: _____

How can you tell? _____

B. *Compare your answers with another student's. If there are any differences, reread the paragraphs to support your answers.*

SAMPLE RATIONALE

Identifying a Writer's Bias

Bias is similar to *point of view* but taken a step further. A biased writer expresses a one-sided opinion or prejudice about a person, group, or idea. Words are used to influence the reader's feelings about the person, group or idea. Biased writing may include some of these characteristics:

- It presents only one side of an argument.
- It includes only facts or examples that support the writer's opinion.
- It uses language intended to influence the reader's emotions (fear, anger, pity, outrage).
- It ridicules other opinions or views.

Bias may be present in many different kinds of writing, including news reporting, political commentary, and even in textbooks. It may involve political or religious opinions, racial or national groups, or other groups, people, or ideas. It is important to recognize bias in writing so that you, the reader, can make a fair judgment about the validity of the writer's ideas.

(Adapted from Advanced Reading Power, *2007, p. 226)*

Directions: A. Read each paragraph and underline the words and phrases that could indicate bias. Then answer the question below. The first one is done for you.

WORLD CUP SOCCER CHAMPIONSHIPS

1.   The World Cup soccer championships have opened this week in Germany. As usual, everyone is trying to predict the winner. Some bet on Brazil, which won the last championship, or Argentina, which seems to be in top form. Then there are the usual European top three: France, Germany, and Italy. But there could also be some surprises. At the European championships two years ago, the finals were played between Portugal and Greece, with Greece winning the cup for the first time in its history. For the upcoming matches at the German stadiums, tickets were sold out long ago. There is some concern about the fans becoming overly enthusiastic or even violent. However, the German police say that measures have been taken to prevent any incidents or to contain them quickly.

Is the writer biased or neutral? *neutral*

How can you tell? *The writer gives only information and facts.*

2.   Every four years, ordinary life stops for millions of people in Europe, Asia, Africa, and Latin America and World Cup soccer begins. In the poorer countries of Africa or South America, this is a rare moment of hope and optimism. If its team wins against a rich country—as Ghana did recently against the United States—the joy is unimaginable, unstoppable. The parties go on for days. In Europe, where the tradition of soccer runs deep, the World Cup matches are a *unifying moment* when the usual political, economic and cultural differences are set aside. On the night of an important match, hardly a car moves on the streets. The sidewalks are empty. Everyone is watching the game. Then if the home team wins, everyone celebrates together. The whole country feels they have gained something vital that makes them stronger and better.

Is the writer biased or neutral? _____

If the writer is biased, is the bias in favor of the topic or against it?

_____

How can you tell? _____

3.   It's time for World Cup championship soccer. Once again, if you happen to live in any of the countries where soccer is the national sport, you'll hear about nothing else for a month. People spend hours discussing the physical condition of the players and their relative merits. On the newspapers or television news programs, the journalists are as *obsessed* as everyone else. People who are normally reasonable become wildly patriotic. If their team is winning, they wave flags, shout, and even sing. You'd think that grown

men and women would realize how foolish they look. But no, when those eleven men start running on the field, nothing else seems to matter. The world around them could go up in smoke and they'd never notice. They're totally involved in the primitive ritual of the game, and all they care about is whether their team will make a goal.

Is the writer biased or neutral? _____

If the writer is biased, is the bias in favor of the topic or against it?

_____

How can you tell? _____

(From Advanced Reading Power, *2007, p. 228)*

B. *Compare your answers with another student's. If you disagree, support your answers by rereading the paragraphs.*

Making Inferences

It is widely agreed that most reading is inferential—that is, most of the time the reader has to go beyond what is written in the text in order to construct its meaning. While many students unconsciously make inferences when they read, they do not always realize that they can use this skill as a strategy for understanding a difficult text. Exercises for developing students' ability to make inferences can be designed in several ways, and the aim should be to encourage students to read "between the lines." In the sample rationale that follows, the example is based on guessing about a conversation.

SAMPLE RATIONALE

Making Inferences

The author of a text rarely tells the reader every detail. For example, in stories the writer may not tell the reader the time or place, and the reader has to guess these things. In other words, the reader has to be a detective to find out the missing information. Read the following little story,

He plunked down $18.00 at the window.

She tried to give him $9.00, but he refused to take it.

So she insisted on buying him a box of popcorn when they got inside.

Where are these people?

What are they talking about?

Which words helped you guess?

Short stories and plays provide excellent sources of examples of the importance of making inferences. The teachers can construct exercises using stories that the students are currently reading. The important point is to design an exercise that asks *only* for information that must be inferred. This is essential for keeping the students' focus on the process of making inferences.

Directions: A. Read this passage from a story titled "A Dark Autumn Evening" by Bea Mikulecky. Then work with another student to infer the answers to the questions below.

Where was that man? Usually he spotted her car from his window and was already down at the door to kiss her and help her with her bags. Even after a year, Kate felt a rush of joy and excitement when she saw him. Because she was away so much, she knew that every homecoming was special to them both.

Impatiently, Kate stowed her coat and shoes in the closet under the stairs, slipped into her moccasins, and began unloading the groceries, calling out again, "I'm home! Where are you?" It was odd that he still had not come down. When everything was put away, she glanced at the week's mail, strewn as usual in the middle of the island—nothing interesting there—poured herself a cup of coffee and headed for the stairs to check whether Andy was working in his office.

But something caught her eye in the corner of the darkened dining room and she stopped short. Someone was sitting at the end of the table. Looking closely, she began to scream—it was Peter! He was handcuffed, his arms twisted awkwardly around the back of the chair, blindfolded, with duct tape across his mouth.

"Oh, Peter! What happened? Where's Andy? Where's Jen?"

He seemed to be conscious, thank goodness, and he strained and twisted in an effort to loosen the grip of the handcuffs. Dropping her coffee, Kate switched on the overhead lights and began to remove the securely tied blindfold and the tape. As soon as the tape came off, Peter shouted, "Thank goodness, you're here! "

For each answer, explain how you can tell.

1. Where is Kate?
2. Does she work nearby?
3. What happened in the story before this passage?
4. Who is Andy? Who is Peter? Who is Jen?
5. What happened to Peter?
6. What do you think will happen after this?

B. *Compare your answers with those of another pair of students. If you disagree, look back at the story to find evidence for your answers.*

INTENSIVE READING LESSON

Making inferences can be fun for the students, depending on the passages that they are working on. The teacher should select several passages from books that the students might like to read. Write inference questions for the passages, and have the students work in groups to answer the questions. Then instruct the groups to form additional inference questions for the stories and ask other groups to answer them.

APPENDICES:

APPENDIX I: *Further Discussion of Selected Topics from* Short Course

APPENDIX II: *Phonemes and Their Spelling*

APPENDIX III: *High Frequency Word Lists*

APPENDIX IV: *Table of Common Collocations in Academic Texts*

APPENDIX V: *Answer Key for Selected Skills Exercises*

APPENDIX I: Further Discussion of Selected Topics from *Short Course*

A BRIEF REVIEW

The methodology presented in this book is based on the premise that learning reading skills means learning new ways of thinking, and that this learning is best accomplished if students focus on one new reading skill at a time and have many opportunities to consolidate their learning through discussing, practicing, and applying the skill. Exercise sequences that a teacher tailors for his or her own classes are the most effective for teaching the skills. Here are useful guidelines for this approach:

1. Select a reading skill.
2. Locate, write, or adapt a set of exercises that focus on that skill in a developmental sequence, beginning at a very simple level.
3. Introduce the skill to your students in a way that demonstrates to them the significance of this skill for reading improvement. (That's your rationale.)
4. Give students many opportunities to work interactively and collaboratively on learning and applying reading skills. When they have to explain their thinking, the students acquire new ways of talking and thinking about textual material. Furthermore, such work acknowledges the social nature of learning.
5. Provide opportunities for the students to apply the new skill in intensive reading lessons, using passages that are interesting, relevant, and accessible. A passage from a reader can work well if it contains information that is interesting to your class.

Teachers Reading Aloud

There are many reasons why teachers should read aloud to their students regularly, regardless of the students' age or language proficiency.

1. Students will benefit from hearing a model of fluent reading.
2. Students can hear stories and tales that might be more difficult for them to read because they contain dialect and complicated paragraphs. (This is where we can introduce Mark Twain and Charles Dickens.)
3. Students can be introduced to a wide range of reading materials. This means, for example, that students who might normally avoid reading fiction might be tempted to choose works of fiction once they have experienced them.
4. Teachers can read poems to their students. This gives students exposure to the phonemes, phrases, and rhymes of English as well as an introduction to themes that are commonly found in English language poetry.
5. Teachers can model a way of reading and interpreting stories that develops literate skills, interpolating elaborative questions along the way.

6. After listening to a story or poem, a group of students will have a shared literacy event that can enhance a sense of classroom community.

7. Last, but certainly not least, students can benefit from reading along silently while the teacher reads aloud. This allows language learners to see and hear the sounds of English phonemes, an essential component of fluent reading.

Students Reading Aloud

Teachers should take care to use student oral reading productively. While some students enjoy reading aloud in English in front of their classmates, others can feel awkward. Erickson (1987) described the latter situation as a "public display of incompetence," truly a humiliating situation for those students.

In fact, most students will concentrate on pronunciation when they read aloud and not on the meaning of the text. Therefore, students should always have an opportunity to read a text silently for comprehension before they are asked to read it aloud.

Reading aloud is effective when students do it in situations where oral reading would be expected, such as choral reading, jazz chants, poems, excerpts from a book that a student has read, and plays. Other kinds of authentic reading aloud include group reports to the class, reading students' own writing to a peer group for feedback, reading a short segment of a text to prove a point, or reading for pronunciation practice.

More about Cloze

Cloze is based on the psychological notion of closure, i.e., if a context is given with missing parts, the mind tends to fill in the missing elements. The cloze procedure was originally used as a measure of readability (reading difficulty) of a text (Taylor, 1953). Over the years, teachers and researchers have employed the cloze procedure for many purposes. How a cloze passage is constructed depends in part on how the teacher intends to use it. For example, here are guidelines for constructing a conventional cloze passage that can be used for determining the student's ability to comprehend a particular text:

1. Select a text suitable for the language level of your students. A text which has been "graded" (assigned a level of difficulty), will provide more useful results.

2. Decide on a deletion rate (every fifth word, sixth word, etc.). Difficulty increases with the frequency of deletions.

3. Leave the first sentence intact.

4. Delete every nth word (e.g., 10th, 7th, 5th). Leave a blank of exactly the same size for every missing word so that the length of the blank is not a clue to the correct word.

5. If the students have never done a close passage before, the teacher should provide practice with a short introductory exercise. Students should be instructed to read past theblanks before trying to fill them in. The class should discuss the introductory exercise and students should feel comfortable with the process before the actual cloze test is administered.

6. Students should be told to try to think of the exact word that the author used in each space. Only the exact words will be scored as correct.

7. Cloze scoring when the exact word is required:
   61% or more correct = independent reading level
   41–60% correct = instructional reading level
   40% or less correct = frustration reading level.

Teachers may want to consult some of the following useful websites on Cloze.

- Cloze Generator is a free program for constructing cloze exercises from any passage that a teacher chooses.
  http://www.oit.ac.jp/ip/~kamiya/mwb/mwb.html
- Tom Cobb's excellent free vocabulary learning website also offer excellent and easy-to-use cloze building directions.
  www.lextutor.ca
- Virtual Language Centre is another rich and varied language-learning website that includes cloze exercises.
  www.edict.com.hk/vlc
- Cloze worksheets already made at many levels are offered at this website.
  www.teach-nology.com/worksheets/language_arts/cloze

Cloze exercises are often used as instructional devices and are frequently used for training students in how to guess word meanings from context. Here are some variations on the conventional cloze passage:

1. Present the passage with conventional deletions but allow any acceptable word as correct.
2. Multiple-choice cloze (Olsen, 1982; Bensoussan, 1983) for testing reading comprehension. For example:

   Directions: Read the passage to the end. Then go back and circle the best words.

   There was a table set out under a tree in front of the house, and the March Hare and the Hatter were having tea at (1) them. (2) it. (3) once. (4) her. A Dormouse was sitting between them, fast (1) runner, (2) quiet, (3) eating, (4) asleep, and the other two were resting their (1) selves (2) comfortably (3) elbows (4) hand on it and talking over its head.

3. Matching cloze. For example:

   Directions: Read this passage. Then go back and write a word in each blank space. Use the words in the box below the passage.

   Malcolm Morris is 29 years old. He lives in Charlotteville, Tobago. Malcolm's town is near the _____. There are few cars in this town, but there are many boats. Malcolm is a _____. Every morning he goes out early in his _____ and gets some fish. In the afternoon he works in his garden. He eats lots of fish and vegetables. He also sells some fish in another town. In the _____ he sometimes works with the other fishermen.

   | fisherman | evening | boat | sea | vegetables |

From *Basic Reading Power*, 1997, p. 113

4. The C-text
   Raatz and Klein-Braley (1984) describe their cloze procedure as follows:

   > "Every second word is deleted. However, in order to ensure that solution is possible at all, we leave the first half of the deleted word standing. If the word has an odd number of letters, we delete exactly half the word plus half a letter. If the word consists only of one letter, then this word is ignored in the counting, and half the following word is deleted . . . Only entirely correct restorations are counted as right." (See Sample Exercise D.8 on page 94.)

5. Rational cloze. A "rational" cloze test is constructed by deleting specific words or types of words. In the following item, the goal is to test macro-level comprehension of a text by deleting words that are signals to text cohesion.

   Directions: Read this paragraph and then choose the best phrase that fits in the text and write the letter in the blank space.

   There are many ways to travel: by land, by sea, and by air. People have been traveling by land and sea for many centuries. But it is (1) _____ that people have been able to travel (2) _____. This is because air travel is (3) _____ man-made techniques and inventions.

   Circle the word or phrase that best fits the text.

	A.	B.	C.	D.
1.	rather strange	also true	a long time	only lately
2.	by air	on foot	by water	on horseback
3.	made difficult by	changing	the result of	the reason for

What Are Schemata?

Schemata are mental structures for representing the general concepts stored in memory. They exist for generalized concepts underlying objects, situations, events, sequences of events, actions, and sequences of actions. Schemata are not single, stand-alone items. A schema contains, as part of its specification, the mental network of interrelationships that an individual develops among the parts of any concept and between concepts. Schemata, in some sense, represent stereotypes of concepts (Rumelhart & Ortony (1977, p. 101).

Here are some examples of types of schemata (Winograd, 1977, pp. 75–76):

1. Schemata concerned with concepts of everyday life. For example: events at a birthday party; eating in a restaurant; taking a bus; getting an ice cream cone; breaking some physical object.

   Other schemata of this type may be associated with concepts of animate or inanimate objects such as: an elephant; a home; a flush toilet; the structure of a device being worked on; spatial representations, such as the way people describe apartment layouts.

2. Schemata involved in communication situations.
   - Distinguishing between "And then he told me I was wrong." and "And then he told me, 'I was wrong.'" and knowing who the "he" and "I" are.
   - Interpersonal schemata: conventions for participating in the communication: "How do you do?"
   - Rhetorical schemata: conventions for laying out a reasoning sequence: for example, language signals such as *therefore, because, so,* and parallel sentences in sequences such as: "He must be here. His light is still on."

3. Schemata for narratives: conventions for stringing together a sequence of statements into a coherent text, for example, simple story forms and conventions, such as mysteries, children's tales, flashbacks, and resolutions.

APPENDIX II: Phonemes and Their Common Spellings

Phonemes are the meaningful sounds of a language. According to McGuinness (2005), fluent reading in English requires knowledge of how phonemes are spelled. As she and others (e.g., Wolf, 2007) have explained, English is an opaque language. That is, unlike Spanish, Italian, and many other languages, English doesn't have a one-to-one correspondence between a sound and its symbol. For instance, the sound /sh/ can be spelled in several ways besides *sh*: *ti* (as in *fiction*); *ce* (as in *ocean*); *si* (as in *tension*). The opaqueness of English is responsible, according to McGuinness, for the slow progress and difficulties demonstrated by many young readers. For students who are learning to read English as a second or foreign language, there is the additional challenge of adapting to this opaque feature of English. Here is McGuinness's chart of phonemes and their common spelling. She recommends that students should first be introduced to the simplest phonemes (those having a single pronunciation).

Consonants

Sound	As in	Basic code spelling
/b/	*big*	<u>b</u>
/d/	*dog*	<u>d</u>
/f/	*fun*	<u>f</u>
/g/	*got*	<u>g</u>
/h/	*hot*	<u>h</u>
/j/	*job*	<u>j</u>
/k/	*kid*	<u>k</u>
/l/	*log*	<u>l</u>
/m/	*man*	<u>m</u>
/n/	*not*	<u>n</u>
/p/	*pig*	<u>p</u>
/r/	*red*	<u>r</u>
/s/	*sat*	<u>s</u>
/t/	*top*	<u>t</u>
/v/	*van*	<u>v</u>
/w/	*win*	<u>w</u>
/z/	*zip*	<u>z</u>

These consonant sounds are spelled with two letters.

/ch/	*chin*	<u>ch</u>
/ng/	*sing*	<u>ng</u>
/sh/	*shop*	<u>sh</u>
/th/	*thin*	<u>th</u>
/th/	*then*	<u>th</u>
/zh/	*vision*	—

These consonant combinations have special spellings.

/ks/	*tax*	<u>x</u>
/kw/	*quit*	<u>qu</u>

Vowels

Sound	As in	Basic code spelling
/a/	*bad*	<u>a</u>
/e/	*bed*	<u>e</u>
/i/	*hit*	<u>i</u>
/o/	*dog*	<u>o</u>
/aw/	*law*	<u>aw</u>
/u/	*but*	<u>u</u>
/ae/	*made*	<u>a-e</u>
/ee/	*see*	<u>ee</u>
/ie/	*time*	<u>i-e</u>
/oe/	*home*	<u>o-e</u>
/ue/	*cute*	<u>u-e</u>
/o͝o/	*look*	<u>oo</u>
/o͞o/	*soon*	<u>oo</u>
ou	*out*	<u>ou</u>
oi	*oil*	<u>oi</u>

Vowel + *r*

Sound	As in	Basic code spelling
/er/	*her*	<u>er</u>
/ah/-/er/	*far*	<u>ar</u>
/oe/-/er/	*for*	<u>or</u>
/e/-/er/	*hair*	<u>air</u>

(*citation:* Diane McGuinness, *Language Development and Learning to Read: The Scientific Study of How Language Development Affects Reading Skill, Table, pages ix-x: English Phonemes and their Basic Code Spellings.* Copyright 2005 Massachusetts Institute of Technology, by permission of the MIT Press.)

2,000 Most Frequent Words in English Language Texts

Source: Adapted from Michael West, A General Service List of English Words. London: Longman. 1936/1953. Available at http://www. lextutor.ca

First Thousand

able	apply	board	cloud	defeat
about	appoint	boat	coal	degree
above	arise	body	coast	demand
accept	arm	book	coin	department
accord	army	both	cold	depend
account	around	box	college	describe
accountable	arrive	boy	colony	desert
across	art	branch	color	desire
act	article	bread	come	destroy
active	as	break	command	detail
actor	ask	bridge	committee	determine
actress	associate	bright	common	develop
actual	at	bring	company	die
add	attack	broad	complete	difference
address	attempt	brother	concern	difficult
admit	average	build	condition	direct
adopt	away	burn	consider	discover
advance	back	business	contain	distance
advantage	bad	but	content	distinguish
adventure	ball	buy	continue	district
affair	bank	by	control	divide
after	bar	call	corn	do
again	base	can	cost	doctor
against	battle	capital	cotton	dog
age	be	captain	could	dollar
agent	bear	car	council	door
ago	beauty	care	count	doubt
agree	because	carry	country	down
air	become	case	course	draw
all	bed	castle	court	dream
allow	before	catch	cover	dress
almost	begin	cause	cross	drink
alone	behind	center	crowd	drive
along	believe	certain	crown	drop
already	belong	chance	cry	dry
also	below	change	current	due
although	beneath	character	cut	duty
always	beside	charge	danger	each
among	best	chief	dark	ear
amount	between	child	date	early
ancient	beyond	choose	daughter	earth
and	big	church	day	east
animal	bill	circle	dead	easy
another	bird	city	deal	eat
answer	black	claim	dear	effect
any	blood	class	decide	efficient
appear	blow	clear	declare	effort
	blue	close	deep	egg

eight	fine	hand	keep	market
either	finish	hang	kill	marry
elect	fire	happen	kind	mass
eleven	first	happy	king	master
else	fish	hard	know	material
empire	fit	hardly	lack	matter
employ	five	have	lady	maybe
end	fix	he	lake	mean
enemy	floor	head	land	measure
English	flow	hear	language	meet
enjoy	flower	heart	large	member
enough	fly	heat	last	memory
enter	follow	heaven	late	mention
equal	food	heavy	latter	mere
escape	for	help	laugh	metal
even	force	here	laughter	middle
evening	foreign	high	law	might
event	forest	hill	lay	mile
ever	forget	history	lead	milk
every	form	hold	learn	million
example	former	home	leave	mind
except	forth	honor	left	miner
exchange	fortune	hope	length	minister
exercise	four	horse	less	minute
exist	free	hot	let	miss
expect	fresh	hour	letter	mister
expense	Friday	house	level	modern
experience	friend	how	library	moment
experiment	from	however	lie	Monday
explain	front	human	life	money
express	full	hundred	lift	month
extend	furnish	husband	light	moon
eye	future	idea	like	moral
face	gain	if	likely	more
fact	game	ill	limit	moreover
factory	garden	important	line	morning
fail	gas	in	lip	most
fair	gate	inch	listen	mother
faith	gather	include	literature	motor
fall	general	increase	little	mountain
familiar	gentle	indeed	live	mouth
family	get	independent	local	move
famous	gift	industry	long	Mrs.
far	girl	influence	look	much
farm	give	instead	lord	music
fast	glad	interest	lose	must
father	glass	into	loss	name
favor	go	introduce	love	nation
fear	god	iron	low	native
feel	gold	it	machine	nature
fellow	good	join	main	near
few	great	joint	make	necessary
field	green	jointed	man	necessity
fight	ground	joy	manner	need
figure	group	judge	manufacture	neighbor
fill	grow	just	many	neither
find	half	justice	mark	never

new
news
newspaper
next
night
nine
no
noble
none
nor
north
not
note
notice
now
number
numerical
numerous
object
observe
occasion
of
off
offer
office
official
often
oh
oil
old
on
once
one
only
open
operate
opinion
opportunity
or
order
ordinary
organize
other
otherwise
ought
out
over
owe
own
page
paint
paper
part
particular
party
pass
past

pay
peace
people
per
perhaps
permit
person
picture
piece
place
plain
plan
plant
play
please
point
political
poor
popular
population
position
possess
possible
post
pound
poverty
power
prepare
present
president
press
pressure
pretty
prevent
price
private
problem
produce
product
profit
progress
promise
proof
proper
property
propose
protect
prove
provide
provision
public
pull
purpose
put
quality
quantity
quarter

queen
question
quite
race
raise
rank
rate
rather
reach
read
ready
real
realize
really
reason
receipt
receive
recent
recognize
record
red
reduce
refuse
regard
relation
relative
religion
remain
remark
remember
reply
report
represent
republic
reserve
respect
rest
result
return
rich
ride
right
ring
rise
river
road
rock
roll
room
rough
round
royal
rule
run
safe
sail
sale

salt
same
Saturday
save
say
scarce
scene
school
science
sea
season
seat
second
secret
secretary
see
seem
sell
send
sense
sensitive
separate
serious
serve
service
set
settle
seven
several
shadow
shake
shall
shape
share
she
shine
ship
shoot
shore
short
should
shoulder
show
side
sight
sign
silence
silver
simple
since
sing
single
sir
sister
sit
situation
six

size
sky
sleep
small
smile
snow
so
social
society
soft
soldier
some
son
soon
sort
soul
sound
south
space
speak
special
speed
spend
spirit
spite
spot
spread
spring
square
stage
stand
standard
star
start
state
station
stay
steel
step
still
stock
stone
stop
store
story
strange
stream
street
strength
strike
strong
struggle
student
study
subject
substance
succeed

such	trade	what	afford	basin
suffer	train	when	afraid	basket
suggest	travel	where	afternoon	bath
summer	tree	whether	agriculture	bathe
sun	trouble	which	ahead	bay
Sunday	true	while	aim	beak
supply	trust	white	airplane	beam
support	try	who	alike	bean
suppose	Tuesday	whole	alive	beard
sure	turn	why	aloud	beast
surface	twelve	wide	altogether	beat
surprise	twenty	wife	ambition	beg
surround	two	wild	amuse	behave
sweet	type	will	anger	behaviour
sword	under	win	angle	bell
system	understand	wind	annoy	belt
table	union	window	anxiety	bend
take	unite	winter	apart	berry
talk	university	wise	apologize	bicycle
tax	unless	wish	apology	billion
teach	until	with	applaud	bind
tear	up	within	applause	birth
tell	upon	without	apple	bit
temple	use	woman	approve	bite
ten	usual	wonder	arch	bitter
term	valley	wood	argue	blade
test	value	word	arrange	blame
than	variety	work	arrest	bless
the	various	world	arrow	blind
then	very	worth	artificial	block
there	vessel	would	ash	boast
therefore	victory	wound	ashamed	boil
they	view	write	aside	bold
thing	village	wrong	asleep	bone
think	virtue	year	astonish	border
thirteen	visit	yes	attend	borrow
thirty	voice	yesterday	attention	bottle
this	vote	yet	attract	bottom
though	wage	yield	audience	bound
thousand	wait	you	aunt	boundary
three	walk	young	autumn	bow
through	wall	youth	avenue	bowl
throw	want		avoid	brain
thursday	war	**Second**	awake	brass
thus	watch	**Thousand**	awkward	brave
till	water		axe	breakfast
time	wave	abroad	baby	breath
to	way	absence	bag	breathe
today	we	absent	baggage	bribe
together	wealth	absolute	bake	brick
ton	wear	absolutely	balance	broadcast
too	Wednesday	accident	band	brown
top	week	accuse	barber	brush
total	welcome	accustom	bare	bucket
touch	well	ache	barely	bunch
toward	west	admire	bargain	bundle
town	western	advertise	barrel	burial
		advice		

burst	comfort	dance	empty	fork
bury	commerce	dare	enclose	formal
bus	companion	deaf	encourage	forward
bush	compare	debt	engine	frame
busy	compete	decay	entertain	freeze
butter	competition	deceive	entire	frequent
button	complain	decrease	envelope	fright
cage	complicate	deed	envy	fruit
cake	compose	deer	especial	fry
calculate	confess	defend	essence	fun
calm	confidence	delay	essential	funeral
camera	confuse	delicate	evil	fur
camp	congratulate	delight	exact	gallon
canal	connect	deliver	examining	gap
cap	conquer	descend	excellent	garage
cape	conscience	deserve	excess	gay
card	conscious	desk	excite	generous
carriage	convenience	despair	excuse	glory
cart	conversation	devil	explode	goat
cat	cook	diamond	explore	govern
cattle	cool	dictionary	extra	grace
caution	copper	dig	extraordinary	gradual
cave	copy	dinner	extreme	grain
cent	cork	dip	fade	gram
century	corner	dirt	faint	grammar
ceremony	correct	disappoint	false	grand
chain	cottage	discipline	fan	grass
chair	cough	discuss	fancy	grateful
chalk	courage	disease	fashion	grave
charm	cousin	disgust	fasten	gray
cheap	cow	dish	fat	grease
cheat	coward	dismiss	fate	greed
check (verb)	crack	disturb	fault	greet
check (noun)	crash	ditch	feast	grind
cheer	cream	dive	feather	guard
cheese	creature	donkey	female	guess
chest	creep	dot	fence	guest
chicken	crime	double	fever	guide
chimney	criminal	dozen	fierce	guilty
christmas	critic	drag	film	gun
civilize	crop	drawer	finger	habit
clay	cruel	drown	firm	hair
clean	crush	drum	flag	hall
clerk	cultivate	duck	flame	hammer
clever	cup	dull	flash	handkerchief
cliff	cupboards	during	flat	handle
climb	cure	dust	flavor	harbor
clock	curious	eager	flesh	harm
cloth	curl	earn	float	harvest
club	curse	earnest	flood	haste
coarse	curtain	ease	flour	hat
coat	curve	edge	fold	hate
coffee	cushion	educate	fond	hay
collar	custom	elastic	fool	heal
collect	customer	elder	foot	health
comb	damage	electric	forbid	heap
combine	damp	elephant	forgive	hello

hesitate	kick	messenger	parcel	prefer
hide	kiss	meter	pardon	prejudice
hinder	kitchen	mild	parent	preserve
hire	knee	mill	park	pretend
hit	kneel	mineral	passage	pride
hole	knife	miserable	passenger	priest
holiday	knock	mistake	paste	print
hollow	knot	mix	path	prison
holy	ladder	model	patient	prize
honest	lamp	moderate	patriotic	probable
hook	lazy	modest	pattern	procession
horizon	leaf	monkey	pause	profession
hospital	lean	motion	paw	program
host	leather	mouse	pearl	prompt
hotel	leg	mud	peculiar	pronounce
humble	lend	multiply	pen	proud
hunger	lesson	murder	pencil	pump
hunt	liberty	mystery	penny	punctual
hurray	lid	nail	perfect	punish
hurry	limb	narrow	perform	pupil
hurt	liquid	neat	permanent	pure
hut	list	neck	persuade	purple
ice	liter	needle	pet	push
ideal	load	neglect	photograph	puzzle
idle	loaf	nephew	pick	qualify
imagine	loan	nest	pig	quarrel
imitate	lock	net	pigeon	quart
immediate	lodging	nice	pile	quick
immense	log	niece	pin	quiet
improve	lone	noise	pinch	rabbit
inform	loose	nonsense	pink	radio
informal	lot	noon	pint	rail
informally	loud	nose	pipe	rain
inn	loyal	noun	pity	rake
inquire	luck	nuisance	plane	rapid
insect	lump	nurse	plaster	rare
inside	lunch	nut	plate	rat
instant	lung	oar	plenty	raw
instrument	mad	obey	plough	ray
insult	mail	ocean	plural	razor
insure	male	offend	pocket	recommend
intend	manage	omit	poem	refer
interfere	map	onward	poison	reflect
international	mat	oppose	police	refresh
interrupt	match	opposite	polish	regret
invent	meal	orange	polite	regular
invite	meantime	organ	pool	rejoice
inward	meanwhile	origin	postpone	relieve
island	meat	ornament	pot	remedy
jaw	mechanic	outline	pour	remind
jealous	medicine	overcome	powder	rent
jewel	melt	pack	practical	repair
joke	mend	pad	practise	repeat
journey	merchant	pain	praise	replace
juice	mercy	pair	pray	reproduce
jump	merry	pale	preach	reputation
key	message	pan	precious	request

rescue	seldom	spit	telegraph	typical
resign	self	splendid	telephone	ugly
resist	sentence	split	temper	umbrella
responsible	severe	spoil	temperature	uncle
restaurant	sew	spoon	tempt	universe
retire	shade	sport	tend	upper
revenge	shallow	staff	tender	upright
review	shame	stain	tent	upset
reward	sharp	stairs	terrible	upward
ribbon	shave	stamp	thank	urge
rice	sheep	steady	theater	vain
rid	sheet	steal	thick	veil
ripe	shelf	steam	thief	verb
risk	shell	steep	thin	verse
rival	shelter	steer	thirst	violent
roar	shield	stem	thorn	vowel
roast	shirt	stick	thorough	voyage
rob	shock	stiff	thread	waist
rod	shoe	sting	threat	wake
roof	shop	stir	throat	wander
root	shout	stocking	thumb	warm
rope	shower	stomach	thunder	warn
rot	shut	storm	ticket	wash
row	sick	stove	tide	waste
rub	signal	straight	tidy	wax
rubber	silk	strap	tie	weak
rubbish	sincere	straw	tight	weapon
rude	sink	stretch	tin	weather
rug	skill	strict	tip	weave
ruin	skin	string	tire	weed
rush	skirt	strip	title	weigh
rust	slave	stripe	tobacco	wet
sacred	slide	stuff	toe	wheat
sacrifice	slight	stupid	tomorrow	wheel
sad	slip	suck	tongue	whip
saddle	slope	sudden	tonight	whisper
sake	slow	sugar	tool	whistle
salary	smell	suit	tooth	wicked
sample	smoke	supper	tough	widow
sand	smooth	suspect	tour	wine
satisfy	snake	suspicion	towel	wing
sauce	soap	swallow	tower	wipe
saucer	sock	swear	toy	wire
saws	soil	sweat	track	witness
scale	solemn	sweep	translate	wool
scatter	solid	swell	trap	worm
scent	solve	swim	tray	worry
scissors	sore	swing	treasure	worse
scold	sorry	sympathy	treat	worship
scorn	soup	tail	tremble	wrap
scrape	sour	tailor	tribe	wreck
scratch	sow	tall	trick	wrist
screen	spade	tame	trip	yard
screw	spare	tap	trunk	yellow
search	spell	taste	tube	zero
seed	spill	taxi	tune	
seize	spin	tea	twist	

Academic Word List

This is a list of the 570 words most frequently encountered in academic texts such as textbooks and professional journals.

Coxhead, Averil. *Academic Word List*. Printed by permission of Averil Coxhead.
"Source: A. Coxhead, Academic Word List, 1998, Victoria University of Wellington, New Zealand. More information available at http://www.victoria.ac.nz/lals/resources/academicwordlist/default.aspx

abandon	attribute	conceive	decade	ensure
abstract	author	concentrate	decline	entity
academy	authority	concept	deduce	environment
access	automate	conclude	define	equate
accommodate	available	concurrent	definite	equip
accompany	aware	conduct	demonstrate	equivalent
accumulate	behalf	confer	denote	erode
accurate	benefit	confine	deny	error
achieve	bias	confirm	depress	establish
acknowledge	bond	conflict	derive	estate
acquire	brief	conform	design	estimate
adapt	bulk	consent	despite	ethic
adequate	capable	consequent	detect	ethnic
adjacent	capacity	considerable	deviate	evaluate
adjust	category	consist	device	eventual
administrate	cease	constant	devote	evident
adult	challenge	constitute	differentiate	evolve
advocate	channel	constrain	dimension	exceed
affect	chapter	construct	diminish	exclude
aggregate	chart	consult	discrete	exhibit
aid	chemical	consume	discriminate	expand
albeit	circumstance	contact	displace	expert
allocate	cite	contemporary	display	explicit
alter	civil	context	dispose	exploit
alternative	clarify	contract	distinct	export
ambiguous	classic	contradict	distort	expose
amend	clause	contrary	distribute	external
analogy	code	contrast	diverse	extract
analyze	coherent	contribute	document	facilitate
annual	coincide	controversy	domain	factor
anticipate	collapse	convene	domestic	feature
apparent	colleague	converse	dominate	federal
append	commence	convert	draft	fee
appreciate	comment	convince	drama	file
approach	commission	cooperate	duration	final
appropriate	commit	coordinate	dynamic	finance
approximate	commodity	core	economy	finite
arbitrary	communicate	corporate	edit	flexible
area	community	correspond	element	fluctuate
aspect	compatible	couple	eliminate	focus
assemble	compensate	create	emerge	format
assess	compile	credit	emphasis	formula
assign	complement	criteria	empirical	forthcoming
assist	complex	crucial	enable	foundation
assume	component	culture	encounter	founded
assure	compound	currency	energy	framework
attach	comprehensive	cycle	enforce	function
attain	comprise	data	enhance	fund
attitude	compute	debate	enormous	fundamental

furthermore	interact	network	principal	route
gender	intermediate	neutral	principle	scenario
generate	internal	nevertheless	prior	schedule
generation	interpret	nonetheless	priority	scheme
globe	interval	norm	proceed	scope
goal	intervene	normal	process	section
grade	intrinsic	notion	professional	sector
grant	invest	notwithstanding	prohibit	secure
guarantee	investigate	nuclear	project	seek
guideline	invoke	objective	promote	select
hence	involve	obtain	proportion	sequence
hierarchy	isolate	obvious	prospect	series
highlight	issue	occupy	protocol	sex
hypothesis	item	occur	psychology	shift
identical	job	odd	publication	significant
identify	journal	offset	publish	similar
ideology	justify	ongoing	purchase	simulate
ignorant	label	option	pursue	site
illustrate	labor	orient	qualitative	so-called
image	layer	outcome	quote	sole
immigrate	lecture	output	radical	somewhat
impact	legal	overall	random	source
implement	legislate	overlap	range	specific
implicate	levy	overseas	ratio	specify
implicit	liberal	panel	rational	sphere
imply	license	paradigm	react	stable
impose	likewise	paragraph	recover	statistic
incentive	link	parallel	refine	status
incidence	locate	parameter	regime	straightforward
incline	logic	participate	region	strategy
income	maintain	partner	register	stress
incorporate	major	passive	regulate	structure
index	manipulate	perceive	reinforce	style
indicate	manual	percent	reject	submit
individual	margin	period	relax	subordinate
induce	mature	persist	release	subsequent
inevitable	maximize	perspective	relevant	subsidy
infer	mechanism	phase	reluctance	substitute
infrastructure	media	phenomenon	rely	successor
inherent	mediate	philosophy	remove	sufficient
inhibit	medical	physical	require	sum
initial	medium	plus	research	summary
initiate	mental	policy	reside	supplement
injure	method	portion	resolve	survey
innovate	migrate	pose	resource	survive
input	military	positive	respond	suspend
insert	minimal	potential	restore	sustain
insight	minimize	practitioner	restrain	symbol
inspect	minimum	precede	restrict	tape
instance	ministry	precise	retain	target
institute	minor	predict	reveal	task
instruct	mode	predominant	revenue	team
integral	modify	preliminary	reverse	technical
integrate	monitor	presume	revise	technique
integrity	motive	previous	revolution	technology
intelligence	mutual	primary	rigid	temporary
intense	negate	prime	role	tense

terminate	tradition	ultimate	valid	vision
text	transfer	undergo	vary	visual
theme	transform	underlie	vehicle	volume
theory	transit	undertake	version	voluntary
thereby	transmit	uniform	via	welfare
thesis	transport	unify	violate	whereas
topic	trend	unique	virtual	whereby
trace	trigger	utilize	visible	widespread

APPENDIX IV: Table of Common Collocations in Academic Texts

SOME COMMON TYPES OF COLLOCATIONS FOUND IN ACADEMIC TEXTS	
Collocations	**Examples**
Adjective + noun	key issues, persistent problems, wide range, further research, current theory, larger context, detailed references, essential information, prior knowledge, practical applications, straightforward approach
Verb + adverb (or adverb + verb)	develop further, demonstrate conclusively, present effectively, explore thoroughly, highly appreciate, successfully complete
Verb + noun	acquire vocabulary, gain awareness, reach a goal, address the issue, raise the question, develop a theory, provide a framework, set the scene, clarify the point
Phrasal verbs	depend on, relate to, focus on, bring together, deal with, consist of, respond to, lead to, serve as, point out
Prepositional phrases	in that case, in any case, on the whole, with regard to, in other words

(From *Advanced Reading Power,* 2007, p. 62. These examples of collocations were compiled by the authors from several academic texts.)

APPENDIX V – *Answer key for selected skills exercises*

PART I

page 4 What is reading? Flying a kite

PART II

None

PART III

A. none

B. 1, page 52
    1. d 2. c 3. d 4. a 5. b 6. d 7. c 8. b

B. 7, page 58
    1. no 2. yes 3. yes 4. no 5. no 6. yes
    7. yes 8. no 9. yes 10. no

B. 8, page 58
    1.c 2.b 3.c 4.b 5.a 6.b

B. 11, page 62
    1. d 2. g 3. b 4. c 5. a 6. f 7. e

C. 1, page 74
    1. no
    2. Linda works part time; they have a large
       family.
    3. Linda
    4. both Linda and Dennis
    5. Who will take care of the children when Linda
       works full time?

C. 2, page 74
    1. F 2. F 3. T

C. 3, page 75
    1.F 2.T 3.T 4.F

C. 4, page 75
    1.b 2.d 3.a 4.c 5.a 6.d 7.a 8.b

C. 8, page 82
    1.c 2.d 3.b 4.a 5.c

D. 8, page 94
    1.F 2.F 3.F

D. 16, page 104
    1. Running 2. Runners 3. races
    4. Boston Marathon 5. winners

D. 17, page 105
1.
    1. human-powered transportation
    2. businessman
    3. pedicabs
    4. pedicabs
    5. pedicabs
    6. people who don't want to walk

2.
    1. drivers of pedicabs
    2. owner
    3. drivers
    4. typical driver
    5. driver
    6. driver
    7. one pedicab driver
    8. driver
    9. driver

D. 18, page 105

    This-tight ensemble
    they-actors
    They-actors
    They-actors
    That-making mistakes
    They-language learners
    they-language learners
    their-language teachers
    they-inhibitions

D. 19, page 106
    1. companies-businesses
    2. outright ban-regulating workers' behavior,
       crackdown, zero-tolerance policies

D. 20, page 107
    1. Mount McKinley, Alaskan mountain,
       snowcapped mountain, mountain
    2. Mr. Kim's house on Beacon Street, house on
       Beacon Street, house in Boston, house
    3. Los Angeles, city in California, city in the
       United States, city on planet earth
    4. Mrs. Brown's tall pine tree, tall pine tree,
       evergreen tree, tree

D. 21, page 108
2. violin, stringed instrument
3. president of the city council, leader
4. hurricane, storm
5. Lemons, oranges, and limes; citrus fruits

D. 22, page 108
Sentence Referent
2. common dangerous dumping practices
2. practices
4. hazardous chemical wastes
5. heavy metals and other byproducts of technology
7. wastes
9. the metal rusting and waste materials leaking into surrounding soil
10. local soil
11. local soil that has been removed
13. the chemical waste reaching the water tables deep in the earth's surface

D. 23, page 110
2. sports   3. languages   4. religious buildings
5. contagious diseases

D. 24, page 110
2. collection: mystery books, novels, biographies, travel books, how-to manuals, science fiction, thrillers, and reference books
3. purchases: groceries, shoes, tires

4. health problems: respiratory problems, premature deaths
5. musical events: concerts in Hatch Shell and on Boston Common, Tanglewood symphony concerts, concerts on ships sailing in Boston Harbor

E. 1, page 118
1. F   2. F   3. T   4. T   5. F

E. 2, page 120
A misogynist is someone who dislikes women.

E. 3, page 121
family, company, war, planes, countries

E. 5, page 122
windows

E. 6, page 122
1. birds   2. fly   3. rivers

E. 7, page 123
1. a   2. d   3. b   4. b   5. c

E. 10, page 128
1. noun, b
2. verb, c

E. 11, page 129

Nouns	Adjectives	Verbs	Adverbs
institute institution	institutional institutionalized	to institute to institutionalize	-------
emphasis	emphasized	to emphasize	-------
-------	primary	-------	primarily
optimum optimization	optimal	to optimize	optimally
conclusion	concluding conclusive	to conclude	conclusively
drama dramatics dramatist	dramatic	to dramatize	dramatically
suitability	suitable	to suit	suitably
abbreviation	abbreviated	to abbreviate	-------

2. emphasis
3. abbreviate
4. suitably
5. primary
6. conclusions
7. dramatic
8. optimal

F. 1, page 136

2. S-company   V-sells
3. S-Kenji   V-stays
4. S-He   V-works
5. S-people   V-use
6 S-people   V-look
7. S-people   V-find
8. S-work   V-is
9. S-It   V-is
10. S-He   V-enjoys

F. 3, page 138
1. a   2. d   3. b   4. d

F. 6, page 143
2. African countries   3. desserts (sweets)
4. types of land transportation

F. 7, page 144

2. Spanish speaking countries
3. buildings; places to work
4. parts of a book
5. European languages
6. science subjects

F. 8, page 144

1. workers in a company or store
2. workers in a bank
3. parts of a computer
4. gardening supplies
5. things to buy in a department store

F. 9, page 145
Answers for 2, 8, and 9 may vary.
2. medical doctors (psychologist)
3. simple tools (wheelbarrow)
4. land forms (bay)
5. boats (surrey)
6. parts of the eye (semicircular canals)
7. containers in a lab (Bunsen burner)

8. Romance languages (Polish)
9. scientists (Michelangelo)
10. horses (boxer)

F. 11, page 147
1. returning a clock – at a store
2. waiting for a famous person- outside a theater or concert hall

F. 12, page 148
1. Yes – Iceland   2. No   3. No   4. Yes- Istanbul

F. 13, page 150
A. 1. c (a-too general, b-too specific)
2. a (b-too specific, c-too general)
3. c (a-too general, b-too specific)
B. drinks; beverages

F. 14, page 151
A. 1. lightning   2. three kinds of clouds   3. fog
B. weather

F. 15, page 152
A. 1. Los Angeles Lakers (Most basketball teams...)
2. Boston Celtics (Boston fans also...)
3. Basketball and money (Other programs during...)
B. basketball

F. 16, page 153
1. Television news can be...
2. Usually only bad news...
3. Many news stories are...

F. 17, page 154
1. The Hawaiian Islands; While the Hawaiian Islands differ from each other, they share many features.
2. Natural history of Hawaii; The islands, in fact, have an interesting and unusual natural history.
3. islands special and unique features; Each of the islands has special and unique features.

F. 18, page 155
1. c   2. a   3. e   4. b

F. 19, page 157
A. 1. b. Clothes can tell a lot about a person.
2. b. Clothes are important when you travel.
3. c. Clothes today are different from the clothes of the 1800s.
B. clothes

F. 20, page 158
    1. c. Choices a. and b. are too specific.
    2. a. Choice b. is too specific and choice c. is not
       stated in the paragraph.
    3. b. Choices a. and c. are too specific.

F. 21, page 160
1. Topic: The giant panda
Main idea: The giant panda is slowly dying out in
China.

2. Topic: The first year of life for a panda
Main idea: For the whole first year of its life, the
panda is completely dependent on its mother.

3. Topic: A mother panda
Main idea: A wild female panda in China was a very
loving and careful mother.

F. 22, page 161
A.
1. Topic Building an ideal society
Main idea: Those who believe in an ideal society can
inspire social change.

2. Topic: Two utopian communities—Fruitlands and
Brook Farm
Main idea: Two utopian communities were formed in
mid-19th century Massachusetts but they only lasted a
short time.

3. Today's utopian communities
Main idea: Today's utopian communities try to inspire
social change in practical ways.

B. Utopian communities
C. People who dreamed of an ideal society in
   America experimented with many forms of
   utopian communities from the 19th century to the
   present time.

G. 1, page 165
Sentences with lists: 2,3,5

G. 2, page 166
Topic: Memo from Jim's boss
Main idea: A memo from Jim's boss gave him <u>many</u>
reasons to feel good about his work.
Key word in the main idea: many

Signal words:	**Details:**
First	Jim learned job quickly.
Also	Jim got along well with others.
In addition	He's very kind and polite to customers.
Finally	He will get a bonus in his paycheck.

3. Topic: Why Mary might quit her job
Main idea: Mary might quit her job because her boss
has many unpleasant characteristics.
Key word in the main idea: many

Signal words:	**Details:**
First	The boss never praises Mary.
Second	The boss interferes with her work and doesn't let her work alone.
Last	The boss is late for work and takes long lunch hours.

G. 3, page 167
1. Topic: changes caused by the use of e-mail
Main idea: The widespread use of electronic mail has
caused numerous changes in the way people relate to
each other.
Key word in the main idea: numerous

Signal words:	**Details:**
First,	People who don't like to use the phone can send a message.
Second,	E-mail is more democratic; no clues about sender from stationery or tone of voice.
Also,	E-mail is instant…no delays.
Last	Messages give no clues about sender's age, gender, or physical appearance.

2. Topic: Newest cell phones
Main idea: The newest cell phones allow the user to
do an amazing number of things.
Key words in the main idea: number of things

Signal words:	**Details:**
still,	can be used to make phone calls
also,	send text messages
In addition,	computers inside to connect with a home computer
Also,	documents can be received by and sent from the phone
a further	can takes still photos and movies and send them to others

G. 5, page 170
Example a.
Main idea: Franklin D. Roosevelt, the thirty-second president of the United States, served his country for <u>most of his life</u>.
<u>Key words in the main idea: for most of his life</u>
<u>(Signal words are given. Details are obvious.)</u>

Example b.
Main idea: Using a digital camera and a computer is an easy and enjoyable way to make good photographs.
Key words in the main idea: way to make
<u>(Signal words are given. Details are obvious.)</u>

G. 6, page 171
1. Main idea: The French <u>began</u> the Vietnam War in 1946 but after 8 years they left the war.
Key word in the main idea: began

Signal words:	Events:
At first, 1946,	War began
By 1953,	French army was in trouble
in 1954	French army left Vietnam

2. Main idea: The second part of the Vietnam War began as a civil war but by 1965 had become an American war.
Key words in the main idea: began, had become

Signal words:	Events:
in 1954,	second part of war began; two governments, North and South Vietnam
from 1954 to 1960	the two governments fought against each other,
By the beginning of 1965,	the North Vietnamese were winning the war
in March 1965,	U.S. government began to help South Vietnam
by July 1965	75,000 American soldiers were fighting in Vietnam

G. 7, page 172
Main idea: When you decide to take a trip, the <u>planning</u> can be fun.
Key word in the main idea: planning

Signal words:	Steps in the process
First,	decide where to go
Next,	look at maps and plan your time
Soon after that,	find out how you will travel and how much it will cost
Then,	learn a few words in the language of the country you will visit
Finally	make a packing list

G. 8, page 173
5,7,3,10,9,2,6,1,4,8

G. 10, page 176
1. both
Topic: Subways in New York City and Paris
Main idea: Subways in NYC and Paris are similar in some ways but there are also striking differences.
Key word in the main idea: similar

Signal Words	Details
both	subways are often crowded
Another likeness	noisy trains
A further similarity	cover a wide area at a low cost to riders
However,	striking differences
While	New York stations tend to be plain/Paris stations are generally attractive
On the other hand,	Paris subways are clean/New York subways less clean

2. Similarities only
Topic: Filled meat pastries in Japan and the Ukraine
Main idea: In Japan and the Ukraine, people have one thing in common: filled meat pastries.
Key words in the main idea: in common

Signal Words	Details
similar	Japanese *gyoza* and Ukrainian *pilmeni*
Both	made of flat dough with meat filling
both	Japanese and Ukrainians eat this dish with sauce

3. Differences only
Topic: Differences before and after the first baby arrives
Main idea: When the first baby arrives in a family, everything changes.
Key words in the main idea: everything changes

Signal Words	Details
but	<u>in the past, needed alarm clock/now baby wakes them</u>
but	parents used to read and watch TV/ now they admire baby
In contrast,	life is more carefully planned
While	used to go out any time/now they need a baby sitter
Unlike	tidy rooms in the past/now full of baby things
difference	conversations are all about the baby

G. 11, page 178

1. What is this paragraph comparing? English and American breakfasts

Main idea: English and American breakfasts are similar in some ways and different in others.

Key words in the main idea: similar, different

Signal Words		Details
Likenesses:	In both	large breakfasts
	In both	may include some meat
Differences:	However	English drink tea/Americans drink coffee
	But	English usually do not eat sweats/Americans do

2. What is this paragraph contrasting? American and Italian breakfasts

Main idea: American breakfasts are very different from breakfasts in Italy.

Key word in the main idea: different

Signal Words	Details
larger	Americans eat larger breakfasts than Italians
But	Americans have several different foods/Italians have bread and coffee
Different from	American coffee is weak/Italian coffee is strong

G. 12, page 179

1. similarities

Main idea: In some ways, college life is similar to high school life.

Signal words:	Details:
In both places,	Success depends on being a good student
like,	College social situation similar to high school
resembles	College activities resemble high school

2. differences

Main idea: The University of Bologna is different from most North American universities.

Signal words:	Details
major difference,	Bologna is very old/American universities are newer
Another difference,	Bologna campus spread out/American campus in one area
Unlike,	American universities have student common areas/Bologna does not.

3. similarities and differences

Main idea: In Russia, special foreign language schools teach the same subjects as regular public schools, but they are different from them in many ways.

Signal words:	Details:
Same,	same subjects in regular schools and special schools
However,	subjects are taught in foreign languages in special schools
Different,	students are selected for the special schools
greatest difference	foreign language abilities are better in special schools

G. 14, page 183

A. 2. < 3. < 4. > 5. < 6. > 7. < 8. <
   9. < 10. >

B. Answers will vary. Explain.

G. 15, page 184

1. Coal-burning factories (C) acid rain. (E)
2. Stricter anti-pollution laws (C) higher prices for consumers. (E)
3. Acid rain (C) death of lakes and streams.(E)
4. Forests have become diseased(E) acid rain. (C)
5. Coal burning (C) higher levels of sulfur dioxide in the air. (E)
6. Sulfur dioxide pollution (C) higher infant death rates. (E)
7. Coal burning (C) the exterior walls of buildings to decay. (E)
8. Strict anti-pollution controls (C) coal miners to lose their jobs (E)

G. 16, page 186

Answers will vary. Students should explain their choices.

G. 17, page 186

1. Topic: Americans buy a lot of vitamins

Main idea: Americans buy a lot of vitamins for several reasons.

Causes	Effects
They want to stay healthy	Buy vitamins
They don't eat health food	Buy vitamins
Advertising of vitamins	Buy vitamins

2. Topic: Uses of aspirin
Main idea: Aspirin is a simple drug that has many useful effects.

Causes	Effects
Using aspirin	Relieves pain
Using aspirin	Lowers fever
Using aspiring	Keeps heart healthy

G.19, page 189

2. After TO;   3. presented CE;
4. worse than CC;   5. not so many CC;
6. were left CE;   7. many SL;   8. SL;
9. inspire CE;   10. although CC;

G. 20, page 189

1. SL (3)   2. TO (5)   3. CC (4)   e. CE (1)

G. 21, page 191
1. Problem: How can you keep fruits and vegetables fresh in a hot climate when you do not have a refrigerator?
Solution: You can make a cooler with sand, a clay pot, and a damp cloth.
Main idea: You can keep fruits and vegetables fresh in a hot climate by make a cooler with sand, a clay pot, and a damp cloth.
2. Problem: How can you slow down the process of aging?
Solution: Eat blueberries every day.
Main idea: Scientists have found that eating blueberries every day slows down the aging process.

G. 22, page 193
2. Concept being defined: Lunar craters
Main idea: Lunar craters are circular depressions that were created by the impact of various objects on the surface of the moon.
Key words in the main idea: *are*
Explanation and description: Lunar craters are deep holes visible from the earth. There are millions of lunar craters from small (a few feet) to large (hundreds of kilometers). Some are surrounded by mountains. They do not change because the moon has no atmosphere.
Signal words for details: none

H. 1, page 196
A. Topic: Chicago's attractions
Topic sentence/Main idea: The City of Chicago, Illinois, is an attractive place to visit because it offers wonderful architecture, many museums, and beautiful parks.
Key words in main idea: *offers wonderful architecture, museums, and parks*
Pattern: Listing

Signal words	Details/Examples
Architecture	skyscrapers were important in history of U.S.buildings
Museums	history, science, and art
Parks	Grant Park

Concluding sentence: Tourists can find plenty to do in Chicago.

B. Topic: Chicago's attractions
Paragraph 1—Thesis statement: Three of the top attractions for tourists in Chicago are the wonderful architecture, many museums, and beautiful parks.
Key words in the thesis statement: three top attractions
Pattern of organization of the essay: listing
Paragraph 2—Topic: architecture
　　　　　　Main idea: One of Chicago's greatest attractions is its architecture, which has played an important role in the history of American buildings
　　　　　　Pattern: time order
Paragraph 3—Topic: museums
　　　　　　Main idea: Chicago is noted for its many museums.
　　　　　　Pattern: Listing
Paragraph 4—Topic: Grant Park
　　　　　　Main idea: Grant Park, located on the lake shore, is a large park with many enjoyable features.
Pattern: Listing
Paragraph 5
Topic: Conclusion
Main idea: Chicago has a lot to offer the tourist.

H. 2, page 199

Topic of this essay: Water sports in Hawaii

Paragraph 1—Thesis statement for this essay: Three sports that are especially popular on the islands are surfing, snorkeling, and scuba diving.

Pattern of organization of this essay: Listing

Signal words that helped you decide on the overall pattern? *Three water sports*

Paragraph 2—Topic: surfing
Main idea: Surfing, the islands' most famous sport, started in Hawaii many years ago
Pattern of organization: sequence

Paragraph 3—Topic: surfing
Main idea: Surfing requires you to do many things at once.
Pattern of organization: sequence

Paragraph 4—Topic: scuba diving and snorkeling
Main idea: Both scuba diving and snorkeling allow you to see under the water, but scuba diving is more difficult and also provides more opportunities to be near sea creatures.
Pattern of organization: Comparison/Contrast

Paragraph 5—Topic: Why Hawaii is good for snorkeling and scuba diving
Main idea: Whether you choose surfing, scuba diving or snorkeling, you will understand why Hawaii is known as a perfect place to enjoy water sports.
Pattern of organization: Cause-effect

H. 3, page 202
2. planets   3. planting a tree
4. preparing for a party

H. 4, page 203

2. Liz came home
3. Geraldo went to work (or school).
4. Anna went shopping.
5. Jeff planted a garden.
6. The islanders got ready for the storm.
7. Piper got ready to do her school work.

H. 5, page 205
1. Alien species of plants and animals have taken over in new areas, changing the landscape and causing problems for people.
2. Tiger mosquitoes, an alien species from Asia, are replacing the common European mosquito and becoming a nuisance in parts of southern Europe.
3. Zebra mussels, another alien species, have spread into the Great Lakes of North America, causing millions of dollars worth of damage.
4. The Indian mongoose, brought to Hawaii to kill rats, is a major threat to the native birds and is costing poultry farmers millions of dollars.

H. 6, page 206
A. Pattern: Cause/effect
Summary: Alien species such as the tiger mosquito, the zebra mussel, and the Indian mongoose have invaded new areas, causing discomfort, environmental damage, the loss of millions of dollars, and threatening native animals.

H. 7, page 207
Step 1.
Overall pattern of organization: sequence

Step 2:

Part 1: Paragraphs 1–2	Topic: Discovery of frozen man
Part 2: Paragraph 3	Topic: Ideas about who the iceman was
Part 3: Paragraph 4	Topic: Disagreement about who should keep the frozen man.
Part 4: Paragraphs 5-6	Topic: Results of research about the frozen man
Part 5: Paragraph 7	Topic: What we can learn from the Iceman about the Bronze Age

Step 3.
Part 1: In 1991, melting ice in the mountains between Austria and Italy revealed the frozen body of a man with some of his clothes and tools.

Part 2: There were many theories about the identity of the frozen man, when he lived, and the cause of his death.

Part 3: Both Italy and Austria wanted to keep the Iceman, but in the end he was moved to a museum in Bolzano, Italy.

Part 4: Scientists have concluded that the Iceman lived about 5,300 years ago during the Bronze Age and that he died from a wound while he was fighting.

Part 5: From the clothes and tools of the Iceman, scientists have learned a great deal about the Bronze Age.

Step 4. Summary:

In 1991, the frozen body of a man with some of his clothes and tools was found in the mountains between Austria and Italy. There were many theories about who he was, when he lived, and the cause of his death. Though both Italy and Austria wanted the Iceman, he was brought to a museum in Italy. Now scientists who have studied the body have concluded that the Iceman died during the Bronze Age (5,300 years ago) from a wound he received while he was fighting. From his clothes and tools, they have learned a great deal about the Bronze Age.

H. 8, page 212
C. The same conditions that are cause frogs to die may someday cause humans to die.
D. Questions will vary. Students should explain why their questions are important.

H. 9, page 214
B. Pay Levels in the United States, 2008
This report presents earnings data from the Current Population Survey (CPS), a national monthly survey of approximately 60,000 households conducted by the U.S. Census Bureau for the U.S. Bureau of Labor Statistics. Information on earnings is collected from one-fourth of the CPS sample each month. Readers should note that the comparisons of earnings in this report are on a broad level and do not control for many factors that can be significant in explaining earnings differences.

In 2008, women who were full-time wage and salary workers had median[1] weekly earnings of $638, or about 80 percent of the $798 median for their male counterparts. In 1979, the first year for which comparable earnings data are available, women earned about 62 percent as much as men. After a gradual rise in the 1980s and 1990s, the women's-to-men's earnings ratio peaked at 81 percent in 2005 and 2006.

Asian women and men earned more than their white, black, and Hispanic counterparts in 2008. Among women, whites ($654) earned 87 percent as much as Asians ($753), while blacks ($554) and Hispanics ($501) earned 74 percent and 67 percent as much, respectively. In comparison, white men ($825) earned 85 percent as much as Asian men ($966), black men ($620) earned 64 percent as much, and Hispanic men ($559), 58 percent.

C. 1. Hispanic women   6. 2005–2006
    2. Asian men   7. Hispanic women
    3. men   8. Asian men
    4. Hispanics
    5. 1979

H. 10, page 217
Answers will vary. Students should be able to explain their answers.

H. 11, page 218
Answers will vary depending on what students find out in their web search.

H. 12, page 219
a. 1. To give information for ESL teachers and students.   2. Yes
b. 1. To tell about the services of an investment company   2. Yes
c. 1. To show the products of a publisher of textbooks   2. Yes
d. 1. To give information about the state of Massachusetts   2. Yes
e. 1. To give language learning activities for teachers and language learners   2. Yes
f. 1. To show what you can buy from a department store company   2. Yes
g. 1. To tell about a music company   2. Yes

H. 13, page 220
Possible answers, but they will vary.
    1. Sites 5 and 6 – they are blogs
    2. Site 2. Government site
    3. Sites 1,2,3, and4
    4. Sites 1 and 2

H. 14, page 220
    1. to inform
    2. She presents facts and explanations about using limited fires to protect forests.

H. 15, page 221
A. 1. Topic: Amount of TV children watch
Point of view about topic: Watching four or more hours of TV is not beneficial.
How can you tell: Author presents negative consequences of watching so much TV.

2. Topic: Fast food and overweight
Point of view about topic: We can't blame fast food restaurants for our health and weight problems.
How can you tell? Author says "We should blame ourselves."

Sample Rationale
Where are these people? At the movies
What are they talking about? Buying tickets
How can you tell? Popcorn

H. 16, page 223
A. 2. biased; in favor; writer makes inferences about emotions of the people and other non-factual aspects of the World Cup.
   3. biased; against; states opinions that can't be proved.

H. 17, page 225
Answers will vary. Students should be asked to explain their answers by citing parts of the story.

BIBLIOGRAPHY

Alderson, J. C. 1984. Reading in a foreign language: a reading problem or a language problem? In *Reading in a Foreign Language,* (ed.) J. C. Alderson and A. H. Urquhart, New York: Longman.

Anderson, N. 1999. *Exploring Second Language Reading: Issues and Strategies.* Boston: Heinle & Heinle.

— 2010. Developing Fluent Readers: Integrating Reading Rate and Comprehension. TESOL Boston, MA.

Anderson, R. C., Hiebert, E. H., Scott, J. A., & Wilkinson, I. A. G. 1985. *Becoming a Nation of Readers.* Washington, DC: National Institute of Education.

Atwell, N. 2007. *The Reading Zone: How to Help Kids Become Skilled, Passionate, Habitual, Critical Readers.* New York: Scholastic.

Baldauf, R. B. and Propst, I. K. 1979. Matching cloze tests for elementary ESL students. *The Reading Teacher, 32*:683-690.

Bamford, J. 1984. Extensive Reading By Means of Graded Readers. *Reading in a Foreign Language* 2 (2) 218-260.

Bander, R.G. 1980. *From Sentence to Paragraph.* New York: Harcourt College Publishers.

Beck, I. L. and McKeown, M. G. 1986. Instructional Research in Reading: A Retrospective. In *Reading Comprehension: From Research to Practice,* (ed.) J. Orasanu. Hillsdale, NJ: Lawrence Erlbaum Associates.

Bensoussan, M. 1983 Multiple choice modification of the cloze procedure using word length and sentence length blanks. *Foreign Language Annals* 16 (3) 189-198.

Besnier, N. 1986. Spoken and Written Language Differences in a Restricted Literacy Setting. Paper presented at the 11th Annual Boston University Conference on Language Development, October 17-19, 1986. Boston, MA.

— 1995. *Literacy, Emotions and Authority: Reading and Writing on a Polynesian Atoll.* Cambridge: Cambridge University Press.

Birch, B. 2002. *English L2 Reading: Getting to the Bottom.* Mahwah, NJ: Lawrence Erlbaum Associates.

Bolger, D, Perfetti, C and Schneider, W. 2005. Cross-cultural Effect on the Brain Revisited: Universal Structures Plus Writing System Variation. *Human Brain Mapping,* 25. 92-104.

Brady, E.C., & Kritsonis, W.A. 2008. Targeting Reading Fluency for ESL Students: A research based and practical application. *The Lamar University Electronic Journal of Student Research,* 7 (Spring)

Bransford, J. D. and Johnson, M. K. 1972. Contextual Prerequisites for Understanding: Some Investigations of Comprehension and Recall. *Journal of Verbal Learning and Verbal Behavior 11, 717-726.*

Brown, A. L. 1978. Knowing When, Where, and How to Remember: A Problem of Metacognition. In *Advances In Instructional Psychology,* (ed.) R. Glaser. Hillsdale, NJ: Lawrence Erlbaum Associates.

— 1980. Metacognitive development and reading. In *Theoretical Issues in Reading Comprehension,* (ed.) R. J. Spiro, B. C. Bruce, and W. F. Brewer. Hillsdale, NJ: Lawrence Erlbaum Associates.

Brown, A. L., Armbruster, B. B., and Baker, L. 1986. The Role of Metacognition in Reading and Studying. In *Reading Comprehension: From Research to Practice,* (ed.) J. Orasanu. Hillsdale, NJ: Lawrence Erlbaum Associates.

Brown, A. L. and Day, J. 1983. Macrorules for summarizing texts: The development of Expertise. *Journal of Verbal Learning and Verbal Behavior* 22.

Carrell, P. L. 1984. The effects of rhetorical organization on ESL readers. *TESOL Quarterly* Vol. 18, #3.

— 1985. Facilitating ESL Reading by Teaching Text Structure. *TESOL Quarterly* 19, #4.

— 1987. Content and Formal Schemata in ESL Reading. *TESOL Quarterly 21, #3.*

— 1987. Text as Interaction: Some implications of text analysis and reading research for ESL composition. In *Writing Across Languages: Analysis of L2 Texts,* (ed.) U. Connor and R. Kaplan. Reading MA: Addison-Wesley Publishing Company.

Carroll, J.B, et al 1971. *American Heritage Word Frequency Book.* Boston: Houghton Mifflin.

Casanave, C. P. 1988. Adding communication to the ESL reading class. *TESOL Newsletter* XII(3).

Cates, G. T. and Swaffar, J. K. 1979. *Language in Education: Theory and Practice #20 Reading in a Second Language.* Washington, DC: Center for Applied Linguistics.

Cazden, C. 1987. The Myth of Autonomous Text. Paper presented at the 12th Annual Boston University Conference on Language Development, October 23-25, 1987. Boston, MA.

Christison, M. and Krahnke, K. 1986. Student Perceptions of Academic Language Study. *TESOL Quarterly 20, #1.*

Clark, D. F. and Nation, L. 1980. Guessing the Meaning of Words from Context: Strategy and Techniques. *System 8, #3.*

Clarke, M. 1979. Reading in Spanish and English. *Language Learning 29*:121-150.

Clyne, M. 1980. Writing, testing and culture. *The Secondary Teacher* 11:13-16.

Coady, J. 1979. A Psycholinguistic Model of the ESL Reader. In *Reading in a Second Language: Hypotheses, Organization and Practice,* (ed.) R. Mackay, B. Barkman, and R. Jordan. Rowley, MA: Newbury House Publishers.

Cobb, T. www.lextutor.ca

Collins, A. and Smith, E. 1980. *Teaching the Process of Reading Comprehension* (Tech. Rep.No. 982) Urbana: University of Illinois, Center for the Study of Reading.

Connor, U. 1996 *Contrastive Rhetoric: Cross-Cultural Aspects of Second-Language Writing.* Cambridge: Cambridge University Press.

Connor, U. and Kaplan, R. (ed.), 1987. *Writing Across Languages: Analysis of L2 Text.* Reading, MA: Addison-Wesley Publishing Company.

Cook-Gumperz, J. (ed.). 1986. *The Social Construction of Literacy.* Cambridge: Cambridge University Press.

Cooper, C. R. and Petrosky, A. R. 1976. A Psycholinguistic View of the Fluent Reading Process. *Journal of Reading 20.*

Cooper, M. 1984. Linguistic Competence of Practiced and Unpracticed Non-native Readers of English. In *Reading in a Foreign Language,* (ed.) J. C. Anderson and A. H. Urquhart. New York: Longman.

Coxhead, A. 2000. A New Academic Word List, *TESOL Quarterly, 34,* 2:213-238.

Coxhead, A. 2006. *Essentials of teaching college vocabulary.* Boston: Houghton Mifflin. (Since 2007 this book is published through Heinle Cengage).

Crow, J. and Quigley, J. 1985. A Semantic Field Approach to Passive Vocabulary Acquisition for Reading Comprehension. *TESOL Quarterly 19, #3.*

Cziko, G. 1978. Differences in first- and second-language reading: the use of syntactic, semantic, and discourse constraints. *Canadian Modern Language Review 34:473-489.*

D' Andrade, R. 1981. The Cultural Part of Cognition. *Cognitive Science 5*:179-195.

Day, R.R. and Bamford, J. 1998. *Extensive Reading in the Second Language Classroom.* Cambridge: Cambridge University Press.

de Castell, S., Luke, A., and Egan, K. (ed.), 1986. *Literacy, Society, and Schooling: A Reader.* Cambridge: Cambridge University Press.

Dubin, F., Eskey, D., and Grabe, W. (ed.), 1986. *Teaching Second Language Reading for Academic Purposes.* Reading, MA: Addison-Wesley Publishing Company.

Edelsky, C. 1986. *Writing in a Bilingual Program: Habia una vez.* Norwood, NJ: Ablex Publishing Company.

Edinburgh Extensive Reading Project: www.jalt-publications.org/tlt/files/97/may/choosing.html).

Eggington, W. G., 1987. Written Academic Discourse in Korean: Implications for Effective Communication. In *Writing Across Languages: Analysis of L2 Text,* (ed.) U. Connor and R. Kaplan. Reading, MA: Addison-Wesley Publishing Company.

Erickson, F. 1987. Paper presented at the 12th Annual Boston University Conference on Language Development. October 23-25, 1987. Boston, MA.

Eskey, D. 1973. A model program for teaching advanced reading to students of English as a foreign language. *Language Learning* 23(2):169-184.

— 1986. Theoretical Foundations. In *Teaching Second Language Reading for Academic Purposes,* (ed.) F. Dubin, D. Eskey and W. Grabe. Reading, MA: AddisonWesley Publishing Company.

Flavell, J. H. and Wellman, H. J. 1977. Metamemory. In *Perspectives on the development of memory and cognition,* (ed.) R. V. Kail and J. W. Hagen. Hillsdale, NJ: Lawrence Erlbaum Associates.

Freebody, P. and Anderson, R. C. 1983. Effects of vocabulary difficulty, text cohesion, and schema availability on reading comprehension. *Reading Research Quarterly 18.*

Fry, E. B. 1978. *Reading Drills for Speed and Comprehension.* Providence, RI: Jamestown Publishers.

— 2000. *Skimming & Scanning: Advanced Level.* Lincolnwood, IL: Jamestown Publishers.

Gee, J. P. 1996 *Social Linguistics and Literacies: Ideology in Discourse 2d. Ed.* 1996. Bristol, PA: Taylor and Francis, Inc.

— 1985. The Narrativization of Experience in the Oral Style. *Journal of Education 167,* #1.

— 1986. Orality and Literacy: From The Savage Mind to Ways With Words. *TESOL Quarterly 20, #4.*

— 1989 Literacy, discourse, and linguistics: Essays by James Paul Gee, special issue of the *Journal of Education,* (ed.) Candace Mitchell. 171

Gipe, J. P. 1978-79. Investigating techniques for teaching word meanings. *Reading Research Quarterly* 14 (4):624-644.

Goodman, K. S. 1970. Reading: A Psycholinguistic Guessing Game. In *Theoretical Models and Processes in Reading,* (ed.) H. Singer and R. B. Ruddell. Newark, DE: International Reading Association.

— 1971. Psycholinguistic Universals in the Reading Process. In *The Psychology of Second Language Learning,* (ed.) P. Pimsleur and T. Quinn. Cambridge: Cambridge University Press.

Goodman, K.S. and Goodman, Y.M. 1977. Learning about psycholinguistic processes by analyzing oral reading. *Harvard Educational Review 403* 317-33.

Grabe. W. 1986. The Transition from Theory to Practice in Teaching Reading. In *Teaching Second Language Reading for Academic Purposes,* (ed.) F. Dubin, D. E. Eskey and W. Grabe. Reading, MA: Addison-Wesley Publishing Co.

— Grabe, W. 1991. Current developments in second language reading research. *TESOL Quarterly, 25, 375–406.*

Graff, H. 1979. *The Literacy Myth: Literacy and Social Structure in the 19th Century City.* New York: Academic Press.

Grellet, F. 1981. *Developing Reading Skills: A Practical Guide to Reading Comprehension Exercises.* Cambridge: Cambridge University Press.

Haber, L. R. and Haber, R. N. 1981. Perceptual Processes in Reading: An Analysis-by Synthesis Model. In *Neuropsychological and Cognitive Processes in Reading,* (ed.) F. Pirozzolo and M. Wittrock. New York: Academic Press.

Hall, W. S., White, T. G. and Guthrie, L. 1986. Skilled Reading and Language Development: Some Key Issues. In *Reading Comprehension: From Research to Practice,* (ed.) J. Orasanu. Hillsdale, NJ: Lawrence Erlbaum Associates.

Halliday, M. A. K., and Ruqaiya Hasan. 1976. *Cohesion in English*. London: Longman.

Harris, D. P. 1966. *Reading Improvement Exercises for Students of English as a Second Language*. Englewood Cliffs, NJ: Prentice-Hall, Inc.

Heath, S. B. 1982. What no bedtime story means. *Language in Society II:*49-76.

— 1983. *Ways With Words*. Cambridge: Cambridge University Press.

— 1984. Literacy or literate skills: Considerations for ESL/EFL learners. In *On Tesol 84*, (ed.) P. Larson, E. L. Judd, and D. S. Messerschmitt. Washington, DC: TESOL.

Helgesen, M. 1997. Bringing those books back to the classroom: Tasks for extensive reading. *The Language Teacher 21.5* 53-54.

Hill, D. 2008. Extensive Reading Programmes. *ELT Journal*, 62 (2) 184-204

Hinds, J. 1987. Reader versus Writer Responsibility: A New Typology. In *Writing Across Languages: Analysis of L2 Text*, (ed.) U. Connor and R. Kaplan. Reading, MA: Addison-Wesley Publishing Company.

Hoffman, D. M. and Heath, S. B. 1986. *Inside Learners*. Stanford University, Stanford, CA.

Hosenfeld, C. 1977. A Preliminary Investigation of the Reading Strategies of Successful and Unsuccessful Second Language Learners. *System 5, #2.*

Hudelson, S. 1981. *Learning to Read in Different Languages*. Washington, DC: Center for Applied Linguistics.

Hudson, T. 1980. The effects of induced schemata on the "short circuit" in L2 reading performance, *Language Learning 32, #1.*

Huey, E. B. 1908. *The Psychology and Pedagogy of Reading*. Cambridge, Mass: MIT Press

Hymes, D. 1981. "In vain I tried to tell you": Essays in Native American Ethnopoetics. Philadelphia: University of Pennsylvania Press. *The International Journal of Corpus Linguistics.*

Jensen, E. 2005. *Teaching with the Brain in Mind*. 2d Ed. Alexandria, VA: Association for Supervision and Curriculum Development (ASCD).

Jiang, Y and Grabe, W. 2010. Promoting Reading Comprehension by Raising Students' Awareness of Text Structure. Presented at TESOL 2010 Boston.

Johns, A. 1981. Necessary English: A Faculty Survey. *TESOL Quarterly* 15, #1.

Johnston, P. H. 1983. *Reading Comprehension Assessment: A Cognitive Basis*. Newark, DE: International Reading Association.

Kaplan, R. 1966. Cultural Thought Patterns and Intercultural Education. *Language Learning 16, #1 & 2.*

Kintsch, W. 1974. *The Representation of Meaning in Memory*. Hilldale, NJ: Lawrence Erlbaum Associates.

Kintsch, W. 1977. On Comprehending Stories. In *Cognitive Processes in Comprehension*, (ed.) M. Just and P. Carpenter. Hillsdale, NJ: Lawrence Erlbaum Associates.

Kintsch, W. and Van Dijk, T.A. 1978. Toward a model of text comprehension and production. *Psychology Review* 85(5) 363-394.

Koda, K. 2004. *Insights into Second Language Reading: A Cross-Linguistic Approach*. New York: Cambridge University Press.

Koda, K. and Zehler, A.M. (ed.) 2008. *Learning to Read Across Languages*. New York: Routledge.

Kolers, P. A. 1973. Three Stages of Reading, in (ed.) F. Smith. *Psycholinguistics and Reading*. New York: Holt, Rinehart and Winston.

Krashen, S. 1985. *Insights and Inquiries*. Hayward, CA: Alemany Press.

Langer, J. A. 1981. From Theory to Practice: A Pre-reading Plan. *Journal of Reading 25:452.*

Langer, J. A. (ed.) 1987. *Language, Literacy, and Culture: Issues of Society and Schooling*. Norwood, NJ: Ablex Publishing Company.

Mackay, R., Barkman, B. and Jordan R. R., (ed.) 1979. *Reading in a Second Language: Hypotheses, Organization, and Practice.* Rowley, MA: Newbury House Publishers.

Mahon. D. 1986. Intermediate Skills: Focusing on Reading Rate Development. In *Teaching Second Language Reading for Academic Purposes,* (ed.) F. Dubin, D. E. Eskey, and W. Grabe. Reading, MA: Addison-Wesley Publishing Company.

Mandler, J. 1984. *Stories, Scripts, and Scenes: Aspects of Schema Theory.* Hillsdale, NJ: Lawrence Erlbaum Associates.

McGuinness, D. 2005 *Language Development and Learning to Read.* Cambridge, MA: MIT Press.

— 2004 *Early Reading Instruction.* Cambridge, MA: MIT Press.

McNeil, J. D. 1987. *Reading Comprehension: New Directions for Classroom Practice.* Second Edition. Glenview, IL: Scott, Foresman and Company.

McNeil, J. D. and Donant, L. 1982. Summarizing strategy for improving reading comprehension. In *New Inquiries in Reading Research Instruction, 31st Yearbook of the National Reading Conference,* (ed.) J. Niles and L. Miller. Rochester, NY: The National Reading Conference.

Meyer, B. 1977. The Structure of Prose: Effects on Learning and Memory and Implication for Educational Practice. In *Schooling and the Acquisition of Knowledge,* (ed.) R. C. Anderson, R. J. Spiro, and W. E. Montague. Hillsdale, NJ: Lawrence Erlbaum Associates.

Meyer, B. and Rice, E. 1987. The interaction of reader strategies and the organization of text. *Text* 2, #1-3.

Michaels, S. 1986. Narrative presentations: An Oral Preparation for Literacy with First Graders. In *The Social Construction of Literacy,* (ed.) J. Cook-Gumperz. Cambridge: Cambridge University Press.

Mikulecky, B. 1984. "Reading Skills Instruction in ESL." In *On TESOL '84,* (ed.) P. Larson, E. L. Judd, and D. S. Messerschmitt. Washington, DC: TESOL.

Mikulecky, B. 1991 "Comprehension Strategies of Bilingual Russian Readers: Processes and Techniques in Russian and in English." Unpublished dissertation, Boston University School of Education.

Miller, W. and Steeber de Orozco, S. 1990. *Reading Faster and Understanding More. Book Two, Third Edition.* New York: HarperCollins Publishers.

Moore, J. et al. 1979. *Reading and Thinking in English.* Oxford: Oxford University Press.

Nagy, W. E., Herman, P, and Anderson, R. 1985. Learning Words from Context Reading *Research Quarterly 20, #2.*

Nation, I.S.P. 2001. *Learning Vocabulary in Another Language.* Cambridge, UK: Cambridge University Press.

Nation, I. S. P. 1997. The language learning benefits of extensive reading. *The Language Teacher, 21*(5), 13–16.

Nespor, J. 1987. The Construction of School Knowledge: A Case Study. *Journal of Education* 169:34-54.

Nuttall, C. 1982. *Teaching Reading Skills in a Foreign Language.* London: Heinemann Educational Books.

Olshavsky, J. 1976. Reading as problem solving: an investigation of strategies. *Reading Research Quarterly 12, #4.*

Olsen, M. 1982. Paper presented at ESL symposium, Newton, MA.

Olson, D. R. 1977. "From Utterance to Text: The Bias of Language in Speech and Writing." *Harvard Education Review* 47.

Ong, W. 1982. *Orality and Literacy: The Technologizing of the Word.* London: Methuen.

Orasanu, J. (ed.) 1986. *Reading Comprehension: From Research to Practice.* Hillsdale, NJ: Lawrence Erlbaum Associates.

Ostler, S. 1987. English in Parallels: A Comparison of English and Arabic Prose. In *Writing Across Languages: Analysis of L2 Text*, (ed.) U. Connor and R. Kaplan. Reading, MA: Addison-Wesley Publishing Company.

Oxford Collocations Dictionary for Students of English. 2002. Oxford: Oxford University Press.

Palinscar, A. S. and Brown, A. L. 1985. Reciprocal teaching of comprehension monitoring activities. In *Reading Education: Foundations for a Literate America*, (ed.) J. Osborn., P. Wilson, and R. C. Anderson. Lexington, MA: Lexington Books.

Pattison, Robert, 1982. *On Literacy: The Politics of the Word from Homer to the Age of Rock.* Oxford: Oxford University Press.

Pearson, P. D. (ed.) 1984. *A Handbook of Reading Research.* New York: Longman.

Pica, T., Young, R. and Doughty, C. 1987. The Impact of Interaction on Comprehension. *TESOL Quarterly* 21, #4.

Raatz, U. and Klein-Braley, C. 1984. The C-Test - A Modification of the Cloze Procedure. In *Occasional Papers: Practice and Problems in Language Testing*, (ed.) T. Culhane, C. Klein-Braley, and D. Stevenson, Cochester, England: University of Essex.

Rayner, K. 1998 Eye Movements in Reading and Information Processing: 20 Years of Research. *Psychology Bulletin.* 24, No. 3. 372-422.

Reynolds, R. E., Taylor, M. A., Steffensen, M. S., Shirey, L. L. and Anderson, R. C. 1982. Cultural Schemata and Reading Comprehension. *Reading Research Quarterly 17.*

Rumelhart, D. E. 1980. Schemata: the building blocks of cognition. In *Theoretical Issues in Reading Comprehension*, (ed.) R. J. Spiro, B. C. Bruce, and W. F. Brewer. Hillsdale, NJ: Lawrence ErIbaum Associates.

Rumelhart, D. E. and Ortony, A. 1977. The representation of knowledge in memory. In *Schooling and the Acquisition of Knowledge*, (ed.) R. C. Anderson, R. J. Spiro, and W. E. Montague. Hillsdale, NJ: Lawrence ErIbaum Associates.

Samuels, S. J. and Kamil, M. L. 1984. Models of the Reading Process. In *Handbook of Reading Research*, (ed.) D. Pearson. New York: Longman.

Scallon R., and Scallon, S. 1981. *Narrative, Literacy, and Face in Interethnic Communication.* Norwood, NJ: Ablex Publishing Company.

Schank, R. C. and Abelson, R. C. 1977. *Scripts, Plans, Goals, and Understanding.* Hillsdale, NJ: Lawrence Erlbaum Associates.

Schieffelin, B. and Cochran-Smith, M. 1984. Learning to Read Culturally: Literacy Before Schooling. In *Awakening to Literacy*, (ed.) H. Goelman, A. Oberg, and F. Smith. Portsmouth, NH: Heinemann Educational Books.

Schieffelin, B. and Ochs, E. 1986. Language Socialization. *Annual Review of Anthropology* 15.

Schlessinger, J. H. 1984. Outside Reading and Oral Reports: Sure-fire Reading Motivation. *Journal of Reading* 28, #3.

Schmitt, N. 2000. *Vocabulary in Language Teaching.* New York: Cambridge University Press.

Schulz, R. A. 1983. From word to meaning: foreign language reading instruction after the elementary course. *The Modern Language Journal* 67(2):127-134.

Scribner, S. and Cole, M. 1981. *The Psychology of Literacy.* Cambridge, MA: Harvard University Press.

Sivell, J. N. 1987. Profile of the ESL extensive reader. Paper presented at the 21st Annual Convention of TESOL. April 21-25, 1987. Miami, Florida.

Smith, F. (ed.) 1973. *Psycholinguistics and Reading.* New York: Holt, Rinehart and Winston.

— 1977 "Making Sense of Reading—And of Reading Instruction," *Harvard Educational Review* 47 (1977): 386-395.

— 1986. *Understanding Reading (Third Ed.)* Hillsdale, NJ: Lawrence Erlbaum Associates.

Smith, S. 1984. *The Theater Arts and the Teaching of Second Languages.* Reading, MA: Addison-Wesley Publishing Company.

Spargo, E. and Williston, G.R. 1980. *Timed Readings.* Providence, RI: Jamestown Publishers.

Stanovich, K. E. 1980. Toward an interactive-compensatory model of individual differences in the development of reading fluency. *Reading Research Quarterly 16*, (1).

Steffenson, M. S., Joag-dev, C. and Anderson, R. C. 1979. A Cross-cultural Perspective on Reading Comprehension. *Reading Research Quarterly 15.*

Stein, N. L. 1986. Critical issues in the development of literacy education: toward a theory of learning and instruction. In *Literacy in American Schools: Learning to Read and Write,* (ed.) N. Stein. Chicago: University of Chicago Press.

Stein, N. L. and Trabasso, T. 1982. What's in a Story: An Approach to Comprehension and Instruction. In *Advances in Instructional Psychology, Volume 2,* (ed.) R. Glaser. Hillsdale, NJ: Lawrence Erlbaum Associates.

Stoller, F. 1986. Reading Lab: Developing Low-level Reading Skills. In *Teaching Second Language Reading for Academic Purposes,* (ed.) F. Dubin, D. Eskey, and W. Grabe. Reading, MA: Addison-Wesley Publishing Company.

Street, B. 1984. *Literacy in Theory and Practice.* Cambridge: Cambridge University Press.

Szabo, S. 2010. Older Children Need Phonemic Awareness Instruction, Too. *TESOL Journal 1:1 March 2010.*

Taguchi, E. and Gorsuch, G. 2002 Transfer Effects of Repeated EFL Reading on Reading New Passages: A Preliminary Investigation. <u>Reading in a Foreign Language</u> 14:(1).

Taylor, W. L. 1953. "Cloze procedure": a new tool for measuring readability. *Journalism Quarterly 30:415-433.*

Thorndike, R. L. 1974. Reading as reasoning. *Reading Research Quarterly.* 9.

Tierney, R. J. and Cunningham, J. W. 1984. Research on Teaching Reading Comprehension. In *Handbook of Reading Research,* (ed.) Pearson D. New York: Longman.

Toussaint Clark C., & Clark I., 2008. Exploring and Exposing a Gap in L2 Research: How Socio-linguistic Roles and Relationships Facilitate or Frustrate Second Language Acquisition. *ATLANTIS. Journal of the Spanish Association of Anglo-American Studies.* 30.1 101–113.

Van Daalen-Kapteijns, M. and Elshou-Mohr, M. 1981. The acquisition of word meaning as a cognitive learning process. *Journal of Verbal Learning and Verbal Behavior* 20:386-399.

Van Dijk, T. and Kintsch, W. 1983. *Strategies of Discourse Comprehension.* New York: Academic Press.

Vygotsky, L. S. 1962. *Thought and Language.* Cambridge, MA: Massachusetts Institute of Technology Press.

Wagner, D. 1987. Does Learning to Read in a Second Language Always Put the Child at a Disadvantage? Some Counter Evidence from Morocco. Paper presented at the 12th Annual Boston University Conference On Language Development. October 23-25, 1987. Boston, MA.

Washburn, K. 2009 Conspiracy Theories: Patterns, Teaching, and Thinking. Edurati Review (blog: http://eduratireview.com/category/cross-disciplinary-thinking/).

Watson-Gegeo, K. and Gegeo, D. 1986. *Language Socialization Across Cultures.* New York: Cambridge University Press.

Wexler, B.E. 2006. *Brain and Culture: Neurobiology, Ideology, and Social Change.* Cambridge, Mass: MIT Press.

Wexler, J. et al. 2008. A Synthesis of Fluency Interventions for Secondary Struggling Readers. *Reading and Writing: An Interdisciplinary Journal, 21* (4) 317-347.

Winograd, T. 1977. A Framework for Understanding Discourse. In *Cognitive Processes in Comprehension*, (ed.) M. A. Just and P. A. Carpenter. Hillsdale, N.J.: Lawrence Erlbaum Associates.

Wolf, M. 2007. *Proust and the Squid: The Story and Science of the Reading Brain.* New York: Harpercollins.

Zupnik, J-Y. 1988. In Teaching Reading Skills. Paper presented at the 22nd Annual TESOL Convention. B. Mikulecky and J. Y. Zupnik. March 9, 1988, Chicago, IL.

INDEX